CW01391053

Mothering Justice

Working with Mothers in Criminal and Social Justice Settings

Edited by Lucy Baldwin

With a Foreword by Vicky Pryce

WATERSIDE PRESS

Mothering Justice
Working with Mothers in Criminal and Social Justice Settings
Edited by Lucy Baldwin

ISBN 978-1-909976-23-8 (Paperback)
ISBN 978-1-910979-02-0 (Epub ebook)
ISBN 978-1-910979-03-7 (Adobe ebook)

Main UK distributor Gardners Books, 1 Whittle Drive, Eastbourne, East Sussex, BN23 6QH. Tel: +44 (0)1323 521777; sales@gardners.com; www.gardners.com

North American distribution Ingram Book Company, One Ingram Blvd, La Vergne, TN 37086, USA. Tel: (+1) 615 793 5000; inquiry@ingramcontent.com

Cataloguing-In-Publication Data A catalogue record for this book can be obtained from the British Library.

Printed by CPI Group, Chippenham, UK.

e-book *Mothering Justice* is available as an ebook and also to subscribers of Myilibrary, Dawsonera, ebrary, and Ebscohost.

Published 2015 by
Waterside Press
Sherfield Gables
Sherfield-on-Loddon
Hook, Hampshire
United Kingdom RG27 0JG

Telephone +44(0)1256 882250
E-mail enquiries@watersidepress.co.uk
Online catalogue WatersidePress.co.uk

Contents

Edited by Lucy Baldwin

Ripples

I watch the birds soaring in the sky
like ever decreasing circles in a river
The higher they fly the smaller they get —
until they disappear
Will this be me? Will I disappear?

The longer I am here the smaller I feel —
like ever decreasing circles in a river.
The memories of my children's faces,
love in their eyes, their touch their smell.
The longer I am here — will my memories fade —
like ever decreasing circles in a river?

My heart, it aches the pain hurting me,
stopping me sleeping, breathing, living
It does not get smaller the longer I am here —
it is nothing like ever decreasing circles in a river
It will not disappear.

Acknowledgements

It is important to thank the authors and contributors, even those who didn't in the end participate as much as was initially hoped—nevertheless you were all part of the journey and the process and are therefore woven into this book too. Special thanks to Susie Atherton, Leila-Zoe Mezoughi and Sinead O'Malley.

All of the contributors are grateful to the women they have worked with who have touched their lives and made this book possible and they thank those women for the insight, understanding and positive professional development gained from that experience. The 'voice' of all of those women is present throughout the book. To them we would like to say, 'You are all now hopefully "part of something" that will contribute positively to the wonderful ongoing work with mothers in and around criminal and social justice.' Thank you: we hope you who made this book possible are 'heard'—in every sense possible.

Finally, I would like to thank my family, my beloved children and partner who have been endlessly patient with my preoccupation. You are all my world. So thanks to Lisa, Christopher and Annie, Matthew and Keely, Meghan and Fred, Jak and my nearly here, loved already, grandson Wilfred Barnaby Francis (We are all beyond excited to meet you!).

All my love

Mum X

P.S. Very special thanks to Bryan Gibson at Waterside for giving us a 'voice', for your patience for your humour, the checked shirt and the singing. Keep on chopping!

Lucy

This book is dedicated to my lost children and grandchildren and those yet to come and to mothers and children the world over, particularly those who are vulnerable, struggling or surviving against the odds.

I would especially like to dedicate it to all of the women and mothers I have worked with professionally over the last 27 years and two in particular 'Maxine' and 'Caroline', wherever you are now, you both — along with everything you taught me as I supported you — have stayed with me.

About the Authors

Author/Editor: Lucy Baldwin BA (Hons), MA, Dip SW, Cert CTS, FHEA
Lucy is a Senior Lecturer in Criminology at De Montfort University. She joined Academia in 2004 after a long career in Social and Criminal Justice. She has practice experience in a variety of fields across Social Services, the Probation Service and Prisons and has worked across a wide range of resources with service user, victim and 'offender'-focussed perspectives. She is undertaking research in the sentencing of mothers and has articles forthcoming relating to proposals for change and managing emotions and trauma in prison as mothers. Her doctoral research is concerned with mothers, custody and emotions. In whatever setting she has been employed she has have been touched by the heart and soul of women, especially the mothers with whom she has worked and the challenges they face. Lucy is a mother of three, stepmother of one — three boys aged 23 to 33 and a daughter aged 21. She also has a grandbaby due around the time this book will be published — very exciting!

Lisa Hackett BA (Hons), MA, Dip SW, AMHP
Lisa is a qualified Social Worker and Approved Mental Health Practitioner (AMHP) and Head of Division of Criminology at De Montfort University. She has 20 years' experience in the field working in residential settings, child protection, fostering, women's aid and adult mental health. She teaches around mental health and diversity, young people and crime and mental health and policing. Lisa has a keen interest in how practitioners interact and work with vulnerable children and adults, and how they use their understanding of 'self' to formulate and develop knowledge, insight and perspective. She plans to undertake research around engaging positively with personality disorders from both a service user and practitioner perspective in order to support the process of desistance. Lisa lives in a busy household with her partner and three sons.

Cassandra Barnes BA (Hons), MA, SW
Cassandra is a qualified Social Worker working as a Senior Social Worker in a duty and assessment team for Children's Services. She is passionate

about child protection and felt 'driven to working in frontline child protection in an attempt to support the change of the stories of children and young people who experience abuse, neglect and deprivation. Her work has a particular focus on supporting children via work with families to break cycles of abuse. Cassandra aims to inform her practice by developing positive working relationships with families, crucially mothers, to assist and support them to effectively and safely parent their children.

Catherine Thompson BA (Law)

Catherine is a Detective Constable within the Domestic Violence Investigation Unit (DAIU) in a busy city police force. She has been a Police Officer for some eight years and worked within the DAIU for around the last three. In this rôle she investigates high risk domestic incidents dealing with both the suspect, interviewing and charging where possible, and the injured party by providing safeguarding assistance. Before moving to this unit she worked within the CID investigating burglaries and robberies and before that was a response officer for 999 calls from members of the public. Before joining the police, Catherine was a member of a city Youth Offending Team for around five years. Whilst in this team she worked with first-time offenders and eventually the prolific, older offender group and their families in order to try and address the underlying reasons for their offending.

Leila Zoe Mezoughi BA (Hons), Barrister-at-Law

Leila graduated with a 1st Class degree (Hons) after winning the Gerard Maye Legal Prize and the Future Lawyer Excellence scholarship to study for the Bar Professional Training Course at City Law School. She has extensive experience in criminal law but a passionate interest in gendered sentencing approaches and gendered rehabilitation provision. She is a qualified 'McKenzie Friend', which involves representing litigants in person, in domestic violence disputes for the National Centre for Domestic Violence. Further to this Leila is a Trustee for Women's Breakout, a charity that represents organizations working with women who have offended and those who are at risk of offending. She has a keen interest in women's rights and was responsible for the UK contribution to Equality Now's Rape Law Research Project. This multi-jurisdictional research was presented to the United Nations with a view to enforcing best practice guidelines for sexual violence laws in all UN countries.

Pamela Windham Stewart BA, MA

Pamela's early life was spent on a Texan ranch, close to the Mexican border, moving to The Netherlands and then to London. She has a passion for Art, which she studied in the USA, returning to London after graduating. Following the births of her three children she re-trained at the London Montessori Centre and spent many happy years teaching and managing a North London nursery. Inspired by her work with children she completed an MA where her dissertation, for which she received a distinction, described her work with mothers and babies in Holloway Prison. Its title, 'Born Inside', is the name she gives her work with mothers and pregnant women in prison. She trained as a Psychoanalytic Psychotherapist and divides her time between her private practice working with individuals and couples as well as supervising and supporting other therapists and her forensic psychotherapy at HM Prisons Holloway and Bronzefield. The Born Inside Project is ongoing at the latter.

Laura Abbot RGN, RM, BA, BSc (Hons), MSc, PGCE, FHEA

Laura is a Senior Lecturer and Admissions Tutor for Pre-registration Midwifery at the University of Hertfordshire. Prior to lecturing, she trained as a nurse and midwife and has 25 years' experience as a health care professional, including working as an Independent Midwife and Supervisor of Midwives. She leads the Complex Social Issues in Maternity and Perinatal Mental Health Modules at master's level and teaches on a number of undergraduate midwifery courses at the university. Laura is undertaking a professional doctorate researching the experience of being a pregnant woman in prison. She has a special interest in providing care for women who may be marginalised or invisible to society and has trained as a 'Birth Companion', supporting pregnant women in prison as a volunteer, visiting women in the ante-natal period, attending their births and visiting women post-natally. In 2014, Laura was awarded funding and the prestigious Jean Davies Award from the Iolanthe Midwifery

Trust and the Royal College of Midwives for her work in addressing inequalities and disadvantages for women and their babies. She lives in Bedfordshire with her husband and three sons.

Susie Atherton, BSc, MSc, PG Dip
Susie was a Senior Lecturer in Criminology at De Montfort University for six years before leaving to complete her PhD in Criminology, exploring how community justice initiatives contribute to community life and social cohesion. Prior to that she worked as a researcher and also in the Home Office and Social Exclusion Unit. Her doctoral research aims to contribute to better understanding of how community conditions can impede or assist the implementation of Community Justice. Susies' teaching has of late focussed around multi-agency working, research and policing. She has taught Criminology and Criminal Justice Policy to undergraduates and practitioner students and has conducted qualitative research in the UK and EU on topics including the resettlement of ex-offenders and services for problematic drug and alcohol users. Her research interests include social capital, community cohesion, gender and interagency communication.

Kayley Galway BA (Hons), MA, Dip SW
Kayley is a qualified Social Worker and works as an Operational Manager in a Criminal Justice Drug and Alcohol Treatment team, with 15 years' experience in this field. She is an Associate Lecturer at Leicester University and teaches on the foundation degree around her area of specialism. She has particular interest in working with 'hard to reach' groups, including homeless and travelling communities. Kayley works in partnership with HM Prison Peterborough and NHS Maternal Medicine Units and is passionate about working with mothers and their families and the importance of complex need interventions. She resides with her partner and three children in Leicestershire and some of the time in Italy.

Sinead O'Malley, BA (Hons), MASW
Sinead is a Doctoral Researcher based at the UNESCO Child and Family Research Centre at the National University of Ireland, Galway, since

2013 but has been working on research with mothers in prison since 2012. She is a qualified Social Worker with professional practice experience in Child Protection and Welfare and Child and Adolescent Mental Health (CAMH), as well as experience working with both the homeless and traveller communities. Sinead teaches around reflective practice. She delivers accredited seminars, information sessions and invited lectures all over Ireland on mothers engaged in the Criminal Justice System for state agencies, NGOs, Masters in Law, Criminology and Social Work students, amongst others. She contributes to this book as a survivor and someone who is passionate about working positively with women with complex histories and needs. She is a wife and most importantly a mother of a six-year-old 'beautiful boy'.

The author of the Foreword
Vicky Pryce is an economist and former Joint Head of the UK Government Economic Service. She is the author of *Prisonomics: Behind Bars in Britain's Failing Prisons* (Biteback Publishing, 2014).

Foreword
Working with Mothers in Social and Criminal Justice Settings

Vicky Price

I absolutely recognise the value and importance of this book and feel sure it will add to and develop understanding in relation to working with mothers in criminal justice.

Many of the difficulties facing women in prison, both in terms of their level of engagement with staff and the management of their own emotions comes from the fact that many are mothers — and as such are struggling to deal with the separation from their children.

The worst impact on the women I met was the loss of control over what goes on with their family once in prison. I saw statistics suggesting that 50 per cent of women who receive a custodial sentence go to court on sentencing day not expecting to be sent to prison and often having left children with neighbours and being completely emotionally and practically unprepared for what comes next. This was certainly the case with those who had to deal with that shock when not being able to communicate easily except through expensive phone calls at restricted times and letters which required stamps they often didn't possess and having to rely on restricted visits. Some four per cent of prisoners lose touch with their families. Sometimes because of the distance families and small children may have to travel but is a particular problem for women given the very small number of women's prisons around the country.

For some though, this loss of contact is deliberate. Either they don't want to expose their families to what has happened to them and the indignity of being in prison, but often also because the pain is too much. On visit days in open prison, women would spend ages getting ready and to look good for the children's visits and once over we (the prisoners collectively) had great difficulty preventing some from cracking-up.

For me that was the most dangerous time. One girl who was visited by her partner and youngest child, an eight-month-old baby, looked animated during the visit, then cried all the way back to the main house and tried to commit suicide that evening. She was then moved back to a closed prison for her own protection.

Of the women with children in prison about a third are single mothers. The issue is stronger for them and self-harm is widespread. I would hear them shout in desperation and cry on the phones, and worry terribly as their children were bullied at school because their mother was in prison. Others were going through the agony of having them taken into care or a partner starting divorce proceedings, impacting on access with children. We were basically spending a lot of our time being amateur counsellors to try and cheer them up, and amateur lawyers to help them navigate the complex environment out there, for which there was usually very little or no help in prison—and less so now with the legal aid cuts.

I was lucky in that my adult children were all supportive and we had regular contact by phone, letters and e-mails and I wasn't staying in prison for long but even I did my best to look on top of the world when they came. I reasoned, rightly, that if I looked good they would go away thinking that things were ok … whatever the truth might be.

The mothers in this book are 'real' in that they represent a voice of women who often go unheard. Their stories are representative of so many others, too many, for whom lack of understanding can have devastating consequences.

Mothering Justice, by examining the reflections of experienced practitioners who work or have worked with mothers, both in custody and other areas where mothers feel vulnerable, judged, scared and exposed—will in my opinion shine a light on positive changes in the field — but will also highlight additional areas where change needs to still occur. The 'Pauses for Thought' in the text will encourage readers to expand their thinking beyond the scope of the book whilst also encouraging critical, informed and compassionate reflection on the women's narratives presented in the book. Furthermore, by describing a range of effective working practices that achieve positive outcomes the book will help a range of professionals who work with mothers to do their job—and to do it well.

Vicky Pryce, September 2015

CHAPTER 1

Why Motherhood? Setting the Scene
A Personal and Professional Reflection

Lucy Baldwin

'Motherhood: All love begins and ends there.' (Robert Browning)

During my many years of practice, in whatever context I have worked, I have often been impressed and inspired by women in general and I find working with women and girls rewarding, something I sincerely hope has always been conveyed to the women I have worked with. However I have always been particularly affected in relation to working with mothers. Mother, motherhood, mothering—are all terms which seem to somehow 'invite' opinions, sometimes judgements, arguably always expectations—and often shared empathy and compassion. Working with vulnerable mothers can be as challenging as it can be rewarding, not least because 'motherhood' and its experience, from both sides, i.e. from that of the child or the mother, is something that is of enormous consequence; psychologically, emotionally and physically to all concerned. I remember all too well being a 'teenage mum', trying to escape a past whilst at the same time trying to forge a future—a future in which no-one expected me to succeed. As with all of us there are aspects of our pasts that inform and shape our futures, we all have our story. I was determined my future would not be 'as predicted' and this perhaps gave me a certain demeanour and determination, most certainly influencing my life choices, both personally and professionally. As a much older and wiser person—as well as being an experienced professional and three times mother—for the most part a single mother—I am able to reflect on when, where and how personal experiences can and do 'leak' into our professional lives or our career choices.

There are many aspects to the successful management of this 'phenomenon' and that is perhaps someone else's book for another time — but I would suggest that significant key aspects to successful and healthy 'professional engagement' very much include open, honest self-reflection and positioned self-awareness. Practitioners in this book provide opportunities for reflection on thoughts, feelings and emotions and practice during work with mothers by including 'Pauses for Thought' in every chapter in the hope that readers will find this thought-provoking, reassuring and productive.

I am lucky in that despite a rocky start there have been some positive and significant people in my life and via those people came opportunities — without which my life would be very different — two such people are my midwife and my health visitor, namely Ann Fox and Mary Maruf. Both met me when I was pregnant with my first child at 16, I became pregnant a month after coming out of hospital following a serious attempt to take my life. Without them this book wouldn't be possible — without them perhaps even life for me wouldn't have been possible. Wherever you both are thank you from the bottom of my heart.

I have witnessed and experienced first-hand the devastating consequences of pain-filled childhoods, abusive relationships and unhealthy coping strategies — adopted often as a means of survival. I have observed and reflected on the challenges this can present to happy, healthy and effective parenting. Later, as a practitioner working with women and mothers I found such issues all too often beset the lives of many of the women who come to the attention of statutory or third sector services or who might enter the criminal justice system (CJS). However, equally as significantly long-lasting and affecting to me has been the positive experience of working with women who tirelessly and valiantly fight to be seen and heard in systems that often appear to want to ignore women's needs, or to punish them further than their disadvantage already does.

I was lucky that when I insisted on leaving hospital less than 48 hours after my first son was born (the norm was a minimum of seven days usually ten in those days!) that my midwife supported me rather than judged my behaviour risky and immature. Or again when I discharged myself from hospital with my second baby on our second day, even though I was still young (just turned 18), that my midwife didn't share the view of the consultant who called it an 'act of wanton rebellion'—instead recognising it as the act of someone who needed to be home to feel safe and needing to be with her other child too. I was lucky I was not judged reckless and I was fortunate that my midwife had no concerns for my ability to parent based on my age or my background—she trusted me, supported me and encouraged me. I was lucky that my health visitor felt the same and was 'who' she was and 'how' she was—and that she was able to know when I needed help—because I would never have asked for it (I'm stubborn that way!), reaching out to me when I needed her instead. Despite being labelled 'clever' I had left school with hardly any qualifications (I truanted for most of secondary school!). My health visitor encouraged me to do my A-levels. I completed three in a year, she then even secured me paid childcare via and old lady and the local vicar—which enabled me to go on to university for my undergraduate degree (Long story—and I'm not religious—but very grateful).

I am very, very aware that my life could have been quite different for me and for my children had it not been for these two people—Fiona Anderson wasn't so lucky. Fiona was a 23-year-old mother of three children all under the age of four: Levina, Addy and Kyden. Despite the involvement of child protection services, Fiona hadn't felt able to engage with professionals or disclose the fact she was struggling to cope—she actively avoided professionals out of fear her children would be taken from her and so she continued to struggle. Until the day when Fiona could apparently struggle no more, and in April 2013 she leapt to her death from a multi-storey car park—whilst eight months pregnant with her daughter, Eve ... and after killing all three of her children. The inquest revealed 'a harrowing insight into the real state of her mental health' and the struggles she had been battling with became apparent in a torn-up letter found in the bin and Fiona's writing on the walls. Despite receiving over 50 visits from services in the three years prior to her death and intermittent service involvement—there had been no mental health assessment—partly due to Fiona's avoidance and reluctance to engage and partly due to system failures and failure to engage the family. After drowning her children Fiona had placed a lipstick kiss on each child and wrote that she loved them on their tummies—she had apologised for *'taking them with her'* but wrote *'a mother never abandons her children.'* (SCR: 2013).

What is all the more tragic is that there were opportunities to support Fiona and her children—indeed the night before her death her ex-partner and her had an altercation in which she injured him with a knife—but he failed to disclose this at the hospital as he was 'trying to protect' Fiona, fearing if he was honest about the attack that the children may be lost to the care system. Issues such as these will be revisited in the Mental Health chapter (*Chapter 2*) and Social Work chapter (which deals with child protection) (*Chapter 3*) of this book, but sadly this situation is not unique. In order to avoid what they fear is the inevitable and unwelcome 'intrusion' of child services, mothers may disengage, minimise their symptoms and fears—or deny them altogether; thus meaning that for some mothers the opportunity to secure real help and positive support is at best delayed, at worst lost. This needs to change, mothers need to feel there is 'support' rather than judgement at the end of a phone call—to be able to admit they are 'struggling'—without that being seen as an admission they are 'failing'.

Dolman *et al* (2013) suggest this is especially the case when a mother has an existing mental health diagnosis. Fear and anxiety exacerbate mental distress, never so painfully demonstrated than by the tragic death of Charlotte Bevan in 2014 who, again, apparently leapt to her death with her four-day-old daughter Zaani. Charlotte, who was living with a diagnosis of schizophrenia and depression, had reportedly stopped taking her medication in order that she could breastfeed. The full inquiry has yet to take place and any one that does will address how far the hospital and Charlotte's care team adhered to the recently updated National Institute for Health and Care Excellence (NICE) guidance relating to working with pregnant and new mothers at risk of mental distress. It will not be surprising should the inquest find there was some issue with multi-agency communication and a 'joined-up approach', which is tragically all too often a feature in most serious case reviews (SCRs) or inquiries. Mothers like Fiona Pilkington, who killed herself and her disabled daughter in 2007 and who features in the Police chapter (*Chapter 4*) alongside Jael Mullings who killed her baby sons despite calls to police in the hours before their deaths stating she was a risk—or Tania Clarence, also in 2014 (who killed her three disabled children and was detained in psychiatric care rather than custody), or indeed Angela Schuman who leapt from the Humber Bridge in 2005 with her two year old daughter Lorraine (both survived). Angela was jailed for attempted murder of her daughter—later released on appeal—though with a no contact order.

All of these women lost children to their own hands, that is true, but in one way or another they were failed by society and systems that are meant to offer protection to vulnerable women, mothers and children. It almost goes without saying that 'lessons must be learned' from each of these tragic cases—but not singularly. Every SCR report I have ever read mentions failure to communicate or failure to share information in some important way. However, often a conclusion will be drawn in each report that due to the 'individual' and particular characteristics of a case 'the tragic outcome could not have been predicted'—meaning 'lessons aren't learnt because 'failings' are seen as 'case specific'. Nonetheless, often what is key is that in many cases the 'common' failings have not only been missed opportunities to support and engage mothers—but there have been many missed opportunities to *'listen'* to the mothers themselves, for the mothers to have a *voice*.

This 'failure to listen' is illustrated by Tania Clarence and her legal representation in court. Tania did in fact have extensive support for her family, up to 60 professionals were 'involved' in her daily life as a mother caring for three disabled children—however her legal team stated poignantly that Mrs Clarence felt pulled this way and that, she felt 'undermined, insecure and patronised'. He went on to say that 'each separate specialist seemed unable to appreciate the *whole*—and it is this "whole" that Mrs Clarence lived.' One person in the sea of professionals involved with her family whom Tania did trust and engage with positively was her social worker, who was with her from the beginning—yet eight weeks before the children's deaths this social worker was removed from the case because her manager felt she was 'getting too involved with the family'—both Tania and the social worker fought the decision and lost—the social worker, an experienced senior practitioner resigned—following a stressful meeting with her new and inexperienced social worker Tania texted her husband stating simply, 'I don't have any hope.' Tania Clarence's 'voice' was not 'heard'.

One of the aims of this book is to assist the reader to think about the presenting issues from the perspective of the mother—to truly try and place the reader, yourself, in her shoes and to think through issues for practice that will produce positive results, even when decisions being made might not be the ones the mothers want—for example being separated from her baby in prison or a mother deciding not to allow her children to visit. How does that then feel for mothers and how can these decisions and the subsequent emotions impact on her ability to engage, to trust or to survive? The 'Pauses for Thought' throughout the text assist the reader to think critically and compassionately about the issues and challenges faced by mothers and practitioner responses to them. For example, if we revisit Fiona, Charlotte and Tania for a moment via 'Pause for Thought'—it becomes apparent how reflection and critical thinking is encouraged throughout each chapter. This book, rather than giving you all of the answers, seeks to encourage you to ask the questions.

‖ Pause for Thought

What could have been done differently to support Fiona?— Do you think her fears were real in relation to losing her children?—What support package would have been best for Fiona and her children? What does her own statement, 'Mothers don't abandon their children' tell us about expectations of mothers? How do you think the fact she was 'struggling' would have made her feel as a mother?

For Charlotte—How must it have felt to her knowing she needed her medication—but also knowing breast milk is best? How do you think her anxiety/dilemma could have been managed? What are your initial thoughts of motherhood and mental illness? What are the dilemmas for mothers and professionals? For Tania—How might she have felt in a 'sea' of 'experts' and professionals?

During my long career I have been lucky enough to work with many professionals who are committed to improving social and justice system responses to vulnerable women and their children. Passion and drive is something I have rarely found lacking in any of the professionals I have come across in relation to working with women and mothers I have had the pleasure to do this with, including those involved in this book; professionals who come from a range of statutory and third sector settings all seeking to affect positive change on both macro and micro-levels for women in criminal justice and related settings. The importance of responding to people as 'individuals', with kindness and respect cannot, I think, be overstated. It is my experience that even when the 'reins' of the 'system' employing said practitioners may prevent workers from working perhaps as freely as they would like, or with less than 'ideal' resources, many of the practitioners I have come across simply as *'people'* have affected change, or at the very least had a significant and positive impact on women and/or mothers they have worked with.

So the purpose of this book is to bring together some of that knowledge and experience to facilitate understanding and assist in the development of professional confidence, professional empathy and 'emotional safety'. This will be achieved by exploration of, and reflection on, a range of emotional and related issues that may arise when working with women and mothers, particularly in the criminal justice system — but equally in a range of other settings. The book is designed to be used almost as a thought-provoking 'companion' text to assist those who work with and are learning to work with women, girls and mothers facing challenges, but additionally to enrich and inform knowledge whilst inspiring further learning. It is hoped this will be facilitated by providing examples drawn from a variety of practice settings together with encouragement for professional and personal reflection via a range of 'Pauses for Thought', offering an opportunity for reflection around experiences, feelings and responses.

It is further hoped the book will add to the practical and experiential rather than purely academic literature surrounding working with women and especially working with women who are mothers. It is a book for practitioners written by practitioners and hopefully to benefit women and mothers by including their voices and experiences.

There are no assumptions made here or in what follows that all of the women 'we' work with will be mothers and nor are we suggesting that women who are not mothers are 'less' in anyway, or indeed that working with non-mothers is any less important. There is simply a wish to highlight 'motherhood' in relation to wider professional engagement — as often it is an aspect of working with women that has a 'centrality' to it. Even if it is not be the 'focus' of the work we undertake in a specific rôle, for example in relation to substance misuse or policing, it is likely that 'mother' status will interact with the intervention and the practitioner somewhere. Arguably, motherhood is an aspect of identity, emotion and sense of self that no practitioner is able to or would want to ignore when working with women. During work with mothers within our specific roles, there may or may not be legal aspects and implications in relation to working with women who are mothers — additionally there may or may not be practical considerations depending on the employing agency we represent, but arguably there will *always* be emotional aspects to working with women who are also mothers. Whether the women have their children with them or not, the impact of those 'emotional' aspects and responses to them — are likely to have at least *some* relevance to how we work and how we ought to work with women who are also mothers. Recognising the importance of working positively with emotions, recognising trauma in order to move forward, especially with mothers, is something that is central to this book and is discussed further in the closing chapters.

Motherhood and Professionals

Motherhood is a rôle many women expect and are expected to play in their lifetime, it is one that has a duality to it, in that often we are mothers alongside being some*thing* else or some*one* else. It is a rôle that paradoxically invites celebration and heightened status for women who sometimes are perceived as 'superior because of their "mother status", e.g. mother knows best' — yet also invites judgement and can be a means to 'reduce' a woman, e.g. 'She doesn't work, she's just a mother.' We see these paradoxes and attitudes reproduced and represented in the media and in society (Johnson and Swanson 2003) — but where and how does the motherhood 'script' fit in professional working relationships with vulnerable women in challenging circumstances?

Obviously, during work with service user mothers, then the focus is on the service user and as previously stated may not be focused on the service user 'as a mother' — but is it ever 'left out' of the picture? When working professionally and engaging with women and mothers as service users, we are often engaging — sometimes as mothers ourselves (and daughters?). Does this have any relevance to how we work, what we think professionally and on the decisions we make? Often part of our work might be dealing with and/or exploring the impact of both positive and negative mothering. We as professionals, but arguably *everyone*, have a list of 'shoulds' and 'should nots' in relation to motherhood — in terms of personal qualities, characteristics and behaviours (Bowlby 1978; Oakley 1979; Kaplan 2013).

It is important therefore to be able to reflect honestly, at least internally, on our own thoughts, feelings and values in relation to being a mother or 'expectations' of motherhood — if only to assist in 'managing' our own internal processing and to ensure our working relationships are not unconsciously governed or affected by our own emotions (as illustrated in the Mental Health chapter (*Chapter 2*) of this book). Much has been written on the expectations and stereotyping of mothers (Kaplan 2013; Oakley 1979; Rich 1992), but not so much on its relevance in relation to professional relationship dynamics and scripts.

Phoenix (1994) suggests that although it is not a lone consideration, nevertheless when working with mothers, being a women and additionally being a mother will lend itself well to the establishing of rapport, trust and ergo quality of the working relationship — but does that also bring other dimensions and dynamics into play too? Would therefore *not* being a mother have any relevance, perceived or real? Would being a male practitioner bring more dimensions into play — for both mothers and the practitioners? However, 'sisterhood' and identification aside Rowe (2011) reminds us that women are not and nor should they be regarded as a homogenous group 'reduced in terms of social identity' neither in expectation, assumptions or rôles.

I have witnessed mothers in the most desperate of situations where everyday life is a struggle or indeed sometimes a fight to survive. Yet in even the bleakest of circumstances those same women may easily be persuaded to smile in the face of adversity — persuaded by the simplest of gestures from their child. I have witnessed and worked with women who have been able to set aside life's challenges and strive to meet the needs of their children and families — sometimes at great cost to themselves. I have seen women fight like tigers for their children — against all odds, whilst simultaneously facing innumerate additional challenges, poverty, mental illness and abuse to name a few. However, equally as significant in my mind, are the 'children' — of *all* ages — felled by the loss, the interruption or the lack of maternal nurturing when this 'triumph over adversity' isn't possible (for whatever reason). I have seen just how devastating it can be to all concerned when the powerful bond associated with motherhood is broken, damaged, imperfectly formed or, for whatever reason, impossible to maintain.

Reflecting on this as a practitioner it has seemed to me that the mother/child relationship 'knows no bounds' in relation to impact and significance — both in a positive way when it is a healthy, loving, nurturing relationship, and in a negative way when, for whatever reason, that relationship is not present, can't be present or is disrupted.

It is important to state this is obviously notwithstanding additional relationships and the significance of 'others' in a child's life, a father figure, a significant rôle model, or grandparents for example — of course they are valuable, important and relevant too, as are a multitude of external, socio-economic and environmental factors — but in my experience as a practitioner (and perhaps also as a mother) none, it seems to me, has such a profound influence over the development of holistic 'wellbeing' as the one between a mother and her child. It is for that reason that 'motherhood' and the importance of appropriately supporting women in this rôle runs as a thread throughout this working companion.

Motherhood, Mothering, Social Expectation and Emotion

Where does this concept of 'motherhood' come from, is it biological or is it environmental? Has society and the development of media and media influence maintained pressure on women to feel a certain way in relation to motherhood and mothering? Nature versus nurture. It's an age-old question and one that all the books in the world will probably not succeed in answering fully, but what *is* known is that, from almost the moment they are born, girls are located in the emotional landscape that will 'expect' them to become mothers one day (Oakley 1974; Mead 1935; Rich 1992; Baldwin 2015c).

Girls are encouraged to be 'mini-mothers', nurturers and carers from the moment they start to play, 'pretend' kitchens, dolls, prams, and shops etc. — arguably these are all toys that provide inevitable signposts along the journey towards 'motherhood' (Thorne 2004; Rich 1992; Oakley 1974). So many aspects of women's identities are tied up with the emotion of birth, motherhood and mothering. Given an acceptance of the presence of such perspectives, pressures and assumptions (Johnson and Swanson 2006) this book aims to explore the potential implications of judgements surrounding the women with whom professionals might work in and around criminal or social justice settings who are mothers.

Arguably motherhood and emotion are two words that can never be separated — they are intertwined and interlinked in whatever capacity we look at either one. How often do we see the words 'No greater love than that of a mother's love'? 'What a joy motherhood is', 'What a beautiful thing it is to witness,' 'How consuming motherhood is', 'How completing and how fulfilling it is.' This may very well all be true — but is this the case for all women? What pressure does this place on them to bear witness to such evocative, emotive language and descriptions of motherhood? Indeed If we do assume or accept this to be true what does this say — or perhaps more to the point what does 'society' say — about women who do not feel this way about motherhood or mothering? Or mothers whose behaviour is 'deemed' to not be putting the needs of their children 'first'? Or those for whom mothering does not come 'naturally', or whose mothering is affected by offending behaviours, 'poor' lifestyle choices or reliance on substances. How easy is it to meet the ideals of being a protective, nurturing, selfless parent when you as a mother face violence, poverty or homelessness for example?

Media representations and references to motherhood are very often presented in either judgemental or glowing terms. Repeatedly when someone well-known or with celebrity status has given birth we are presented with headlines or lead comments such as, 'I have never felt love like it' or 'I wasn't prepared for the emotion of it all' and 'My feelings for this little person have overwhelmed me.' This is not withstanding the barrage of idealised motherhood 'truths' presented in mothering and pregnancy guidebooks or latterly internet sites such as mumsnet.com. Constant exposure to messages such as this are arguably not lost on any of us (Kaplan 2013). There is an acceptance and knowledge, but more than that an *expectation* that becoming a mother, or perhaps rather giving birth, will result in feelings as described above (Woolf 1994; Rich 1970). Furthermore that this feeling alone will facilitate good parenting and is so powerful that it assumes superiority and therefore takes precedence over a multitude of socio-economic factors and/or environmental ones.

How does this idealisation and expectation impact on vulnerable women? Does this often just feel like additional pressure to women and girls who become mothers in the midst of often already disadvantaged lives? — Do all of these assumptions about motherhood and how mothers 'should' behave simply add to the emotional 'baggage' women have to deal with in relation to coping? If women and mothers engaged in services surrounding the criminal justice and related settings are already dealing with the wealth of emotions described above in relation to their rôle as mothers, how might those emotions be magnified if we add in fear of judgement, stigma, and fear of consequences — together with feelings of failure or guilt? Therefore in reflections of working with mothers, and within recommendations for future working with mothers we need to encompass and explore the emotional ramifications and manifestations related to 'motherhood' in order to facilitate comprehensive, empathic and effective working practices.

Emotion, Judgement, Mothers and 'Systems'

It is often presented (particularly in 'popular' media) that mothers whose 'actions' by way of committing crimes or who live in or amongst chaos or substance misuse are placing the 'needs' of their children secondary to their own. Do 'we' (society in general, practitioners) judge such mothers more harshly than women in similar circumstances who do not have children? If 'we' are mothers ourselves do 'we' judge more harshly? Are mothers the harshest critics of other mothers? Does that judgement have an impact? If so what is it and how does it manifest itself? And more importantly in relation to this book, how do these emotions, feelings and perceptions impact on our engagement with mothers, on mothers themselves—and us as practitioners? Do we sufficiently acknowledge, appreciate or explore this? Do women and girls who are mothers 'fear' or 'expect' this judgement in their engagement with practitioners—and, if so, how does that feel? Layder suggests:

> 'We don't and cant "do" personal relationships on our own. To a large extent, how we respond or deal with a friend or a lover, or even a stranger, will depend upon how we think they will respond to us.' (Layder, 2004:1)

Such fears, perceptions and expectations are often compounded by issues pertaining to diversity. If a mother feels emotionally vulnerable already because of aforementioned influences, then how might those feelings seem even more prohibitive and overwhelming in the midst of cultural, language, socio-economic, age and power differentials in relation to engaging with practitioners and professionals? The Hibiscus organization works with foreign nationals (of which there is a significant proportion in the female prison estate) reports that many women, out of shame, will not even let relatives know they are in prison—often choosing to let their children and families believe they are missing or dead rather than 'inflict' cultural shame and therefore community rejection on them.

Wilson and Huntington (2006) suggest that teenage or 'too young' and especially young and single mothers are often perceived to be the 'mothers of future delinquents', not a new suggestion. Zedner (2010) suggests this was a common preoccupation in Victorian England (as referred to in the Prison chapter (*Chapter 6*)) additionally a perspective reflected in political ideologies and popular media, particularly related to single mothers and 'broken families' whom, as stated by politicians and Prime Ministers of the time, apparently 'Cannot represent traditional family values' (Daly 1994). Carlen (1983) and Bosworth (1999) suggest female 'lawbreakers' already experience higher levels of stigma than comparable males, and Sharpe (2015) goes further than this, arguing that in the case of young women who are also mothers that this stigma is only intensified. In her paper 'Precarious Identities: Young Motherhood, Desistance and Stigma' (*Ibid*), Sharpe found that *all* of the participants in her study revealed that they had experienced 'gendered stigma' and that this was judged against a range of 'conventional identity scripts'—like that of 'mother'. She goes on to suggest that expectations and perceptions of potential judgement or stigmatisation in young and vulnerable mothers can actually lead to reluctance or refusal to engage in services or access support. She gives the example of 'Anna', a young mother vulnerable to re-offending who would not attend a local supportive resource and who stated to her:

> 'I used to get into loads of trouble with the police, and there's loads of coppers here in [home town] that have had babies—at the Sure Start centre there's these two coppers who have both nicked me loads in the past—so they sit there and look down their noses at me.' (Sharpe, 2015, 1-16:8)

Sharpe suggests that having a label as a 'law breaker' adversely affects the 'good mother' identity but additionally that the combination of 'young age' and offending behaviour attracts additional judgement and disapproval. Her paper suggests that stigma relating both to status as 'lawbreaker' and 'mother' often means that women continue to 'endure judgement of maternal deficiency' even in the absence of recent offending or anti-social behaviour. Again this raises questions and concerns about potential willingness/unwillingness to engage of mothers, especially young mothers—who are fearful of the consequences of that judgement—real or imagined, cognitive or physical. This is revisited in the Social Work chapter (*Chapter 3*) and Mental Health chapter (*Chapter 2*) you may be reminded of Fiona, mentioned earlier in this chapter.

Layder (2004) suggests 'understanding' and awareness of 'dual rôle' for professionals and service users is important—in relation to all work with people but especially in agencies such as prison or probation and social work whom Layder (*Ibid*) suggests will have a 'service' response but will arguably also have a 'personal' response—and perhaps it is that personal response that mothers, especially young mothers, fear just as much. Whether only perceived, imagined and internally processed, rather than real—based on actual experience of professionals and externally expressed—it is perhaps easy to see how this might have an impact on interactions, engagement and professional relationships.

Judgement, stigma and consequential emotion share significance not just in relation to interactions with practitioners, but additionally within service user or prison populations in relation to each other. Enos (2001) refers to a female offender convicted of offences related to property who felt that, as she had offended to increase her wealth and therefore improve her children's lifestyle she did not believe that her own offending conflicted with 'good mothering'. Yet the same woman was disparaging of other mothers, particularly those whose offences were drug-related stating:

> 'You can be a good mother and be involved in crime and shoplifting and stuff, but with drugs—that's another thing.' Enos (2001:118)

Even within disadvantaged and vulnerable groups there is a hierarchy of offences regarded as in conflict with mothering—with obviously child cruelty and sexual offences against children being the 'lowest' (as described in the Psychotherapist chapter (*Chapter 7*)). Research evidences the impact of formal controls in relation to women and mothers whose lives enter or skirt around the CJS (Carlen 1983; Epstein 2012; Caddle and Crisp 1997)—with particular focus on the consequences of imprisonment for women and their children. However Sharpe (2015) suggests (and I concur) that 'the effects of informal labelling and stigma from peers', wider society and therefore practitioners can be equally as significant—not least because of the 'enduring judgements of maternal deficiency,' which she suggests often remain long after crime, supervision and offending behaviour have been left behind. For many the emotional impact and fear of judgement remains.

I would argue that working 'emotionally' with women, creating a place of 'emotional safety' especially for women who are mothers and grandmothers (because of the heightened expectations) is key to enabling women to reach the point where they are able to engage. Once women have been supported in or enabled to process the concept of emotional management, tracing some of the emotional management strategies (coping mechanisms) that may have led to particular 'choices' they have 'made', i.e. taking drugs to block out the emotional pain of past abuse (which may then lead to criminal convictions), women are then more able to work within trauma-informed practice models, desistance models and cycle-breaking models (This is re-visited in the closing chapter). Arguably this can *only* be achieved if women regard themselves as 'emotionally safe' with the people working with them.

What can we do as practitioners to counteract barriers or address these issues in order to facilitate positive and effective working relationships and therefore emotional safety and emotional management?

Arguably the very fact of being associated with criminal justice and related agencies as a mother service user leaves women vulnerable to feeling stigma and the emotional consequences of stigma (Corston 2007). Presumably, on no-one's list in a 'Good Parenting Guide' would be the suggestions 'Go to prison,' 'Lead a chaotic life,' 'Misuse substances.' Following on logically, and taking at least some of the feelings described above in relation to motherhood as read, then just the very act of committing a crime, and certainly being sent to prison or needing the assistance/ intervention of related services arguably means a mother might feel she immediately falls short of the 'perfect mother' expectation (expectations of self, wider society, etc.). Indeed, with regard to multi-agency and child protective responses it can actually mean that a mother effectively does fall short of the 'good enough' mother expectation and can result in the loss of her children—as illustrated in the chapters on Social Work (*Chapter 3*), Mental Health (*Chapter 2*) and Substance Misuse (*Chapter*

10). For many mothers it is not only fear of judgement in relation to their parenting skills but additionally fear of *consequences* that may prevent them seeking advice, guidance and support.

If a mother finds herself in custody these feelings are magnified even further. Baroness Corston (2007) highlighted this very fact and suggested that simply being imprisoned as a mother would lead to feelings of anxiety, guilt and inadequacy as mothers—are women who do find themselves behind bars therefore seen by others automatically as 'bad' mothers too? Indeed do the women judge themselves to be only and irretrievably 'bad mothers'? Corston (2007) suggests wearing or being subject to this assumption/label is, understandably damaging to self-esteem and self-worth, stating:

> 'Many women still define themselves and are defined by others by their rôle in the family. It is an important component in our self-identity and self-esteem. To become a prisoner is almost by definition to become a bad mother.' Corston (2007:2.17:20)

For many women in prison incarceration is the first time they have been separated from their children for any length of time, and many of those children do not remain in the care of the family or the family home (Reed 2014). In fact only five per cent of children of incarcerated mothers remain in the family home and 14 per cent go directly into the care of the local authority (*Ibid*). Obviously this has an emotional impact on all concerned as found by Corston (2007) who highlighted that:

> 'For many women the experience of prison is made worse because they are anxious all the time about their children's wellbeing—and even their whereabouts.' Corston (2007.3.25:33)

This has implications for working practices when engaging with mothers in criminal justice and related settings. Given what we 'know' about the backgrounds and experiences of many women who become enmeshed in them, in relation to childhood abuse, domestic abuse, mental health issues and discrimination (Carlen 1985). Mothers in the CJS and related settings, particularly custody are often dealing with issues and anxiety related to offending behaviour 'on top' of the emotional fallout of pain-filled lives. So to then have the worry of being or to actually be separated from one's children either via custody or mandatory intervention, one really doesn't have to leap too far into the hearts and minds of others to hold some imagining of what this might feel like. The Prison chapter (*Chapter 6*) explores these issues in more detail. For some mothers in prison having children is the only experience they have of 'pure love' given and taken (Devlin 1998), for others motherhood is simply a further example of something they have 'failed at' by the very fact they are in prison or are separated from their children (Corston 2007). Either way I would suggest there is likely to be some kind of emotional impact and consequently emotional management—arguably both on the part of the mothers and therefore on the part of the practitioner/professionals too.

The effective management of emotions and the consequences surrounding these issues is dealt with wonderfully in some services. Motherhood, parenting and all that goes with it is given focus and credence ensuring the surrounding issues are embedded into productive, effective work with women who are mothers (see 'Birth Companions' in the Midwife chapter (*Chapter 8*) and the 'Born Inside Project' in the Psychotherapist chapter (*Chapter 7*) for example). Perhaps it could be argued however that this is something that could be dealt with more fully, more consistently and therefore more effectively.

As will be illustrated throughout this book many women who are in prison or leaving prison have complex needs, often as a result of multiple traumatic experiences—key to working positively with women throughout the CJS is aiming to promote a climate of emotional safety. This will be revisited in the closing chapter of the book where the explicit links between 'emotional management', emotional safety and trauma-informed practice are made.

Mothering, Guilt and Interventions

Aside from the wider societal expectations of women, maternal expectation is high from the moment pregnancy is confirmed (Annandale 1998). Opinions about good and bad mothering arguably present themselves before children are even born; pregnancy generates similar fears and elicits similar judgement as motherhood does. The internal management and processing of many of the emotions related to fear of judgement, fear of consequences, fear of failure and guilt described above often begins in pregnancy.

Sutherland (2010) *et al* suggest most if not all mothers 'do' guilt as a result of expectation and 'failure to match up to mothering ideals'. Imagine how it must feel to be incarcerated 'by your own hand' and be separated from your children? Or to give birth whilst in prison? To have a child with you in prison—then to have that child taken from you per- haps when the Mother and Baby Unit age limit is reached and the child is removed screaming from you? How and where does the emotional fallout of such events present? Or to lose a child because of substance misuse or because of lifestyle choices—how does that feel? Years after such events, how does it still feel? Obviously there is an argument in relation to 'choices', but for many reasons—beyond the scope of this book—some choices are more challenging than others, some feel impos- sible to make and others are simply not available to all—but that doesn't necessarily remove the 'emotions' or the 'trauma' of a situation. Emo- tions that will arguably come into play in the interactions between the practitioner and the 'mother', irrespective of her status as a law breaker. The Prison chapter (*Chapter 6*) and Psychotherapist chapter (*Chapter 7*) in particular illustrate that pain is quite simply just pain.

Enos (2001) suggests that sometimes, especially in custodial settings, emotional responses are misread and recorded according to percep- tion—sometimes having disastrous consequences in relation to maternal capability assessments for example.

> 'They [prison staff] think that I don't hang them up [pictures of her chil- dren] because I couldn't be bothered. That hurts me. For me, it hurts for me to see my kids in pictures and stuff and I'm not there. You know what I'm saying? I can't look at them. I feel so guilty. I can't look at their pictures and not feel so guilty.' Enos (2011:110)

Additionally Gannon and Cortoni (2010) found that in their experience of working with imprisoned women, apparent 'emotionless' responses, rather than being evidence of embedded deviancy was in fact merely a coping mechanism adopted to facilitate the 'survival' and management of guilt, shame and stigma—achieved by shutting-off all emotional responses. During an interview a woman who had spent four years in prison and four under supervision told me she never once had a conversation with anyone either in prison or whilst on probation for four years following her sentence about how she was 'coping' away from her children or how it was going re-establishing a relationship on release:

> 'Mostly because I couldn't, I needed to be in control of my emotions: about missing my kids, how I felt about myself and all the stuff to do with domestic abuse—I had to constrain them in order to cope, if I told people I was struggling they would see that as heightening my risk—meaning they could keep me away from my kids longer—so why would I tell them?—But also because no-one ever asked.' Ursula (2015)

My response to this was one of shock, how could it be that no-one thought to ask about this? As Ursula tells us herself in the Prison chapter (*Chapter 6*), being a mother is central to her world so to not enquire about her relationship with her five children during the most stressful period in her life is the epitome of ignoring a giant elephant in the room.

As Worrell (1999), Carlen (1988) and Sharpe (2015) *et al* suggest, simply being linked to 'chaotic' or 'offending lifestyles' is enough to attract at least stigma and labels related to 'bad mothering'. Baroness Corston (2007) discusses the impact in relation to guilt and anxiety that many women then feel—particularly those who might end up losing their children altogether—suggesting this is particularly the case for women in custody and is an obvious factor in relation to mental ill-health—but perhaps particularly for mothers and grandmothers in prison.

Building on research and knowledge like Rotkirch (2009) and Sutherland (2010) in relation to mothering and guilt, this perhaps raises questions of how mothers such as those described above 'manage' the burden of guilt, of judgement—how this feels for mothers is explored throughout the book.

Court for many is a place of 'shame' and guilt, where one's 'wrong-doing' is aired and one's flaws and misdemeanours and mistakes are effectively 'on show'. Court alone for many women is a traumatising experience (Pryce 2013). Pryce (*Ibid*) suggests that many women are re-traumatised by what they hear in court about themselves as evidenced in the Courts chapter (*Chapter 5*) and 'Nina's letter to her daughter in the Prison chapter (*Chapter 6*).

Judges' summings-up in relation to sentencing women with children often do not only pass 'judgement' in relation to sentence but also in relation to mothering skills (Baldwin 2015c). So is it naïve to think prison staff or others working with women in prison or on release do not have an emotional response to mothers' crimes, or indeed some crimes more than others—and that mothers themselves don't 'know' and fear this in their interactions with the professionals they come across.

A judge summing up a recent child sexual abuse case in which a mother was charged alongside a male stated:

> 'That you were manipulated by [her male co-defendant] is obvious. But you are a mother, your infant only ten-months-old. A mother naturally loves, protects, shields, nurtures and cherishes. Your infant would have trusted you implicitly. You totally betrayed that trust.'

Or, in the case of a mother who was jailed alongside her adult daughters—but who received a sentence almost twice as long—despite all three being charged with a similar number of offences and to the same value, the judge sentencing the mother stated:

> 'You are the villain of the piece. It is your fault your daughters are in court. Some mother.'

So was this woman's sentence longer because of the 'seriousness' of her crime—or was it because she wasn't a 'perfect mother'? This will be further explored in the Courts chapter (*Chapter 5*).

Is it perhaps predictable that mothers in prison feel often compounded by 'normal' feelings of guilt, firstly just because of the separation from their children but additionally, and arguably especially, if their own children were to suffer or fall into wayward ways, possibly as a direct result of their own incarceration?

'My son got in a fight and was sentenced to custody whilst I was in prison—that is a direct result of me going to prison—it wouldn't have happened if I was outside—I was meant to stop things like that happening—I failed him.' Ursula (2015)

For Ursula, she isn't just serving her sentence for her crime but an additional one as a mother which for her she feels 'has no end', stating she felt she will 'forever be looking at her children through the lens of a mother who went to prison' — constantly checking if her childrens' choices and experiences are 'affected' by her sentence. Do fathers who go to prison feel the same? Is it the same? What needs to be offered long term to support parents who have been to prison and are post licence?

We 'know' statistically that children of mothers in prison are more likely to enter the care system and because of that are more likely to become victims of crime themselves or fall into offending behaviour pathways of their own (Reed 2014). What must it feel like if as a mother you feel all of those consequences are because of you? Where do those emotions go? How are they expressed? Are they understood? Do they impact on the sentence 'management' of women? Baldwin (2015c and e) in her doctoral research suggests that this is something that is indeed a highly relevant factor in relation to how mothers in custody 'manage' their sentences and arguably how far mothers are actually 'able' to comply with sentence planning targets and interventions whilst in the midst of this emotional tornado. Women, mothers and grandmothers need to be in a place of 'emotional safety' before they can fully engage with such things as offending behaviour programmes or courses which try to address root causes of addictions to substances. Early findings of the research suggest that women very much feel that courses which only 'scratch the surface' of their emotions do more harm than good and therefore often they will avoid them in order to maintain control of their emotional wellbeing. We will come back to this in the closing chapters, but it is explored within the Community Supervision chapter (*Chapter 9*) also.

Many scholars and practitioners have long argued for gendered approaches to punishment in relation to working with female offenders and female service users in social and criminal justice settings (Hedderman 2014; Carlen and Worrall 2004; McIvor 2004; Minson 2012; Epstein 2012; Baldwin 2015a, *et al*). Discussions with fellow practitioners and contributors to this book confirmed that 'motherhood' is something that has had, if one will excuse the paradox, a 'discreet prominence' in their engagement with women and girls they have encountered. Most, though not all, of the contributors to this book are mothers, not all are of the same socio-economic backgrounds and not all are heterosexual—but all have felt that the mother role, mother identity, expectations of mothers and the consequent emotions are something worthy of explicit discussion in relation to practice.

This working companion came about because as previously stated all felt the significance and importance of motherhood and its presence in their working experiences even when not the fundamental 'focus' of their particular intervention. Each chapter could have been a 'book' in itself and it was frustrating to not be able to cover more. Despite this it is hoped the collection will offer opportunities for reflection and some guidance in relation to working with mothers based on experience and heed from the voices of women who have been in exactly these positions (both from a service user and practitioner perspective).

However, given all of the above, it remains important to note, as Rowe (2011) in her paper 'Narratives of Self and Identity' takes the opportunity to remind us, that women in prison, even mothers in prison are not a homogenous group—nor should they be researched or regarded as such. This remains valid in relation to all women and mothers who for one reason or another become engaged in one or more services related to social or criminal justice or the third sector. Rowe (*Ibid*) reflects on the position that women ought not to be 'reduced in terms of social identity' neither in expectation, assumption or rôles (Jones 1993: Bosworth 1999). The intention of this book isn't to suggest a 'one size fits all' approach to working with mothers, quite the opposite—it seeks instead to provide additional support for the view that individual experiences and emotions are valid and relevant to effective working with women, girls and mothers and grandmothers.

We hope the book will be used to facilitate the understanding and empathy of students and professionals alike, particularly in relation to both the emotional impact of prison for mothers and their families—which is where my own passions lie—but additionally in relation to contributing to effective, empathic and productive work with women across a range of settings.

You will 'meet' a number of women and the people who work with them. We have aimed to include a cross-section of women with a range of issues and a range of professionals with differing perspectives and backgrounds. In terms of the identities of the individual women in the book, none are wholly based on any one individual but are an amalgamation of many women who I and others have worked with during our many combined years of practice (Well over a hundred years of experience between us!). Many professional scenarios described have been created for the purpose of facilitating learning and understanding, but again are based around real life experiences. We have by no means been able to cover every profession or agency that works effectively with women nor have we been able here to address every single issue or challenge that the women we work with face. All of the 'women' (mothers) chosen for inclusion either have been in the CJS or are vulnerable to entering it—either due to substance misuse, offending behaviour, coercion or circumstance, however not all are in or have been to prison. The focus is really the 'lived experience' and 'emotions' of mothers and how this affects the interplay between mothers and practitioners—and more importantly perhaps practitioners with mothers—and how best to move forward positively.

It is hoped the book will go some way towards assisting practice by developing and encouraging understanding and reinforcing that even if not everything we do as 'professionals' is deemed 'successful' even simply 'how we are' and how we engage with people we work with on a basic human level can still have a profound and significant impact on individuals' lives.

CHAPTER 2

Working With Women and Mothers Experiencing Mental Distress
Creating a 'Safe Place' for Constructive Conversations

Lisa Hackett

'Anyone ever told you you were bad? Like really bad, like you were the problem? They all say it about me; my mum, her boyfriends, social workers, doctors, the police and psychiatrists. My personality is wrong, bad, disordered; I was born faulty.' (Joy)

Overview and Purpose

This chapter seeks to explore how professionals can work with women and mothers experiencing mental health distress, which takes into account their needs and strengths as oppose to their 'deeds' and risks. That is not to say that behaviour that emerges from mental health distress can be ignored or minimised, but that it is managed appropriately, proportionately and not punitively as a result of historical links, connections and stereotypes around the ideals of womanhood and motherhood.

I have tried to avoid the use of the term 'problem' in relation to mental health, i.e. 'a mental health problem', as I believe it communicates a sense of needing to 'solve' or 'fix' something. Such connotations are problematic when applied in an uncritical way, and have the potential to stigmatise and blame women and mothers for their circumstances if they do not respond in the way that has been expected following an intervention or plan. Women experiencing mental distress do not need 'fixing'. They require our professional support and understanding together with an ability to recognise the particular challenges that they face in terms of stigma and discrimination. Mental distress conveys a more balanced and accurate term in the sense of my experience of working with women and mothers exhibiting a range of symptoms in keeping with various mental health concerns and medical diagnosis.

One of the fundamental aims of this chapter, alongside highlighting the complexity and inter-relatedness of mental distress, is to create an opportunity for consideration of how *you* feel about mental distress, and how you interact with women and mothers exhibiting symptoms of this. Taking time to reflect and think critically about this topic is essential as it allows the space to consider your own practice and interactions and what is informing them. Lishman (1994:56) supports this process by noting that 'entering into the lives of people who are in distress, conflict or trouble requires not only technical competence, but qualities of integrity, genuineness and self-awareness.'

To facilitate this space for reflection, the chapter focuses on considering reflexivity; how we can consider women and mother's experiencing mental distress from a supportive, informed and self-aware perspective that is in contrast to an approach that stigmatises; and how we can safeguard against stigma and prejudice by considering and locating our own feelings about women mothers and mental health. Specific attention is paid to the medical and social models of mental health and in order to identify some of the issues that need to be considered for good practice, understanding and support to flourish.

Reflective questions via 'Pause for Thought' and case studies are used, allowing you to interact with your own thoughts and feelings, locate where they have come from and how they impact on your interactions with mothers experiencing mental distress. The case studies are located in my experiences of assessing women and mothers under the Mental Health Act 1983 (amended 2007) for possible detention in hospital. They are composites of actual cases and not based on one single case. The themes and practice issues that emerge are not however unique to this context and can be, and ought to be, considered and utilised by all who come into contact with women and mothers experiencing mental distress.

The chapter is written within an acknowledged frame of reference in which continued cuts to mental health services alongside longstanding social inequality and injustice, particularly for women and mothers, vulnerable or otherwise, in itself presents significant challenges for those seeking to work positively with women on an individual basis. Nevertheless it remains important to continue to strive for positive and supportive engagement with women and mothers experiencing mental distress.

There's No Health Without Mental Health

There can be no doubt that 'good' mental health can be affected by a range of individual, biological, and socio-economic and environmental factors. Not everyone faces the same challenges and subsequently challenges to mental health. Living with discrimination, disadvantage, victimisation, addictions, homelessness or domestic abuse will obviously bear some relevance to our mental wellness.

Nevertheless our mental health is something that we all need to safeguard and be supported in safeguarding; it is crucial to how we are able to function and interact in society; it tends to determine how we are perceived by others and also how we are treated by friends, family, employers and professionals. Acknowledgement of this has translated into political and social catchphrases such as 'There's No Health without Mental Health' published in 2011 and endorsed by the then Coalition government urging that, 'Mental Health is everyone's business' and that a 'Call to action is needed' (HM Government 2011:5).

Whilst this earnest message and worthwhile plea is to be commended in terms of its acknowledgement that good mental health and resilience are fundamental to our physical health, relationships, employment chances and potential; it gives no consideration of the fact that women's and arguably especially mothers' relationships with, or indeed their willingness to discuss their mental health, is a complex and often uncharted area of their private and public life. This often hidden aspect of ourselves and our reluctance for it to emerge can be rooted in historical negative associations of women and 'madness', which are also linked to sexuality, deviancy and criminality or a fear of judgement of its impact on our ability to 'mother'. The reality for mothers experiencing mental distress is that they are 'othered', seen differently to non-mentally ill mothers and often perceived as deviating against their nature by selfishly letting their own emotions get in the way of their (natural) parenting duties (Rich 1995). Additionally, the reality for mothers in the criminal and social justice systems is that they are often disadvantaged as a result of discrimination, inequality, weakened socio-economic positions, and victimisation (Carlen and Worrall 2004; Corston 2007; Baldwin 2015a) — all relevant factors when it comes to mental wellbeing.

We all have mental health. It is a continuum that none of us can avoid and yet this reality of 'othering' for mothers experiencing mental distress is, according to De Beauvoir (1949), unavoidable in human thought. She argued that societies create a concept of the 'other' by constructing social categories as binary opposites. This helps to develop a sense of identity, clarifies social positions and offers people a sense of belonging.

> 'Thus it is that no group ever sets itself up as the One without at once setting up the Other over against itself.' (De Beauvoir 1949:6)

She argued that 'woman' is set up as the other of 'man', making masculinity a norm by which social ideas about humanity are defined and developed. Developing categories of otherness entails the polarisation of groups, which generally translates into the formation of relationships between the 'norm group', and the 'others', which are unequal. Other feminists including Firestone (1972) developed this further by arguing that patriarchal structures imposed on women have caused gender inequalities played out *through* biology and the physical, social and psychological disadvantages imposed by pregnancy, childbirth, and subsequent child-rearing.

Social stigma, fear and a lack of understanding about mental health and our own feelings and responses to it are often the real issues when working with women and for mothers experiencing mental distress. Indeed many mothers who are experiencing mental distress additionally experience the very real fear that reporting feelings of anxiety, depression and/or struggling to cope, addiction — even to non-mental health service professionals such as post-natal midwives and health visitors — may trigger either an informal or formal assessment from children's services. The first chapter of *Mothering Justice* suggests:

'In order to avoid what they fear is the inevitable and unwelcome "intrusion" of child services; mothers may disengage, minimise their symptoms and fears or deny them altogether. Thus meaning for some mothers the opportunity to secure real help and positive support is at best delayed at worst lost.' (Baldwin 2015d).

It is however important to reiterate that intervention can also be an opportunity to work positively with people suffering mental distress and a means to ensuring an individual has access to appropriate sources of support. This can be particularly important in relation to mothers and may mean the 'difference between a family staying together with support or even the difference between life or death for mothers children' (Baldwin 2015d); as is tragically demonstrated in such poignant cases as those mentioned in that chapter.

Pause for Thought

Think back to Fiona Anderson, Charlotte Bevan and Tania Clarence for example in *Chapter 1* and perhaps to your reaction to their stories.

In addition, perhaps practitioners often 'expect' more of mothers in terms of the parental and caring role, therefore our expectations are at times unrealistically high and governed by cultural and societal beliefs about the 'ideal' of mother which we can all unconsciously subscribe to.

Pause for Thought — 'Othering'

Consider how mothers with mental health issues are 'othered' in your own particular area of work? What kind of thinking, theories and legislation supports this process and enables it to occur? What more personal assumptions, expectations and associations run in parallel to motherhood that again enable 'othering' to occur? What do you need to do to safeguard against the 'othering' of mothers experiencing mental distress? What government policies and societal pressure can hinder 'safeguarding'?

What generally, however, separates the mentally 'well' from the 'unwell' are simply different formative experiences, differences in resilience and coping strategies, differences in biology, opportunity, circumstances, disasters, loss and social and economic conditions. Perhaps it could be suggested we have more in common with one another in terms of our experiences of oppression than we care to think we do. Essentially we are separated by 'luck', by dint of where, how and the families we were born into, should you see it that way.

History's Imprint

Hysteria was the first label to be given to women experiencing mental distress. The *Kahun Papri* (a collection of Egyptian texts written in the second millennium BC) 'identifies the cause of hysterical disorders in spontaneous uterus movement within the female body' (Tasca, *et al* 2012:111). This explicit linking of 'madness' to a woman's physiology set in motion the feminisation of mental health, whereby a woman's mental distress became firmly located in cultural and historical notions of womanhood and motherhood (being the weaker sex, being more vulnerable and emotional compared to men). Indeed the diagnostic criteria for borderline personality disorder remains focused on 'instability' and 'impulsivity' mirroring the earlier links to a woman's 'spontaneous uterus' and thus reinforcing ties to biology. Hysteria was also fairly arbitrarily applied to women who appeared to be deviating against embedded societal beliefs of women (and arguably especially mothers) that defined how they should behave and live. This gave rise to concerns about a woman's 'wantonness' which translated into a lack of femininity and deviation from expected social norms. Such links led Chesler (1989:115) to conclude that:

> 'Women by definition, are viewed as psychiatrically impaired—whether they accept or reject the female rôle—simply because they are women'.

Two broad treatments for women and their 'madness' emerged; one located in demonology, the other in science. The first sought to provide cure by 'treating' women via sex or sexual abstinence, punishment and purification via herbs and fire, and/or removal of the womb in order to 'remove the hysteria' (Indeed the term hysterectomy comes from the association of 'madness' emanating from the womb); whereas the second sought to *clinically* study the disease. These dominant patriarchal approaches to mental health still resonate today offering-up views that women are weaker and more vulnerable to mental health disorders *because* of their inherent biological and specifically hormonal pre-dispositions; thereby suggesting that women are easily influenced by organic degeneration and susceptible to the supernatural making them somehow guilty and implicit in their own 'madness'. Society fears women who deviate from gender specific rôles and behaviour, thus making women who display ongoing signs of mental distress a target of perceived non-compliance, in relation to embedded stereotypes around womanhood and motherhood, and therefore in need of treatment, cure and ultimately control.

Mothers who find themselves in contact with the criminal justice or health and social care systems as a result of their mental health are still, perhaps arguably more so, vulnerable to these associations. They are at risk of being treated and assessed based on anxieties and fear about 'what they might do' (e.g. deviate from societal norms) and whom they might 'do it to' such as their children, rather than 'what they need' to regain a more healthy and settled mental state (Baldwin 2015d; Quamby 2011). (See also the case study on Hope later in this chapter).

Pause for Thought — Considering the sources of our knowledge:

Reflect on where your knowledge about women, mothers and mental health comes from — Consider your thoughts on women having a biological disposition that lends itself to mental health problems? As women do we challenge or perpetuate the 'myth' of hormones? — Consider how you feel about the term 'deviant women'. What does this mean to you? Is it related to or influenced by a cultural or a historical context? — Particularly in respect of sexual or maternal conduct for example?

The importance of taking time to reflect on such questions is essential to working positively with women experiencing mental distress, because how *we* feel about mental health is *crucial* to our interactions with women experiencing mental distress. How we feel about women who display mental distress, specifically mothers, needs to be considered. One's ability to interact ethically, without prejudice and to engage supportively and positively with women (with or without children) requires that we examine our own fears, values, stereotypes and views. This notion of reflexivity allows practitioners to engage with their own feelings, understand where their views are coming from and how much of what they feel is based on their own experiences and frustrations—and to what extent these may be influencing their responses, feelings and decisions. Self-awareness is crucial to your perceptions of 'risk' and how it can be managed. However, often when children are a feature in mental health work with women, the professional burden of making the 'right' decision can feel heavier and (unconsciously) subject to influence by some of the historical issues already discussed together with knowledge of cases when things have 'gone wrong'. Additionally, when working from a multi-agency perspective (i.e. where many agencies are involved with one mother) there can be 'competing priorities' that have a further impact in relation to mothers and their outcomes in terms of support or treatment.

The following questions are useful to ask yourself when working with mothers experiencing mental distress:

Pause for Thought—Acknowledging yourself:

How do you feel about mental illness?

Why do you feel angry/sad/frustrated with this case?

Where do your feelings stem from?

Do you have expectations of this mother based on your expectations of all mothers?

What is influencing your decisions?

Are you conflicted /challenged by what is best for the mother and what is best for the child—How can the needs of both be met?

Mental Health and the Law

It is worth spending some time considering the powers that mental health legislation contains in England and Wales (chiefly within the Mental Health Act 1983 (MHA 1983) as amended). An adult can be detained against their will if they have committed a crime, seeking asylum (and are being held at a detention centre) *or* if they are deemed so mentally unwell that they pose an unacceptable level of risk to themselves or others. It is worth spending some time considering this fact; that people experiencing mental distress (and asylum seekers trying to find a safe space, though that is for another book) can lose their liberty in in a similar way to people who have committed a crime.

The MHA 1983 sets out the legal grounds on which a person can be admitted, detained and treated in hospital against their wishes. Because the 1983 Act has different sections, this process is often referred to as 'being sectioned'. However, in reality it ought to be described as undergoing an assessment with a view to securing an appropriate outcome (that is also the least restrictive). This distinction is important because language has power, awareness of power has particular significance in situations such as MHA assessment where there is an absolute 'imbalance of power' present in the relationship between the people being assessed and the persons responsible for the assessment. The 1983 Act, although it may feel prohibitive and oppressive, particularly to those detained against their will, is also 'protective', and covers the rights a patient has, how a patient can leave hospital and what aftercare they can and should receive. However in practice how far the majority of psychiatric patients really understand their rights in relation to detention is arguably questionable and something which organizations such as Re-Think Mental Illness and MIND seek to address. People who are compulsorily detained ('sectioned' in common parlance) under the MHA have the right to have an independent mental health advocate (IMHA) and to appeal against their detention at a Mental Health Review Tribunal (following admittance into hospital). In reality, very few exercise this right.

To consider whether someone needs to be in psychiatric hospital under a formal sectioning (detained *against their will*, but in their best interests) the assessment has to be completed by *two* doctors one of whom has to be a specialist registrar in psychiatry and an adult mental health practitioner (AMHP). An AMHP is usually (though since the 2007 amendments not confined to) a social worker who has undertaken additional specialist training in the field of mental health. The role of the AMHP is to bring an independent special perspective to any given assessment. A person cannot be sectioned without the agreement of the AMHP who must make the application and ensure that the person is conveyed to hospital safely and securely.

A section 2 application entails being detained for a period of assessment for *up to* 28 days whereas a section 3 application involves detention for a period of treatment for *up to six* months. It is possible for both a section 2 or 3 order to be 'discharged' earlier or extended (although section 2 would generally be converted to a section 3 if compulsory detention were still felt necessary). Leaving the psychiatric hospital under either of these sections is not permitted until someone, usually a psychiatrist, deems it fit for the individual to do so. Alternatively, following a period of enforced assessment and treatment a person may decide to remain in hospital informally. An 'informal patient' is one who may have been *admitted* into psychiatric hospital in a *voluntary* capacity, i.e. they have agreed to go to hospital and have the capacity to consent (in an informed way) to this, or they may have become an 'informal' patient when their section expired or was discharged. Other than support in the community, informal admission would be the 'least restrictive' option and one that has to be considered in any assessment (section 4 MHA 1983).

Alternatively, someone may be detained for only a short period, for example 72 hours under an emergency section 4 (that section is used where there are considered to be grounds for detention but insufficient time to meet the criteria for a section 2 or section 3 order in terms of practitioners being available for example). A section 4 cannot be renewed and would need to be converted under an appropriate section prior to the expiry of the 72 hours or else the person concerned must be discharged. Additionally, a person may be detained by the police under a 'place of safety order' (section 136). A place of safety has traditionally been a police cell or a hospital, psychiatric or otherwise.

The aim of such legislation is to allow people to be kept safe whilst their mental health is assessed and/or treated. The magnitude of being being detained under the MHA (commonly known as 'being sectioned') should, however, never be underestimated. The loss of liberty and stigmatising effects of can have far-reaching impacts in terms of employment, separation from children, driving and international travel restrictions and should never be influenced by unfair perceptions of mothers and mental illness or seen as a quick fix to a presenting 'problem' or a means of securing access to services.

Medical Versus Social: Competing Priorities and Perspectives

There are two broad perspectives that locate and treat mental distress; the medical model; and the social model. Historically these have been somewhat mutually exclusive; though in more recent years there has been a shift towards integration (Royal College of Nursing 2014; Priest 2012). The push for integration of health and social care services remains firmly on the agenda and the concept of multi-agency working is embedded in knowledge, if not always in practice (Home Office 2013). Key elements of the MHA 1983 can be related to inter-agency guidelines for effective practice related to aftercare (section 117) and the Care Programme Approach (CPA). Further details and an overview of CPA can be found using the *Student Online Resource Bank* in the *Appendix* to this book. This multi-agency integrated approach has to be regarded as essential, especially in relation to mothers and children — perhaps particularly important when the needs of the mother may contradict or be complicated by the needs of the child (This is referred to in more detail in the Social Work chapter (which deals with child protection) (*Chapter 3*)). The benefits of a multi-agency approach is that it has created some space for the forging of relationships between professionals and the opportunity for professionals to be more open to one anothers' organizational aims, objectives, perspectives and culture. I have delivered safeguarding training to senior safeguarding leads in the NHS and they informed me (anecdotally) that they had seen success in the Multi Agency Safeguarding Hubs (MASHs) that were now operational in their areas. They have found that the sharing and pooling of expertise of health and social care is invaluable when safeguarding children and adults and understanding their needs. Indeed a continued commitment and appetite for such working structures will hopefully provide more safeguards for children and identify support for mothers who may be experiencing mental distress. This is crucial to preventing a repeat of cases similar to that of Fiona Pilkington (Equality and Human Right Commission 2014) whose case mentioned in *Chapter 1* is further discussed in the Police chapter (*Chapter 4*)—again highlighting the importance placed on inter-agency working and communication.

Arguably, the medical model of mental illness locates the 'problem' within the individual in terms of the presence (or absence) of pathology. It seeks to treat the 'problem' with medical interventions (drugs and therapies) to cure the patient. The 'expert' is usually the doctor and not the patient. The focus is on the individual who experiences the problem, rather than the wider circumstances that may have led to the problem. Such an approach can lead to 'victim blaming' and a 'colour and culture blind' approach that negates the impact of racism and subsequent manifestations of structural inequalities in social, political, employment and health arenas (Thompson 2011). Indeed Bushfield (1996) and Fernando (2010) note an individual focus as proposed by the medical model effectively hides patriarchal and racist processes that underpin the structures of services designed to support women experiencing mental distress.

A social model of mental illness looks at wider societal structures and processes which impact on a woman's mental health. Specifically, it considers how patriarchy, abuse, victimisation and socialisation can impact of a woman's mental health, further compounded by ideas and ideals of motherhood. Indeed Ussher (1991) argues that women's experience of distress and oppression gets unfairly constructed as mental disorder.

> 'Women are not mad merely because of our hormones, our genes, our faulty learning, our cognition or our unconscious desires. Our madness is not an illness; it is disguised as such by the legally worded classifications meted out to women. And why is it women who are mad? Why is it that it has always been women? Is this madness actually the result of misogyny, as many feminists would claim, and are the symptoms not madness at all, but anger or outrage?' (Ussher 1991:6)

As noted earlier, these models do not have to be mutually opposing and practitioners need to be aware of the potential dangers of following either one too rigidly. It is important to consider the histories and contexts of the women and mothers that we are working with and understand that these cannot be divorced from their presenting symptoms. According to Thompson (2011:138):

'An uncritical acceptance of mental health problems can therefore be seen as highly problematic in terms of the potential for discrimination and oppression.'

Pause for Thought — Which 'fit'?

Reflect on which model fits best for you and why?

Reflect on which model fits best with your organization?

Consider how you can integrate the two models in your practice — What are the challenges to such integration?

The potential impact of an uncritical acceptance of the information of a mother's presentation, or the ridged application of a given model is evidenced in the next section which utilises three case studies to demonstrate areas of good practice and to explore some of the themes that have already emerged in this chapter.

Case Studies — An Opportunity to Apply Your Thoughts

The case study examples are located in my experiences of assessing women and mothers under the MHA 1983 for possible detention in hospital. They are composites of actual cases and are not based on one single case. The themes and practice issues that emerge are not, however, unique to this context and can be considered and utilised by all who come into contact with women and mothers experiencing mental distress. The key issue here is to encourage critical interaction and reflections in relation to the information presented, and to locate your thinking in a reflective perspective that encompasses self-awareness, particularly in terms of your responses to the questions that have already been posed.

Hope: Meaning a feeling of expectation and desire for a particular thing to happen

One of my first assessments as an adult mental health practitioner (AMHP) involved undertaking a Mental Health Act assessment on 'Hope' a white woman in her 30s who had a diagnosis of schizophrenia and lived alone with her two-year-old daughter. Her brother had called in expressing concerns that his sister was not compliant with her medication and appeared to be experiencing a relapse. He was familiar with the system and requested a Mental Health Act assessment on the basis that he felt his sister needed to be in a psychiatric hospital.

Hope was assessed at her brother's home where she had been staying since he had noticed that she first appeared to be relapsing (around a week ago). During the assessment she expressed that the Devil was talking to her and asking her to select a family member to kill. She said that he had advised her that if she did not do this he would select one and do it for her; she said that she was scared for her daughter whom she 'loved most in the world.' All eyes went to her two-year-old daughter who was whizzing around the room on a little trike singing loudly and bashing into furniture. Immediately we were all engaged in an unspoken risk assessment that we had to protect this child from her mother; this became the focus.

What became clear was that Hope's ability to contribute to the assessment further was compromised (in our minds) by the level of risk she appeared to present. Her insight into her condition and desire to protect her child, despite the fact she had after all agreed to move in with her brother when requested, and she had had agreed to the assessment and engaged honestly with us during it expressing her fears, was lost and minimised as we focussed on her potential 'deeds' and potential risk of harm rather than her strengths. The psychiatrists felt that a section 3 was appropriate as she had a clear and longstanding diagnosis and was clearly evidencing a relapse which meant treatment (section 3) rather than assessment (section 2) was needed. For Hope, 'treatment' at home was not considered appropriate due to her advanced state of relapse and practical considerations around her remaining at her brother's home and his ability to support her fully due to his work pattern. The fact that informal admission was not considered initially was on reflection unusual.

Hope had insight into the fact that her mental health was deteriorating, she wanted and needed a safe place, and she was able to give informed consent. The decision around an informal admission was heavily debated by those of us involved in the assessment, but eventually it was this option we took forward. She remained in hospital informally for a little under two months and her brother, his wife and extended family cared for her daughter. She was reunited with her daughter on discharge and supported by her family, social services and a community psychiatric nurse (CPN) to gradually assume full-time care of her daughter.

▍▍ Pause for Thought — Competing Priorities

Why might the psychiatrist have initially preferred the section 3 option?
Reflect on any fears you may have about mothers harming their children. What are they based on and what factors influence them?
How do you manage and balance your fears about risk with the some-times competing needs and rights of a mother and her child(ren)?
How might this have 'played out' had Hope been detained formally rather than informally? What does this show us about the power of professionals?

Idi: A Zimbabwean girl's name meaning truth (the quality or state of being true)

Idi is a black mother of two in her 30s from Zimbabwe, who had been arrested by the police for public disorder and criminal damage. She had been reported to the police by neighbours, as a result of her walking up-and-down the street pulling windscreen wipers from cars. She had also resisted arrest. Once processed through police custody, concerns emerged about her mental health. She was reported to be talking to herself, unable to follow a coherent conversation and suspicious of all who tried to engage with her.

A Mental Health Act assessment was requested following assessment by the forensic medical examiner (FME—police doctor). The feedback from the FME was that she appeared to be experiencing psychosis and possibly showed signs of schizophrenia. There was limited information available as she had only been in the UK for one year.

She would not come out of her cell to meet with us despite our coaxing her and so the interview took place inside her cell, a far from ideal scenario. Idi remained standing in the corner, pressed up against the wall throughout. During interview she presented as responding to internal stimuli and was guarded and thought disordered, (i.e. appeared to be responding to an internal dialogue). Much of what she said was difficult to follow, but she made reference to feeling persecuted ('people were after her') and said that her family in Zimbabwe had been murdered by 'the Freemasons'. Idi said that they were coming for her and her children (girls eight and 13). She was suspicious of who we were and disbelieving of us even when given our ID badges to examine.

After the interview the discussion with the doctors was around the risks Idi posed to herself and others, specifically her children with a clear focus on aspects of her presentation that could be linked to evidence of a mental disorder (medical model). Moving the focus to her social, personal and potential historical experiences enabled a more holistic assessment to take place (social model). Being open to the idea that she had experienced brutality in Zimbabwe, and that members of her family had indeed died, was crucial to ensuring oppression and discrimination did not flourish. Her fear of us and persecutory thoughts were likely to be based in reality and we had to be open and give consideration to this, or else fall into a culture and colour blind approach. Rates of diagnosis in terms of schizophrenia for black people are disproportionate compared to white people and they are more likely to be medicated for any type of mental disorder than white people (Fernando 1991; Fearon et al 2006; Bhugra and Gupta 2010).

Idi was detained under section 2 MHA 1983 and admitted to hospital. Support at home was not felt to be appropriate given her advanced mental distress; she appeared to be experiencing an acute psychotic episode. She would not consent to an informal admission and her capacity to do this was felt to be very limited at the time of assessment. She had no known history of mental disorder or diagnosis and so 'assessment' (section 2) rather than 'treatment' (section 3) was required. Her children, who had been looked after by a neighbour since the point of her arrest, were placed in foster care as no-one else could be identified to care for them (the neighbour was unable to do so beyond the immediacy of the situation).

Idi remained in hospital for 28 days during which time she was referred to the local Community Mental Health Team (CMHT) and supports were put in place for her discharge for both her and her children, in the form of social work home visits, access to counselling and an allocated mental health practitioner via the CMHT. During her stay in hospital, she had telephone contact with her children, letters, pictures and drawings were exchanged and two visits were facilitated by social services. In hospital she disclosed sexual abuse, oppression and homelessness in Zimbabwe linked to the fact she had been raped. She was diagnosed with an episode of psychosis and post-traumatic stress disorder and reunited with her children upon discharge.

‖ Pause for Thought

Consider the impact of factors such as abuse, migration, displacement and the need for asylum on mental health grounds.

Reflect on how Idi may have felt during the assessment in terms of a Mental Health Act assessment possibly adding to trauma — What can/ should be done to minimise further trauma and fear?

What positive supports would assist Idi and her children in order to avoid relapse or in the event of relapse?

Joy: Meaning a feeling of great pleasure and happiness

The opening quote at the start of this chapter is from Joy a white British mother in her 20s with three children. At the time of my assessment she was pregnant with her fourth baby. All three children were in care and there were plans for her new born to be removed at birth. Joy was well-known to the police, mental health and social care services. She experienced a chaotic and abusive childhood that was punctuated by periods in care. As a child she was diagnosed with attachment and conduct disorder, which later progressed into a diagnosis of personality disorder around her 18th-birthday.

▌▌ Pause for Thought

Personality disorder is not usually diagnosed in children and young people; conduct disorder is the more usual diagnosis for under-18s. A level of vigilance is always required when being alerted to children having a conduct disorder as it can often be a precursor to a personality disorder diagnosis later in life.

Joy was regularly picked-up and detained under a section 136 by the police. Section 136 contains a police power under the MHA 1983 which allows a police officer to move 'a person who is in a place to which the public have access, to a place of safety, if the person appears to the police officer to be suffering from a mental disorder and to be in need of immediate care and control, if the police officer believes it necessary in the interests of that person or for the protection of others' (and see Mental Health Code of Practice 2015:114). The person is taken to a place of safety where they are assessed within a maximum of 72 hours, by the same procedure under the Mental Health Act 1983 as already outlined earlier in this chapter.

Joy would go to various car parks, bridges and the train station and threaten to jump from the buildings or else onto the train tracks. She would call the police who would arrive on the scene and use their powers under section 136 to remove her from danger and take her to a place of safety. During this process, she would lash out physically, spit and be verbally abusive. These events (at the time) happened up to four times a month.

As has already been noted in this chapter, working with mothers with a diagnosis of personality disorder can be challenging. Historically (and to a lesser extent nowadays) mental health and social care professionals have felt that dealing with personality disorder obscured the 'real work' of treating people with discrete mental illnesses. As such 'Individuals living under the label of personality disorder were frequently excluded from health services and often were explicitly disliked by practitioners' (Pickersgil 2013:33).

Papers such as Lewis and Appleby's (1998) 'Personality Disorder: The Patients Psychiatrists Dislike' highlighted this disdain. Their study examined psychiatrists' attitudes towards personality disorder, and noted that patients characterised with these disorders were described as 'manipulative, attention-seeking, and annoying' (Lewis and Appleby 1998:45). My experience in interactions with police, probation and mental health practitioners would also suggest that such views still need to be challenged .

There was however a slow sea change helped by policy documents such as 'Personality Disorder: No Longer a Diagnosis for Exclusion' (National Institute for Mental Health in England 2003) and the removal of the so-called 'treatability' test, following the 2007 amendments to the MHA 1983. The treatability test required the relevant decision-maker to determine whether medical treatment was 'likely to alleviate or prevent deterioration in the patient's condition' (MHA 1983:23).

People with a diagnosis of personality disorder often fell outside of the treatability test measure as it was felt that hospital admission and medication would be unlikely to impact on or alleviate their symptoms since they were more located in behaviour rather than *genuine* mental illness. The amended MHA (since 2007) brought the definition of mental illness into one single category of 'any disorder or disability of the mind', allowing space for those with a diagnosis of personality disorder to be encompassed by the Act.

Nevertheless, the cycle of presenting behaviour can be as physically wearing for professionals as it can be challenging to service users, and can lead to a feeling of helplessness that quickly moves to frustration. In teams that I have worked in we have tried hard to locate this cyclical behaviour in the context of a 'search for a secure place'. This is arguably not because the women or mothers 'fail', but often about the mother's need to test out relationships and the activation of (protective) well-entrenched behavioural patterns of responding to situations, challenge, relationships and life events in ways that may not be 'safe' for her or for her children (As noted in the Psychotherapist chapter (*Chapter 7*)).

Mothers with a personality disorder diagnosis can have the potential to 'split teams' and align themselves with particular staff at particular times, though usually after a 'falling-out' with one member of the team. Positive feedback in social work is often not forthcoming. To have a service user tell you that you are 'much better' than 'that other member of staff they saw last week, month or year' who 'did not understand them' can be seductive but can cause team disharmony. If I was being honest and posed some of the above reflective questions to myself I would say I felt very distressed by Joy's case history, but this was becoming replaced by frustration with the repeat requests for a MHA assessment often late at night that offered no positive outcome or behavioural pattern change. I was starting to (albeit unconsciously) buy into views that she was wasting time and resources and that she was simply not fit for the task of 'mothering'. My interactions, and ultimately decisions, in relation to her were being influenced by my own feelings and those of my team.

Such honest dialogue with oneself (and ones colleagues) is challenging, it is however what makes us human; it is not about feeling bad about one's feelings or thoughts, it is about being self-aware and ensuring that we safeguard our actions and decisions so that they are not unduly and unethically influenced by our prejudices, perceptions and experiences.

It was during my fourth MHA assessment of Joy in around nine weeks that Joy told me she was 'born faulty'. This was in response to me explaining to her that I really wanted to try and understand why she was in this cycle of threatening to kill herself, calling the police and then being detained, but that I needed her help to help us to understand her and her actions. She silenced the room with her response that she was 'born, bad, disordered and faulty' there were no immediate responses or cries of, 'But that's not true' (even though we knew it was not); such a response seemed utterly disingenuous in the face of such certainty.

The magnitude of what she said in terms of her experience of being told that she was 'bad, faulty and a problem' from those tasked with caring for her, coupled with a professional diagnosis of being personality disordered, that she took to have reinforced these beliefs left us all searching for a positive way forward. It was a stark reminder of the fallibility of professionals and of the many missed opportunities to provide additional and comprehensive support for Joy.

Joy's fourth child was adopted. She has had no further children. She continues to self-harm, call the police and threaten suicide. She continues to try and survive in the face of adversity, misunderstanding, and limited support networks and cuts to mental health services.

|| Pause for Thought

What do you think the future will hold for Joy? What do you think the future will hold for Joy's children? What would help Joy most do you think?

For many women like Joy, this pattern ultimately extends and ends with prosecutions and sooner or later prison. Spitting and assaulting police officers are offences for which she may eventually be imprisoned, probably for a very short but incredibly disruptive sentence during which, and as a result of which, she is likely to face further issues that may impact on her mental distress, such as homelessness. The Prison Reform Trust and the Corston Report (2007) both highlight the number of women in prison with mental health needs or personality disorder such as Joy. The positive management of women and mothers with such complex needs provides prison staff with similar challenges faced by those supporting women and mothers in the community — the need for positive, reflexive and engaging interventions and conversations remains vital — despite being in what is often described as a 'secure setting'.

One might question just how safe and 'secure' women in prison feel. Women like Joy don't leave their mental health needs at the gate — since 1991 (and as at the time of writing) 102 women have committed suicide in prison, many of them mothers. Furthermore 46 per cent of women in prison, like Joy, have previously attempted suicide at some point in their lives. Many women in prison or released are 'dealing with complex issues as a result of the fallout of pain-filled lives on top of anxieties about and separation from their children' (Baldwin 2015a, 179.10: 197-198). The

Prison Reform Trust highlights that, like Joy, 14 per cent of imprisoned mothers lose their children to local authority care and for many of those it will be months or years before they can be reunited—sometimes if ever.

Best Hopes: Continued Commitment to Reflective Practice and Constructive Conversation

There is no easy or 'one size fits all' solution or way of working with mothers experiencing mental distress. Such women are not a homogenous group; their experiences are located, as previously stated, within the private and political spheres of their lives and often defined by the interplay between their age, ethnicity, social class, sexuality and economic positions. My best hope was that this chapter was designed for you to develop your own insights and to locate the impact of your own experiences and beliefs in terms of how you view and interact with mothers experiencing mental distress as a fellow human being but importantly as a practitioner—where arguably you hold power.

It is hoped the chapter has secured a commitment in you to developing 'constructive conversations', building on best practice and ensuring that reflexivity is an essential and embedded component of your working life. It is only by asking yourself questions about how you feel, why you feel and what is impacting on your feelings that you can create a safe place to practice both for you and those that you come into contact with. In addition, engaging with women's personal narratives and experiences is essential in the field of mental health to safeguard against oppression and discrimination. Fine (1993) sums up the importance of being 'real' in our 'work' by telling us to:

> 'Watch me with my women friends, my son, his father, my niece or my mother, and you will see what feels most authentic to me. These very moments which construct who I am when I am most me, remain remote from the psychological studies of individuals or even groups.' (1992:16)

CHAPTER 3

Damned if You Do, Damned if You Don't
Frontline Social Worker Perspective

Cassandra Barnes

This chapter presents an insight into the challenges faced when working from a child protection social work perspective with vulnerable mothers. It reflects the position of the social worker and endeavours to explore the perspective of the mother. The chapter aims to highlight the significance of positive, open and honest relationships between mothers and social workers, exploring the impact of factors such as power and fear, which can be inevitable features in a relationship between a child protection social worker and a mother. It is less a description of legislation, policy and rôle and more a reflection on how, in situations that are often emotionally charged, it remains possible to 'practice positively' with mothers whilst still fulfilling a statutory responsibility to protect children.

The gives a brief historical perspective in relation to child protection social work. It then reflectively explores the relationship between child protection social workers and mothers. Case studies and opportunities to 'Pause for Thought' are used to encourage critical practice, reflection and to challenge the reader to empathise with mothers and social workers who meet in extremely difficult situations. In addition it offers tips for good practice and identifies gaps in service provision or missed opportunities to work positively with mothers and children which are found in contemporary child protection social work practice.

The enormity of effects social work decisions and interventions have on children's and mothers' lives is precisely why research into effective practice is highly pertinent (Holland 2010). Only then will social work intervention increase in effectiveness and improve outcomes for the children and families who come into contact with social care services (Horwath 2009).

'It is a matter for politicians to decide what risks to a child their country's child protection agencies should prioritise, but the experience in Britain shows how a shift in emphasis can have quite unintended consequences for practice.' (Munro 2008: 61)

Contemporary social work practice, in line with political paradigms, places significant focus on the need for combining child protection with supporting families (Featherstone *et al*, 2013). This has been debated in policy, research and academia, with arguments being made across the spectrum. Society will always need a social work system but that system has to believe people, parents and especially mothers can and do 'change.' Often the most difficult decisions as a social worker involve determining an acceptable timeframe for a child to 'wait' for such changes to occur particularly in a culture of cuts to service provision which can mean supportive services to mothers might not be available or may be delayed.

Social work practice is shifting towards the importance of early intervention and family support in order to protect children (Department of Education 2011; HM Government 2013). It is widely accepted, not least within the Children Act 1989, that children are best placed within their family (HMSO 1998). 'In all but the extreme cases the birth family is seen as the best place for a child to be nurtured' (Munro 2008:1). Removing children from their mothers is a highly contested subject, with service user and pressure groups advocating increasing support to ensure mothers are well-equipped to meet their child(ren)'s need(s) (Aldgate and Statham 2001; Turney *et al*, 2011). The statutory guidance 'Working Together to Safeguard Children' (2013, 2015) advocates the significance of early help across services. Early help is more effective in promoting the welfare of children than reacting later (D of E 2015). This means that within the government and social work field it is accepted that providing access to services to support positive family functioning is more effective than attempting to rectify the impact of parenting when mothers have not had access to such support. Despite this, practice focuses on the sections within legislation that address children at risk of significant harm more intensively than those provisions that focus on supporting families (Parton 2002). The deaths of Victoria Climbié and

Peter Connelly reinforced a child protection orientation that has arguably led to the lowering of child protection thresholds (Platt 2006; Laming 2003). Furthermore, the Public Law Outline changes in 2014 halved the care proceedings timescale from 52 to 26 weeks. Mothers will inevitably be penalised with the permanent removal of their children given that six months is not sufficient for them to make, evidence and maintain necessary positive change.

Social work at its core is required to be undertaken in an anti-oppressive non-judgemental manner. It is key that social workers are mindful of cultural and class idiosyncrasies; basing assessments on factors which, when considered collectively, take into account socio-economic, cultural and individual circumstances, but that do not leave a child in an evidentially vulnerable position. Having no statutory definition of significant harm allows practitioners to exercise discretion to view children's needs within the context of their social environment and consider their resilience. A definition of 'significant harm' within legislation would result in some unnecessary interventions leading to the oppression of mothers whilst other children's experiences would go unnoticed leaving them in risky situations. Furthermore, changes to the notions of childhood, parenting and abuse over time can be adopted by social workers within their assessments and interact with the underpinnings of a worker's personal and professional values.

Pause for Thought

What is your personal view on child discipline? Would you 'smack' your child? Were you smacked as a child? What are the difficulties for social workers in defining the invisible line that once crossed becomes 'too hard'... Would you struggle with this concept as a social worker? As a mother would you know where the 'official' line was?

As social workers are also members of society, their views and values are also subject to change, evolution and interplay with their professional value-base.

'Mothers, it can be said, are child protection. Throughout its history, there has always been one corollary to the aim of keeping children safe: improving how women mother their children.' (Ferguson 2011:137)

'Motherhood' is a social construct formed throughout generations, subject to cultural influence telling us how to mother a child. Our experiences of mothering shape our identities as mothers and as successful women. Failing as a mother is to fail as a woman and to fail as a woman is to fail in society (Bloomfield *et al*, 2005). The emotions attached to such successes or failures interact and inform our future experiences and the cycle continues (Rutman *et al*, 2002). For example, failing as a mother often leads to depression, low self-worth and demotivation leaving women vulnerable to manipulation, exploitation and further 'failings' (*Ibid*).

In order to strive for change, we must understand the current function of the system; recognising the experiences of mothers in receipt of statutory service provision in a climate of cuts to services is critical to evaluating shortfalls in practice (Rutman *et al*, 2002). Developing different ways to engage mothers assists with this understanding. A common denominator between mothers and social workers is that both strive to achieve the child's best interests. Without support, positive engagement, motivation and commitment of the mother, whom a significant proportion of the intervention targets, these interests will not be achieved. Whilst the pathway to accomplishing this can cause friction and disagreement, the social worker and mother at least have a mutual goal.

Removing children from their mothers is a difficult, challenging and emotional task. There will never be a time when having to do this is not experienced thus. Key to working positively with mothers during this period is to spend time building relationships, being honest and transparent about your thoughts and professional opinions, and basing these on evidence. Explaining this as often as possible, and in different ways, will also help. This is particularly crucial when considering the diverse needs of mothers; mothers whose first language is different to your own, mothers who abuse substances or alcohol and are not always able to hear messages, mothers who have learning difficulties or mental health issues and require messages to be delivered via a medium they will understand, and teenage mothers who have not themselves worked through developmental stages in adolescence before becoming responsible for a child themselves (Sugarman 2001).

> **║ Pause for Thought**
>
> Think about what it must feel like to have a child taken, or to take a crying child from, their mother. How should the 'aftermath' for mother and social worker be dealt with? What would help or hinder this? Does this happen?

Knowledge is Power

Mothers need to know why your view differs from their own, they need to know what led you to that decision, and these decisions need to be based on tangible evidence. Giving mothers specific examples of why you feel they are unable, at this point, to meet their child's needs is essential. For example, it is far harder to understand, 'You can't meet Scott's emotional or physical needs and so the only option is for someone else to do this' than 'Scott is showing evidence of emotional distress through his night terrors, soiling and hurting himself at school and this worries us. There are too many times when Scott is not fed enough and he has been stealing and storing food in school. Scott has also told that he is scared at home and doesn't know how to cope with these feelings. We need to all work together to understand what's important to Scott and how to support him to grow up happy and healthy'.

Whilst I am not suggesting social workers lead with the former approach, the example is used to show that mothers who understand why you are worried for their child and can give factual evidence for this are much more able to understand the actions proposed by the social worker. Leading with a positive would improve this further; too often, understandably, mothers focus on negative aspects of their parenting. Social workers must highlight good elements of a mother's parenting so that motivation to change can be harnessed.

Honest, open communication and, wherever appropriate, involvement in the decision-making process is key to the most positive management of challenging situations for mothers and social workers.

> ## ▮▮ Pause for Thought
>
> Why do you think mothers 'hear' criticism first in parenting assessments? What might social workers (SWs) do to counter this? How differently might the mother experience the two approaches outlined above? How will it help the mother if the SW opens with a positive? If ultimately Scott is going to be removed from her care, do you think it's right that good aspects of her parenting are highlighted? Why? Is there an element of false hope? Or is this an early way to focus Scott's mother on positive parenting when considering whether she has subsequent children?

Without exploring where a mother's issues stem from, you cannot work openly to address them. Only then will mothers begin to trust and be honest with social workers. The power imbalance in the relationship is a barrier to commencing any meaningful intervention (Forrester, Westlake and Glynn 2012). For example, people misusing substances often do so as a coping mechanism for a range of challenging issues, frequently including their own abuse experiences. Mothers may 'block out pain' this way, however this isn't in the child's best interests due to emotional unavailability, physical risks of harm, risky associations and so on. With this recognition comes guilt from mothers who feel they are failing; in order to cope with these failing feelings, further substance use follows and the cycle continues.

> ## ▮▮ Pause for Thought
>
> Think of the 'competing priorities' from the Mental Health chapter (*Chapter 2*), how easily can such issues be resolved and managed? Think of the 'good enough' parenting mentioned in the Psychotherapist chapter (*Chapter 7*)—What falls inside and outside the criteria of 'good

enough'... to you personally and as a statutory body? Can/should they be different?

'Describing an action as abusive always includes a moral judgement' (Munro 2008:56), hence social workers need to reflect on their personal and professional values that influence their perception of the situation (Platt 2006). Mothers, in comparison to workers, are powerless in the relationship (Forrester, Westlake and Glynn 2012). Ultimately the local authority and the courts have the final decision in respect to children's experiences. This threatening relationship demonstrates structural oppression and coercion into meeting the goals set by the local authority.

The social expectation of a 'mother' and the automatic feelings of failure by mothers who have social work intervention can have dramatic consequences on a mother's ability to parent effectively. Women are expected to care for their children despite the difficulties they endure (Ferguson 2011). To feel like a failing mother brings intense emotions that can lead to depression and/or anxiety. These feelings, particularly in relation to substance misuse or severe depression, can lead to mothers harming or being unable to care for their children resulting in statutory intervention.

Pause for Thought

Think about Clare in the Psychotherapist chapter (*Chapter 7*) or Fiona and Charlotte in *Chapter 1* of this book.

Whilst research and academia evidence the need for support services for mothers to improve their ability to meet their own and their children's needs, there continue to be gaps in provision. Where services exist, there are waiting lists, high thresholds and at times minimal packages of support; all factors which compound the difficulties faced by mothers and prolong their journey to positive change.

The Fear of the Knock on the Door

I am the first social worker that knocks on the door of a family following a referral raising concerns about a child. My task is to consider the strengths and assess the risk to the child in its current environment, which then informs my recommendation of intervention and support. This cannot be done without effective relationship-building with mothers and children. Often within a multi-agency setting, the assessment and intervention is informed by mothers relationships with professionals which can lead to debates of how best to support her whilst prioritising the safety her of child(ren).

> 'Mothering is central to occupational constructions of women in child protection work. The focus on the child as client has resulted in a tendency for social workers to respond to mothers only in relation to their impact on children, not as complex subjects in their own right.' (Featherstone 1999, in Scourfield 2000:78)

My statutory responsibility ultimately lies with the protection of the child. This may result in competing and conflicting priorities within a presenting situation. The needs of the mother may differ to the needs of the child; one party's needs may indeed be compounded by the other (Featherstone 1999). For example, a mother may need a residential substance misuse detox in order to effectively parent, but the child may need reinforcement and secure attachment to its mother and both cannot occur simultaneously. An important aspect of working to resolve such issues is to ensure mothers have independent representation of their needs thereby facilitating an open multi-faceted approach in which integrated services can work together. Independent support for mothers can be vital, particularly where there is mistrust and fear on the part of the mother. It must be remembered that many mothers involved with statutory services do not 'trust' easily, particularly those who have experienced a lifetime of breaches of that trust (Baldwin 2015d).

Pause for Thought

How might social workers overcome the initial defensiveness of mothers? What will help 'lowering of barriers' of mothers? What factors are relevant regarding reluctance to engage with social workers — and how do SWs address this? What experiences might mothers have had that might be motivational barriers? Why might some mothers agree to make changes and then achieve this/not achieve this? What would you do to address this with the mother? Think back to Fiona Anderson and Charlotte Bevan. How could they have been enabled to have different outcomes?

Building positive relationships is essential when supporting mothers to trust you, despite the situation that brings you together. It is difficult when, understandably, mothers are fearful of children's services intervention, which can affect the level of information they disclose and the subsequent transparency of the relationship (Waterhouse and McGhee 2009). I have learned the importance of this from witnessing the knock-on effects of implementing the wrong or perhaps less effective decisions in the early stages of contact with families. For example, decisions being based on a wrongly perceived lack of cooperation from mothers which is actually an understandable fear of letting down barriers.

Samantha: A 22-year-old single mother of Charlie six, Lily four

Samantha has struggled to bond with her daughter, Lily (aged four), after she suffered post-natal depression. Samantha previously had a child, Charlie (six) removed from her care due to substance misuse, anti-social behaviour and neglect. She concealed her pregnancy with Lily from professionals due to fear they would report this to Children's Services. Samantha was six months pregnant when Children's Services became aware of it. Due to the previous concerns that led Charlie to be removed, assessments were undertaken to plan for Lily's birth and decide where best, and with what support, she would be cared for. Previous assessments that led Charlie to be adopted were used and this informed care planning. Lily was removed at birth and contact with Samantha was supervised. Her situation had changed since Charlie was removed; whilst often such mothers enter a downward spiral of depression, victimisation and in some cases, more prolific substance misuse, Samantha had reduced her substance use. Whilst this was considered, the impact of her capacity and evidenced ability to maintain change did not appear to significantly affect decision-making—which perhaps requires further reflection on the part of Children's Services. Lily was eventually returned home to her mother with a package of support when she was six-months-old. However, the lasting impact on Samantha and Lily's relationship can be observed within the difficult emotional attachment and Samantha's confidence as a parent, which is compounded by the numerous assessments labelling this as being inadequate. Children's Services failed Lily and Samantha by not utilising the four month window of opportunity from learning about the pregnancy until Lily's birth to assess her current situation and ability to parent, which could have prevented Lily and Samantha being separated once Lily was born.

▌▌ Pause for Thought

If history tells us how to predict the future, do you think decisions can be made from previous reports and assessments? Why do you think this? Do you think this was the right decision? What is a defensible decision? What do practitioners need to support their decisions? Can you imagine how Samantha must have felt—what are the possible future implications—for her and for Lily?

Given 'the way the initial contact is handled has long-term effects on the family's relationships with professionals' (Munro 2008:1), the first home visit with a mother is crucial to building a long-term partnership. Much of my rôle consists of supporting mothers like Samantha in their understanding, learning and insight of their child(ren)'s needs. This itself is a form of intervention; an opportunity to support mothers whilst assessing risk using the power of the professional relationship. Such relationships can propel and motivate mothers into recognising the need for change and focusing their efforts into achieving this for their children and themselves.

Social work will always fulfil a contradictory rôle in society, thus making debates regarding the approach to support and intervention highly pertinent (Garrett 2003; Holland 2010). The most part of my day is not filled with removing children, contrary to media depiction and, more importantly, to most mother's views and fears. Social working with families is exactly that; *with* families. Children are connected to their nuclear and wider families and the adults within these networks learned their own coping, social and parenting skills as children themselves. To understand a mother completely, you must first understand the child within. It is only deserving that when making life-changing decisions about a child, you have all available information and understanding about the child's experiences and potential to be parented. To do this, you need a thorough, critical, reflective and analytical perspective of the mother. To achieve this without having built a relationship with her would be impossible.

It's Not Always a Happy Ending

In circumstances where a mother cannot instil positive change sufficiently in the child's timeframe there are increasingly difficult hurdles to overcome within the working relationship. Such situations require the social worker to explain specifically the evidence that has led to that viewpoint. Mothers need not to feel powerless; this is crucial in working effectively together. If they feel that whatever they say or do won't have any positive effect on the outcomes for their child they understandably are more likely to feel defeated and disengage. Information about the observed impact of parenting on the child can be helpful when supporting parents understanding about how to minimise these effects and build resilience. The physical timelines, intervention and environments from the child's perspective to do this will often provide a platform that denotes the child cannot achieve this in their current environment. Using skills to support mothers to reach similar conclusions in this way is difficult, however remembering to talk about the situation, environment and circumstances her child *needs* to achieve this will support this understanding. This approach supports positive separation which works by encouraging mothers to communicate to their child that it is in their best interests to be cared for by another (Lishman 1991) but that this in no way means they love them less, arguably more. This, though desirable is not always possible due to the immense pain being experienced by mothers and lack of support offered to help them achieve this.

Often, and as is good practice, with mothers whose child is subject to care proceedings and child protection procedures, an advocacy service is sought to work alongside her and support her to communicate her views and understand the situation from an independent perspective (Westad and McConnell 2012). Such agencies are instrumental to mothers' ability to break the repeating cycle a mother may be living in, particularly following the removal of a child. Advocacy agencies support a mother's insight into the situation that led to her child being removed and this is crucial to her sense of being and therefore ability to bring about change. Advocacy and third sector services can remain involved with mothers when children's services have withdrawn (due to the child being removed), and continue working with her in order that when she has subsequent children or is reunited with her child she is enabled to more effectively care for them. They may support her through the separation and continue to work, sometimes with multi-agency involvement, through issues such as self-harm, substance misuse, offending behaviour, relationship issues and lifestyle choices.

▌▌ Pause for Thought

Again, think how different things may have been for Clare (see the Psychotherapist chapter (*Chapter 7*)) and the eight children she had removed if she had had access to this service?

I have often heard from mothers whom I have built positive working relationships with statements similar to 'It's not you I'm angry with, it's the system' or 'I know it's not you doing this.' It is important not to disassociate yourself from the organization and system that governs you, whether that be statutory services or otherwise. However, it is helpful for mothers to have someone/somewhere to vent their negativity towards and it is often beneficial for this not to be their social worker in order to prevent a 'me versus her/him' situation and support a more effective relationship—particularly given the possibility of future involvement with additional children.

> ## ┃┃ Pause for Thought
>
> Is it easier for mothers to internalise or externalise pain and anger (direct towards the system and the social worker (SW)). Why?—What are the dangers of this? How might this feel to SWs if anger is directed at the 'system' rather than themselves?
>
> Think about worker accountability and professionalism but also how the worker wants to maintain positive relationships with mothers. It's important to recognise that 'positive working relationships' need to be just that ... *working*. A relationship that is not honest, available for challenge and constructive criticism in either direction is not positively working. Think about being the mother; if you have had a child removed, how difficult might it be for you to engage positively with children's services again? Particularly if you didn't agree with the removal?
>
> How must it feel to 'have no choice' but to engage or to have to 'prove' you are a capable parent?

It is widely accepted that the most successful indicator of future harm is the presence of past harm (Munro 2008). It must be noted however that such conclusions are reached in the context of contemporary society where mothers are failed by society in the lack of support to effect positive change. No clearer is this issue than when examining the approaches to the removal of subsequent children at birth from their mothers after they have had a previous child removed.

> ## ┃┃ Pause for Thought
>
> Think of Clare and Tilly in the Psychotherapist chapter (*Chapter 7*); had Claire not been in prison and been able to 'evidence' that she had 'changed', realistically it is very likely that Tilly would have been taken into care too?

Any expert assessment conducted within original care proceedings can be drawn upon in subsequent proceedings in order to 'speed up the process of removal'. Often this leaves practitioners facing an emotional dilemma and mothers feeling powerless and voiceless. This highlights the issue of giving a mother 'time' to evidence change against the need to locate the baby in a secure and loving environment. Much like Danielle see later in the chapter), social workers too often feel 'damned if they do and damned if they don't'.

Melissa: Mother of Brian, nine-months-old when removed from her

Brian was removed from Melissa and placed for adoption. The bottom line reason was neglect which included a plethora of unmet basic care needs such as giving him too much or too little milk and food, lack of bathing, proper feeding, failure to change his nappy resulting in sore and painful rashes, lack of supervision meaning Brian incurred a range of injuries from falls or playing with dangerous household objects (bleach, scissors, lighters) and unwise decisions about childcare (leaving him with a range of young people and adults and staying away overnight for long periods). Melissa was a young mother; she fell pregnant at 16 and had no contact with Brian's father, with whom she experienced domestic abuse.

Melissa fell pregnant two months after Brian was placed for adoption to a man with whom she had been in a relationship for two weeks and known for four. She was hurting and was desperate to try to fill the 'hole' in her life left by Brian's removal. Melissa felt she hadn't appreciated him until it was too late. After he was placed for adoption Children's Services stopped working with her—she received little support to manage emotionally or to understand why decisions had been made; in effect Melissa was not prepared or supported to *bring about* change in the event (likelihood) that she mothered subsequent children. Melissa's circumstances hadn't changed; she remained involved with the same network, lived in the same flat, and had limited support from her family only now she had the added factors of immense sadness and feelings of severe depression.

> ## ▌▌ Pause for Thought
>
> What do you think should happen to Melissa's baby? What do you think would be different this time to when Melissa had Brian? What support do you think Melissa needs to bring about change? What support do you think she should have already had? How can professionals work together to stop the cycle of repeat removals of children from their mothers? Given the widely accepted understanding that children in local authority care achieve less positive outcomes than children who remain with their birth family safely, where do you think Melissa's children would best be placed? What do you think will happen to Melissa's children when they become adults or parents themselves?

'My baby is due in three months, so how am I going to live in a single person's night shelter? They (Social Services) have said that if I am still living there when the baby is born that it will be taken off me...that's your answer to that?' (Chase *et al*, 2008)

Young parents report a tendency for social workers to scrutinise care leaver's parenting capacities through the lens of child protection, rather than assessing their needs for support. Child protection assessments are commonly experienced as confusing, intimidating and disempowering, with some young parents complaining that social workers tended to appear on the scene just before the birth of their child in an almost predatory manner (Chase *et al*, 2008).

Chase suggests more attention could be paid to training social workers in sensitising them to the impact of past care experiences on care leavers' adult relationships and parenting. Training to allow social workers to reflect critically on their attitudes to young parents might also be appropriate (*Ibid*). In particular, evidence indicates that better assessments of the support needs of young parents, including young fathers, who are in or leaving care is warranted. Social work practice in relation to pre- and post-birth assessments of looked after young parents should be reviewed to develop a less threatening and more supportive process, particularly in light of the fact that a quarter of girls leaving care already have a child or are pregnant (Chase *et al*, 2013).

Early intervention constitutes universal and targeted services that aim to change the course of parenting and children's experiences rather than react under crisis when children have been adversely affected. For example, accessible mother and baby/toddler groups that support the development of reciprocal relationships between a mother and her child through effective communication, non-verbally initially before moving into verbal communication as the child grows older. This will support mothers to communicate to their child that they are heard, listened to and can manage the child's emotions such as crying, feeling unsafe in new environments and being unsure of unfamiliar faces. The mother can offer containment to their child and this form of positive communication helps the child build trust and a sense of security that helps them feel able to explore their environment and learn positively. Early intervention services are vast and far-reaching; they span agencies including mental health, housing, children's centres, health, schools and police. However with government spending cuts in social care, early intervention services are not prioritised resulting in a gap in service provision for mothers to develop positive parenting strategies and be afforded the opportunities to break the cycle of abuse. Herein lies a deflating feeling that mothers are often failed twice by society; once as a child and again as a mother (Sharpe 2015).

Holland (2010) notes that social workers who prioritise relationship-building within their own communities can help mothers to sustain positive change. The presence of social workers within the community contributes to ongoing support for mothers (*Ibid*). This occurs through developing a common investment in achieving outcomes; if a social worker gives some of themselves to their community and the mothers who live there—a more together approach to achieving change is felt. Mothers who feel that social workers genuinely care about the outcome are more invested into developing positive working relationships. Such community responses to supporting mothers originate from third sector organizations and those with charitable or lottery funding initiatives. Whilst these services are beneficial, they are delivered sporadically across the country. Such initiatives attempt to fill the gap caused by cuts to public sector funding. Arguably, social work origins stem from community-based support services however societal changes and demands to focus on child protection from the public and fuelled by the media have resulted in a 'fire-fighting' response to child protection work. Practice now sees overworked, inexperienced and unsupported social workers with high caseloads and minimal services to draw upon resulting in dangerous decision-making that are service, rather than service-user led—which has a direct impact on mothers and their children.

Pause for Thought

Think about mothers and social work through history — How was it different? Should political paradigms influence decision-making in child protection? Think about how the media and public opinion shape political movements and then the effect this has on social work. What role does the media have in the portrayal of social workers? — Does this 'feed the fear' of mothers? — How /Why?

Child protection social workers can work positively with mothers — assisting them in accessing services such as sponsored nursery places, positive parenting courses, and support groups for parents with disabilities, workshops to understand attention deficit hyperactivity disorder (ADHD) and autism, housing advocacy, emotional relationship-building with their babies and many more. Social work powers within the Children Act 1989 encourage such support to families. However with budget cuts to local authorities, social workers too often find themselves being forced only to carry out their legislative duties (mandatory) rather than use their powers (voluntary) to support families. Herein lies the challenge that society, workers and more importantly mothers face when attempting to break the cycle, and reduce the impact, of deprivation.

Breaking the Cycle of Abuse

Lessons from the Cleveland Enquiry are still being learned nearly 30 years on. The report in 1988 highlighted the need for a multi-agency approach to diagnosing child abuse, specifically child sexual abuse. Over the course of a few months, more than 120 children were diagnosed with having suffered sexual abuse in Cleveland by two paediatricians based on a physical examination of anal dilation. Although it later transpired that many of the children were found to have suffered abuse, most of them were returned to their families after it became apparent that this indicator of sexual abuse was not accurate on its own. High profile deaths and the introduction of ChildLine at the time of the crisis led to increased reporting of sexual abuse and a risk-averse culture amongst social workers who were wary of leaving children in potentially abusive situations. It is known that 90 per cent (Barnardos 2015) of children who are sexually abused are abused by someone who is known to them which means that reporting abuse can be even harder.

But what does this mean for mothers? If the child knows the abuser, it is highly likely that the mother does also. Many mothers may have fallen victim to the same perpetrator themselves, and because of a lived experience of their own which may have involved abusive relationships can mean some mothers are not always best able to protect themselves or their children. Being risk-averse results in more drastic action being taken to ensure the child's safety, which can be to the detriment of a robust offer of support to mothers in order to keep the child safe at home. This results in families being fearful of asking for help — drawing attention to their difficulties and thereby raising the risk children may be removed (Waterhouse and McGhee 2009). This notion is seen by social workers universally and is a difficult barrier to overcome when working with mothers, particularly when working with mothers experiencing domestic rather than sexual abuse.

Danielle: A 31-year-old mother of one, Owen seven

Owen was subject to child protection planning for nine months aged four due to witnessing domestic abuse between his biological parents. Danielle was supported to flee to a refuge with him following a sustained period of domestic abuse, which initially she had tried to hide from friends, family and services. She found Owen's behaviour difficult, and struggled to implement consistent boundaries. Danielle grew-up in a house with few boundaries and, where any existed, they were enforced by violence. Part of the support programme was to assist her in recognising that she had to demonstrate her ability to 'protect' Owen, which included making sure he did not witness further domestic abuse. She spiralled into depression and her self-esteem plummeted. With intervention and support she was enabled to develop local support networks and a reciprocal relationship with Owen, aided by her understanding of her need to be emotionally available to Owen whilst being a positive rôle model who is able to parent with safe discipline. Positive intervention resulted in Danielle feeling a sense of achievement and increased positive self-esteem and eventually statutory services withdrew from the family.

A referral was submitted to Children's Services a year later by a member of the initial refuge that Danielle fled to, with information suggesting Owen's father had moved back to the family home. Once traced and during the home visit, concerns were discussed with her when she appeared honest and denied any contact with Owen's father. I spoke with Owen alone in his room about his family life; he did not mention his Dad. To evidence this further I took a look around the house. I found dad hiding in the cupboard under the stairs. After I dealt with the initial concerns and stabilised the situation

I revisited Danielle and we talked about why she had been dishonest. She stated she was scared; her experience of child protection planning previously made her fearful of being honest about the current situation. She said that she felt she had failed and that social workers would assess this negatively perhaps meaning she'd lose Owen. Danielle told me that whilst she made positive changes previously, she worries she can't sustain them and now that Owen is older he wants to see his dad so she can't keep them separated. She said, 'I'm damned if I do and I'm damned if I don't' meaning that if she rekindled her relationship with his dad social workers would disapprove and, if she didn't, then Owen would blame her.

> ## ▌▌ Pause for Thought
>
> Can you understand why Danielle was dishonest? What must it feel like for Danielle to have been assessed, monitored and reviewed for nine months to then have the threat of another social worker at her door? In what ways do you think social workers can overcome this barrier?

Whilst Danielle was dishonest initially about her situation, her ability to reflect and explain her thought processes aided a better working relationship from this point and we agreed an appropriate plan of support (which offered protection to Owen) without convening a further child protection conference. This support included an agreed contact plan between Owen and his father that was overseen by wider family and that minimised the risk of domestic incidents. She stated she found it difficult to implement a boundary with Owen's father that was to allow him in their lives for Owen but not to re-enter a relationship with him. Therefore supporting Danielle to build skills and confidence in this area was implemented, alongside work with Owen's father that married up with this. After six months of voluntary intervention, Children's Services withdrew from the family once again.

Sangita: A married mother of three, two sons aged five and six and a daughter aged three-and-a-half

Married for seven years Sangita has experienced domestic abuse from her husband from the outset. She is a practising Muslim and we discussed her perceived cultural *expectations* of her as a wife, which were impacting on the children's experiences, namely their witnessing of abuse. She felt she failed as a wife for disclosing the abuse to professionals and was a betrayer of her culture and religion for considering separation. Sangita also felt she failed as a mother for 'allowing' children to witness abuse for a number of years.

Often mothers suffering domestic abuse are judged for their inability to 'prioritise' their children and protect them from the abuser; this singular viewpoint demonstrates a lack of understanding of the complexities of domestic abuse and the difficulties in recognising this as a manipulated and abused mother (Lapierre, 2010).

Supporting mothers experiencing domestic abuse involves building trust between the worker and mother; workers cannot support mothers without the full facts and mothers cannot be honest with workers easily without trusting that the workers' actions and decisions will benefit herself/themselves and child(ren).

Mothers experiencing abuse are victims; their pathway to defining themselves in this situation needs exploration before appropriate support can be offered. Women, mothers in abusive relationships often have low self-esteem, self-worth and lack belief that they deserve an abuse-free relationship or the belief that this is possible. Women are manipulated by their abuser to become dependent on them, isolated from their networks and can be groomed into feeling that they are deserving, moreover lucky, to be in the 'relationship'. When working with such mothers, it is often one of the first tasks to provide an objective view, often using comparisons/examples of abuse free people within their own network such as sisters, mothers, aunts to bring the 'story to life'.

▌▌ Pause for Thought

Is it fair to conclude that Sangita failed to protect her children from domestic abuse? Why is the onus placed on Sangita and not on her husband? When thinking about Sangita within the context of her culture, network and religion, what should she do? What should I have done to support Sangita and protect her children? Do you think it's acceptable for social workers to involve themselves in marital issues in this case? Why is this? How would your view change if Sangita's family did not practise any religion and were white British?

The most common response by others when they learn you are a social worker is 'I don't know how you could do that, I couldn't, I'd be too emotional.' Often when delving further into these views you find yourself trying to convince people you are not cold-hearted, despite the fact you face real-life child abuse and neglect. What is far less common, are the discussions you have about empathy for mothers. I have had people say,

'As a mother, I couldn't do your job, I couldn't face a mother who would do that to their children.' There are a number of issues to reflect on here; does this mean that social workers without children cannot understand or empathise wholly with the child or indeed their mother? Does this affect their ability to be a social worker? What about male social workers? And further because your empathy for mothers who aren't meeting their children's needs is so great when you are a mother yourself, does this affect the social workers who are mothers and their effectiveness in their rôle? Taking this further, I have often been asked by mothers whether I have children myself and frequently been told I was in no position to make recommendations if I did not. As a non-mother, it would be difficult and naïve of me to profess I do know the experiences of mothers. In the same respect I would be unable to do the same for a person abusing illicit substances or managing their bipolar effective disorder. So what does this mean for social workers working with mothers?

Often less confident or experienced practitioners may profess to be mothers in an attempt to connect with mothers in the most important area of their life. The notion of 'sisterhood' between mothers highlights the pressure at times to feel accepted into the group. Which in this case is not only dishonest, but potentially dangerous when considering collusive practice, alongside manipulation of practitioners and over-identification. All of these impact on the quality of relationships that are built to achieve positive outcomes for children, the key remains honesty, transparency and respect.

Sometimes building relationships with mothers is particularly challenging when there are reminders of the effects of the abuse their child has experienced. A mother of a child with foetal alcohol syndrome for example may feel constantly reminded of her not being able to prioritise the needs of her unborn baby or a multiple system failure by society and services to enable and support her to do so. Early-on into my studies I reflected on the idea that everyone is a product of their experiences. This understanding results in not being able to feel anything but empathy for mothers whose experiences and lack of support from society as child, and as a mother, has resulted in her own child experiencing abuse. Whilst this does not equate to the view that 'everyone who has been abused, will go on to abuse,' it does highlight that often a mother's experience of abuse as a child will impinge on her opportunities for positive development of parenting which can result in women needing support when they become mothers (Rutman *et al*, 2002). Society fails when such support is not readily available. Combine this with systems theory to understand the behaviour and cognitions of mothers in the wider context of their own experiences of childhood and being mothered, and you find some prediction of the consequences for their children should they not be supported to develop and learn positive mothering skills (Payne 2005).

A mother's emotions influence her parenting which can then impact on her child's lived experiences. A depressed mother overwhelmed by her feelings is less emotionally available to her child, which can result a lack of containment impacting on development and the cycle continues; the mother's feelings of failure increase, her depression worsens given the child's negative experiences and the child's needs continue not to be fully met. This example is over-simplified and is impacted by a range of other factors such as significant others within the child's life, the mother's support network and her own experience as a child influencing her understanding of parenting. Nevertheless, it demonstrates the potential consequences of societal expectations on mothers who feel they are not, and cannot, meet these. This cyclical effect can be observed in other situations such as mothers addicted to substances or alcohol. Moreover mothers experiencing domestic abuse are vulnerable to experiencing feelings of double failure; as a woman and as a mother.

Adopting an approach to work with a mother depends on the issues within that particular case. For example a mother of a child sexually abused by their father needs support to accept the terms of their child's abuse and the consequences of this with respect to the mother's relationship status. Mothers often experience grief symptoms akin to bereavement and loss theories and social workers need to support mothers through these phases whilst ensuring the child's needs are being met (Hooper 1992, in Ferguson 2011).

Serious case reviews (SCRs) and research inform us that mothers who have abused their children rarely present with a single issue; there are likely to be parenting alone, using alcohol or substances and have experienced abuse in their own childhood and domestic abuse in the past or present. A shadowy male often remains on the periphery of the family and most live in disadvantaged environments. These factors contribute to children expressing challenging behaviour. Ferguson and O'Reilly (2001) found that 67 per cent of children entering care originate from these backgrounds. Yet this chapter has highlighted that social work continues to oppress mothers through overlooking their poverty and reinforcing maternalism, to the notion that women are made to mother by the very fact they are biologically determined to do so. As a result of this, mothers are often left responsible for the neglect of men (Ferguson 2011; Scourfield 2000). Abuse by mothers most often takes place in the context of the difficulties of mothering in patriarchal conditions where little support is available for women who parent in poverty and are held accountable if things go wrong (Ferguson 2011).

It has been highlighted in this chapter that policy decisions are often influenced by knee-jerk responses to a SCRs followed by media and public demands rather than implemented to reflect the needs of mothers and their children. Within this context of oppression, the dynamic of the social work relationship with mothers reinforces a further power imbalance that serves to compound and validate mothers pre-existing fears of children's services. This consequentially makes a difficult task of transparent, honest and reciprocal positive working relationship-building even harder to achieve. Not only does this fail children, but their mothers also and the cycle of abuse continues. Society and indeed social workers must recognise the need for a focus on service provision for mothers within early intervention to prevent a continuation of deprivation, abuse and broken families governed by the state.

A failure to do so is a failure to children, families and mothers.

CHAPTER 4

Policing Mothers
Intervention, Protection and Prevention

Lucy Baldwin, Susie Atherton and Catherine Thompson

'Last year one officer came out and his radio was going and I heard him say "It's a DV, we'll be a few minutes and we'll go to the next job." And I thought—"Thanks a lot, that's my life."' (HMIC 2014:50)

Introduction

This chapter explores issues faced by women and mothers, as victims, survivors and law breakers in the context of contact with the police. It aims to provide an illustration of when, how and why women, particularly mothers, have cause to engage with the police—the challenges they face together with the challenges of overcoming barriers to positive effective support. It is informed by case studies and in particular an account of a mother describing domestic violence (DV). It is important to acknowledge that domestic abuse doesn't occur only from males to females, it happens between all ages, genders and combinations. In this chapter, however, in line with the focus of the book discussions are centred around women and mothers—which statistically, in the majority of cases, occurs largely at the hands of males and towards females. Vignettes and case studies used in the chapter are composites of cases known to the authors, or cases in the public domain and are based on reflective and collective experience. They are considered in the context of various issues raised at individual levels, along with offering space for critical reflection in relation to positive intervention and responses between mothers and police.

The chapter highlights mothers as 'victims' but who may become dually identified as perpetrators, for example in domestic abuse situations women and mothers may have been emotionally and financially bonded to their abusive partner, are or have been dealing with a constant threat of violence to themselves, but may have on one occasion, often the 'last' occasion retaliated. Jordan (2013) found that a previous lived experience of domestic abuse may be considered a 'risk' in relation to the potential for women to go on to become law breakers. However it must be remembered that where this occurs it often occurs in a context of lack of support and protection which can be exacerbated by contact with the police and other authorities. Case studies highlight that, while no two women's or mothers' circumstances can be considered the same, there is often a clear pattern of behaviour exhibited by the abuser. The chapter encourages the reader to critically reflect on the cases studies from a non-judgemental perspective whilst additionally reflecting on the challenges faced by women and mothers when their lived experience involves domestic abuse. To provide context there is a brief historical nod to police responses to domestic abuse. Policy and practice responses are highlighted, with reference to cases together with opportunities for critical reflection via 'Pauses for Thought'.

The chapter does not focus solely on domestic abuse. However, given that one of the chapter authors specialises in working with women, mothers and domestic abuse—and the fact that, still, two women every week die from domestic abuse related incidents—the majority mothers—the authors felt sufficiently justified for domestic abuse to feature significantly in the chapter, particularly given the wider context of the book.

In addition, filicide (where mothers kill their child(ren) is presented via case study with opportunities to reflect on the circumstances surrounding such events, and with particular reference to the context of policing. However, as highlighted in *Chapter 1* it is rarely a 'failing' of only one service that ends in the death of child(ren) at the hands of their mothers.

As well as in *Chapter 1*, the Courts chapter (*Chapter 5*) outlines some of the challenges women, girls and mothers face when they misuse substances and/or commit petty offences and the consequences for them in relation to themselves, their child(ren) and social and criminal justice settings. Given that other chapters are asking readers to critically reflect on less serious or drugs-related offences this chapter is in the main given over to exploring the more serious occasions when mothers come into contact with police. It must be reiterated, however, that women generally are not heavily represented at the 'top end' of this type of criminal behaviour and although these are the kinds of cases that attract media attention they are nevertheless rare and extreme in terms of the overall picture of crime and crimes committed by women—the majority of female offending is located at the lower end of the risk spectrum, with 84 per cent of women in prison convicted of non-violent offences (Prison Reform Trust 2014). Women's and especially mother's offending is often centred around providing for their child(ren) and is a reaction to poverty or perceived 'need' or related to acquisitive crime and in turn related to substance misuse (Carlen 1998; McCoy 2001; Corston 2007). Fraud, theft and handling stolen goods make up the largest part of women's offending/prosecutions with other examples found in prostitution, non-payment of fines, breached orders and the truanting of their child(ren) (Carlen 2002; Reed 2014; Baldwin 2015a).

As mentioned in the opening chapter it is often found following serious case reviews and official inquiries that tragedies are a result of unique circumstances and therefore 'cannot be predicted.' But, often with the benefit of hindsight, even without the ability to predict, more often than not it *is* possible to reflect and identify 'missed opportunities' for support and positive intervention. One such case follows next.

Jael Mullings: A 21-year-old black mother of two boys

Romario, two, and his four-month-old brother Delayno were killed in their home in Manchester in 2008 after their mother Jael Mullings suffered a psychotic episode. The coroner, Nigel Meadows, said police were guilty of 'gross failings' for not taking a concerned call from the mother's GP surgery seriously enough when the call centre was busy. Staff at the practice dialed 999 on the day of the tragedy after Miss Mullings had phoned them in an agitated state. Despite the fact that the GP described the situation as 'an absolute emergency', and had stated she was 'extremely concerned about the welfare of the children' additionally describing Jael as being in a 'very acute psychotic state', police call handlers only gave the call a grade two status meaning officers only had to respond within an hour—had it been given a higher priority officers would have been sent to the address within ten minutes. By the time officers arrived Miss Mullings had left the house and the police left without returning until several hours later. However, Jael came home 40 minutes later and stabbed her two boys to death. The coroner concluded the children were unlawfully killed but that 'police neglect had contributed to their deaths.'

During the formal inquest three years later it was revealed Miss Mullings had been struggling to cope and was experiencing depression and psychotic thoughts, she self-reported she was using cannabis to "mask her symptoms"—however it only made things worse (Cannabis is known to exacerbate paranoia and psychosis). She pleaded guilty to manslaughter on the grounds of diminished responsibility in April 2009 and was detained in a secure hospital indefinitely. She was suffering a psychotic episode at the time of the tragedy and believed she was being pursued by the Devil.

The formal inquest heard that, on the day Romario and Delayno were killed, police radio staff were 'overwhelmed' by up to 80 emergency and urgent jobs in the north Manchester division.

An Independent Complaints Commission (IPCC) investigation raised concerns with regard to how the calls were handled and graded in the police control room that day, and a report in 2010 found 'basic errors' in call handling and a 'lack of resources' at the disposal of radio operators. The family's solicitor, Alex Preston said, 'The police had the opportunity to intervene and to take the boys and Jael to safety.' However, Dawn Copley, assistant chief constable of Greater Manchester Police (GMP), said she was 'puzzled' by the verdict as two IPCC investigations had found no evidence of any misconduct in the way in which calls were handled. She added: 'GMP is asked to deal with an increasing number of calls to-and-from people who are suffering from mental illness. We are urgently talking to the Health Service and the Home Office about our additional responsibilities in these cases and how best to deal with and protect people who are vulnerable.'

Nasim Malik, author of the 2010 IPCC report is clear that there were no specific failings in Jael's case that could be classed as 'police misconduct', however concerns were raised in relation to attitudes and timings of the response. No-one attended the address of Jael and her boys for 90 minutes after that first call and although the officers began a local search, this was interrupted by a shift change and was not resumed. After an initial call at 1.17 pm, it was not until after 5 pm when the children were found to have been harmed—having been discovered by their uncle and grandmother who had taken a taxi to Jael's, after Jael had turned-up alone, injured and distressed at her mother's home (she had made an attempt to stab herself in the heart but failed). Malik states in the report that there were concerns in relation to the attitude of police who it seems felt this was not a 'police matter' but a medical one:

'I appreciate there are times when the police service is seen as a service of last resort. When nobody else will deal with someone who is suffering mental health issues then the problem is left at the hands of the police. I agree that there are times when it is far more important for someone to receive medical attention than be taken into police custody. The IPCC has voiced concerns before that police custody suites are often dumping grounds for people that no-one else wants to deal with. Our research has shown that police cells are used disproportionately, and often inappropriately, as a place of safety for people with mental health problems. However in this case there were real concerns about the welfare of two small children. That was a job for the police to deal with in the first instance. The basis for any effective policing response to an incident such as this one has to be a primary assumption of good faith about the account of the person reporting it. It is not clear this primary assumption of good faith was evident in the response of all the officers and staff to this incident. In fact the responses of some of the officers and staff demonstrated a poor grasp of the problem or a poor understanding of mental health issues.' (IPCC Malik 2010:7-8)

The IPCC concluded there were no misconduct issues, but as with most other serious care reviews recommended, 'lessons must be learned'.

> **‖ Pause for Thought**
>
> What support did Jael need and when to prevent this tragedy? Given that the inquest revealed she was a single mother struggling with financial difficulties and mental health issues — especially following the recent birth of her baby — where could help and support have come from? Why might Jael have been afraid to ask for help? — Do you think the police 'failed' Jael and her boys — before this day — and what other missed opportunities might there have been to support Jael? — Was she 'heard'?

The Mental Health chapter (*Chapter 2*) highlights how police time can be 'swallowed-up' by dealing with mental health (and those involving substance misuse and alcohol) related issues and cases like Jael's and others such as one in Bexleyheath in 2011 when Nicola Edgington killed grandmother Sally Hodkins. Nicola had stated to police it was her intention to kill someone and claimed to have previously killed her own mother — police removed Nicola to a place of safety (under section 136 Mental Health Act 1883 as amended: see Mental Health chapter (*Chapter 2*), but did not check her claim against existing databases. Nicola ultimately left the hospital as she was not legally detained and indeed did kill Mrs Hodkins, an innocent bystander, additionally seriously injuring another person — it later transpired she had indeed killed her mother six years earlier, was diagnosed as paranoid schizophrenic and was in the community under psychiatric supervision. Baldwin (2015d) suggests it is cases such as this that highlight the 'blurred lines' between one service and another — as discussed in the first and last chapter of this book; often because of the lived experiences and complexities of need many of the people, and therefore mothers and grandmothers who come to the attention of one service, are also involved with another. More effective (but always appropriate) communication between the services is often key to actually taking forward the often vague assertion of 'lessons must be learned.'

Not the focus of this chapter, but certainly of significance in relation to Jael, is the drive for police forces to work literally alongside mental health services in order to more effectively support people with mental health issues who may come into contact with police. Police have the power to remove someone from a public place (not their own home) to a 'place of safety'. Historically that place of safety has often been a police cell—not ideal for any party concerned. Leicestershire Police have piloted a hugely successful scheme that involves a designated specialist police officer responding via a 'triage car' to calls like the one received in relation to Jael (or as per Nicola too) where there is an obvious mental health aspect—but the officer is accompanied by a designated non-police mental health professional such as a community psychiatric nurse (CPN) or in some instance an approved mental health professional (AMHP) or social worker—who will by definition have access to mental health records and databases. If further detention is required then the designated place of safety will be a pre-agreed space in the local psychiatric hospital—where the police too have a base. Subsequent detentions under the MHA 1983 are down 40 per cent and the scheme has been deemed so successful it is to be piloted in other areas with Department of Health funding, with Leicestershire's model as one model of good practice to follow. Had this scheme been in place nationally things may have been very different for Jael and her boys and for Nicola, Mrs Hodkins and her devastated family.

As with any other agency, the police do not always 'get it right' or manage to work together as cooperatively and successfully as achieved via the triage car. Again, as with other agencies it is the high profile cases ending in tragedy that generally 'make the press'. Good work undertaken daily by thousands of individual officers or forces as collectives often goes unnoticed by those not directly involved. So although this chapter is highlighting some negative aspects and 'failings' in police work we would like to think they will be seen as a tip of an iceberg—but with the hidden and larger part involving successful outcomes—perhaps paradoxically, successful policing is 'evidenced' by its lack of 'visibility'.

However, the police can and do get it wrong, 'invisibility' can become a negative as is painfully highlighted by reports such as 'Hidden in Plain Sight' (2011) commissioned by the Equality and Human Rights Commission (EHRC), which looked into disability related harassment—partially triggered by the case of Fiona Pilkington, a 38-year-old mother who killed herself and her disabled daughter. Mothers' law-breaking is often, though not always, linked to their experiences of victimisation of other crimes as can be sadly illustrated by Fiona's lived experiences. Prior to her death there where themes of under-protection and disregard for her's and her family's needs — ultimately leading to tragic events which subsequent inquiries show may have been prevented.

Fiona Pilkington: A 38-year-old white mother of two, a disabled daughter and teenage son

> Fiona Pilkington killed herself and her 18-year-old daughter Francecca. She had endured a sustained period of harassment, abuse and torment — directed at her and her two children, her daughter who was classed as disabled and her son who had 'special needs' and learning difficulties. Francecca's complex needs were becoming more challenging and Fiona struggled to cope as Francecca matured, her son had learning difficulties and was a regular target of known youths, and had even been attacked with a knife and locked in a shed by them. Fiona contacted police by phone by letter and in person, even contacting her MP in order to find some peace from the harassment. Fiona's mother moved in with the family as a result of the sustained harassment and she too was targeted. The family had to change the way they lived and shopped and everything was organized around periods when they felt it would be 'safe' to leave the house. She became depressed and anxious, ending one of her letters to police: 'I've had enough. I just want to be able to have a life'. On 27th October 2007 Fiona drove her car to a lay-by and set it alight with her and her daughter inside.

The IPCC concluded the level of service given to Fiona and her family by Leicestershire Police 'fell far below the level expected' (2011:1210), despite there being systems in place to address the needs of victims of persistent harassment. The report concluded police officers' assessments were based on opinions about the area in which Fiona lived, not on reports Fiona provided describing her experiences (2011:1214). Instead of implementing the Protection from Harassment Act 1997 fully to make arrests after repeated incidences of harassment, officers classed the behaviour as 'anti-social', including the shed/knife incident, relying on the local council to take action. Additionally, police did not share all relevant information about the level of offending against Fiona and her family—indeed a key theme for this case was the lack of 'oversight', i.e. the incidences were treated separately, rather than as a sustained campaign of abuse. The report noted the particular challenges facing Fiona as a mother, in that her daughter Francecca, who was disabled, faced an uncertain future. Highlighting this may have contributed to Fiona's decision to take her's and her daughter's lives. The trauma from long-term harassment and the lack of support from the police and local authority was not effectively managed or fully understood. The report concludes, predictably that 'lessons must be learned,' and states that this case may raise awareness about the impact of anti-social behaviour and the consequences of a lack of action or information sharing (Now legally required under section 17 of the Crime and Disorder Act 1998).

Pause for Thought

Do you think the police failed Fiona and Francecca? How could other agencies have helped Fiona and her family? In what way might cuts to services have affected the outcomes of this case? What particular areas of policing have been 'cut'? Is it possible to prioritise which parts of policing are more important than others? What would be top—what would be at the bottom? What were the factors influencing the police's intervention—could it have come sooner? What do you think the 'attitude' might have been towards Fiona and her family? Was Fiona 'heard'?

Mothers as Victims and Perpetrators—Where is the Line?

To understand the complex and stressful situations facing mothers who break the law, it is important to consider complex circumstances which highlight how mothers can be in vulnerable and dangerous situations exacerbating their status as 'victims', but that may also lead them to break the law. This includes domestic violence in which mothers may not only be facing threats to themselves but also to their child(ren). Issues such as these are reflected via the mothers and child(ren) in this chapter and all present examples of where police and other services 'failed' them or missed opportunities to support them.

Isad: A 30-year-old British Asian mother of four children, aged six, four, three years, and four months

Isad had been married at 18 to a man she met on her wedding day and who had been chosen by her parents. Her husband beat her for the first time on her wedding night telling her he was disappointed, she was ugly and he wished he hadn't married her. From then she was beaten regularly, several times requiring hospital treatment, always making excuses for her injuries. Isad begged her family to help her in the first year, but they refused, telling her divorce would bring shame on the family and was not an option, additionally that she was disrespectful for breaking the confidentiality of her marriage. Isad 'accepted' her life as it was, believing that as long as her husband beat her he would not harm her children — she was regularly told she was nothing, she was worthless, that she might be thrown in the street or sent to India without her children. One day her eldest daughter was serving her father dinner and she dropped food on him, he began to beat his six-year-old child. Isad took the knife from the tray and stabbed her husband in the neck, screaming to her child to get out of the house with the babies. Isad rang the police, was arrested and remanded — the children were taken into care as the family refused to take them in because of the shame.

Pause for Thought

What sentence do you think Isad ought to have? — Do you think this ought to be regarded as murder or manslaughter — how would the court view this? Would it be viewed differently if it were a man? — Do you think if Isad is sentenced to custody her children should be adopted? Where/how do you think signs this may be occurring might have been seen? What are the challenges for addressing domestic abuse in varied cultures? — How can cultural 'barriers' be overcome? — Should they be? What might have helped Isad within her community? What role might the police have in preventative or supportive work in specific communities? Where else is domestic abuse less 'visible'? — Why?

Violence in the home is unacceptable for anyone but certain groups are more likely to experience this than others: women, mothers and child(ren) are in such a group (Women's Aid 2014). Police and social services can and do work together in order to protect vulnerable mothers and child(ren). Historically, the response to domestic abuse by the police service has been at best, variable and at worst, inadequate (Dobash and Dobash 1980; Hanmer and Saunders 1984). Police as a whole receive a phone call related to domestic abuse every minute, that's 1,440 calls every day (Women's Refuge 2015) and yet only 35 per cent of domestic violence incidents are reported to the police (Home Office 2002; Stanko 2000); two women are killed every week at the hands of a partner or ex-partner (Office for National Statistics 2015). This is not a small issue.

Although there is no doubt that policing of domestic abuse is a high profile aspect of contemporary policing it is perhaps pertinent to critically reflect on this history of attitude and response to domestic abuse, over time. Police forces are ultimately made up of individuals from wider society, and like wider society their 'make up' and attitudes have over time mirrored sexist, patriarchal and masculine ideals (Westmarland 2001). Although women had been permitted into the police since the early-1900s, up until the 1940s women had to leave the force if they married or got pregnant. It was not until the 1970s when the separate 'Women's Service' was dissolved and it became possible (in theory) for women to expand their police work from working mainly with prostitutes, women, rape victims and child(ren). However it was some time yet before uniform, kit and opportunities for women in the police came to match those of males — although arguably this is still not achieved with women under-represented in higher positions within policing and specialist teams (Home Office 2010). The disbanding of the Women's Service in 1969 resulted in more male officers becoming involved in what had previously been 'women's police work'. Heidensohn (1995) found that higher value is placed' on police work that involves catching 'real villains' and that 'domestics' were seen as 'rubbish work' (1995; 220).

Research undertaken in the 1980s and 1990s found the police service to have a distinct organizational culture, one which socialised new officers and reinforced and reproduced various characteristics over generations (Reiner 1992; Waddington 1999). A significant element of this culture is machismo and sexist attitudes towards women's place in the police station and the rôles they must assume—where as a result they become 'de-feminised' and 'de-professionalised' (Martin 1980; Jones 1986; Heidensohn 1992). Hoyle (2000) suggested that despite the fact that 'domestic violence' was now firmly in the operational domain the attitude of some officers was still that it was peripheral to 'real policing'.

Not surprisingly, particularly in the 1970s and 1980s the reputation of the police in relation to dealing with domestic violence was not good—poignantly and realistically illustrated by the words of the song *Behind the Wall*, released by Tracy Chapman in 1988 and is the epitome of how domestic violence attitudes and responses of the time (listen to the words: there is a link in the *Student Online Resource Bank* in the *Appendix* to this book). Consequently, as well as the well-documented reluctance of women to report domestic abuse for a multitude of complex reasons (some of which are discussed below)—there was also the perception that it was 'pointless' and 'would only make things worse' (Horely 1988), which may very well have been a reality of the time. In a review of police intervention of the time, Dobash and Dobash (1992) found evidence of arrest being an 'unlikely response,' also that officers did not want to remain with the victim for longer than they felt necessary, perhaps intervening by temporarily removing the perpetrator to 'cool off.' Time spent with victims was often used to dissuade them from taking further action, 'given the challenges with prosecution and reluctant witnesses' (*Ibid*).

Domestic abuse accounts for approximately 15 per cent of violent crime, and has the highest rate of repeat victimisation (Home Office 2002; Kershaw *et al*, 2008; House of Commons Home Affairs Committee 2008), with victims being assaulted on average 35 times (often over periods as long as two year) before reporting an offence (McGibbon, Cooper and Kelly 1989; Dobash and Dobash 1979; Pahl 1989). In addition, 30 per cent of incidences of domestic violence start or escalate as women become mothers, in pregnancy (Department of Health 2004) generating higher rates of foetal deaths than gestational diabetes or pre-eclampsia (Friend 1998). Figures from the NSPCC (2011) reveal that in the UK, 25 per cent of children have witnessed domestic abuse, and up to 62 per cent of children living in homes where domestic violence occurs have themselves been harmed. We know that children who have witnessed domestic abuse are more likely to have behavioural issues that may later bring them into contact with police, and are statistically more likely to grow up to be perpetrators or victims themselves (SafeLives 2015). Hence the huge importance of prevention, early intervention, and protection to achieve this it is vital for women and mothers to feel positively supported and to feel able to seek help advice and guidance without judgement or fear of further controlling responses in which they feel they have no voice or choices.

Historically, the prevalent police attitude, partly borne out of frustration but nevertheless unhelpful, judgemental and simplistic, was one of 'Why doesn't she just leave?' Understanding why 'she doesn't' is an important part of contemporary policing. Women's Aid (2014) examined the barriers and challenges women face when leaving violent relationships; revealing for many a significant factor was simply having nowhere else to go (88 per cent), along with being financially dependent on their partner (77 per cent) and fearful of further violence (44 per cent). This fear is often well-founded as can be demonstrated by the many women, mothers and children who have been killed following disclosure to police or 'positive action' undertaken by the police — further demonstrating and emphasising the need for systemic protection for women and children (76 per cent of women who did leave abuse partners reported that violence occurred after separation and police contact). Continued abuse included verbal/emotional abuse, threats towards themselves and their children, physical and sexual violence (Humphreys and Thiara 2002). Women's Aid (2014) reported a significant proportion of women (23 per cent) disclosing post-separation abuse not only in the form of physical abuse, but also, stalking and harassment (physically and via text or social networks), public humiliation and threats or damage to her new partner and property.

Significantly and in addition to the external factors described above—what is often forgotten in popular reflection, in relation to barriers to leaving are the internal factors that act like 'invisible chains' for women whose lived experience has been abusive relationships—possibly for much of her life—factors which destroy a women's confidence and self-esteem—especially if she has 'lost' her children or asked relatives to care for them to protect them—or her children have witnessed the violence—all these things can and do 'confirm' to a mother that she is a bad person, sometimes making her feel she doesn't 'deserve any better'—or sometimes making her feel almost paralysed by numbness with no energy, drive or will to fight to overcome the very real obstacles to 'leaving'. Living with and surviving domestic abuse actually requires a huge strength, that often those who abuse have tried very hard to break down—women and mothers need support in channelling the strength they drew on to live with and survive domestic abuse into strength to leave it behind. Key to this is access to support (in a climate of cuts to services this is not as easy as it sounds)—but also access to support that will create a space of 'emotional safety' (Baldwin 2015c and f) where women can begin to feel 'safe' enough to disclose (if they want to). Very often this support comes from the third sector specialist organizations who deal with those extricating themselves from domestic abuse and who can and do support the police in working partnerships.

▌▌ Pause for Thought

What are your honest thoughts about mothers and abusive relationships? Do you think mothers who 'stay' are the same as mothers 'unable to leave'… if not why not—if so why so? How might growing-up in an abusive household impact on women and violent relationships? Do you think 'it' can happen to anyone—to you? Think that through. Why? How might these 'thoughts' affect working with mothers living with violence?

The Home Office circular 60/1990 directing police forces to improve domestic violence responses, together with academic, feminist and women's rights activists all demanding change led to a shift in thinking and for forces to adopt a more 'proactive' response to domestic abuse (West-marland 2001). Since then there have been a number of legislative, policy and practice changes in relation to domestic abuse. Prior to 1994, because of old law relating to 'conjugal rights' shockingly men could not be charged with marital rape, only sexual assault until the law was changed under section 142 of the Criminal Justice and Public Order Act 1994, and more recently the Sexual Offences Act 2003 has expanded this to other forms of sexual assault. This more proactive response to domestic abuse for many forces meant adopting a policy of 'Positive Action'. This has occurred alongside an announcement by Theresa May, Home Secretary, to add a new offence of coercive control under domestic abuse legislation, in recognition of this as a pre-cursor to physical violence and also examples of behaviour women experience post-separation.

Positive Action was introduced as a way to strengthen the law and, it was felt, to reduce the burden of responsibility from victimised women in relation to deciding to prosecute. It felt this policy gave police the ability to act on behalf of victims of domestic abuse, who may report a crime, but later wish to withdraw their complaint, despite clearly still being at risk. A report by Refuge (2014) highlighted concerns with this policy, which, on the face of it, appears to ensure victims are protected and perpetrators are dealt with; feminist thought offers the view that it can however be seen as yet another patriarchal and inherently sexist policy which sees women as 'only vulnerable' and is yet something else that takes away their own choice, autonomy and voice—another means of control. Arguably, pro-arrest policies were implemented with the aim of overcoming victims' reluctance to prosecute, and for specialist teams to investigate cases. There is a clear assumption that arrest is required for further action and support to be implemented. However insufficient attention is often paid to the risks for victims, there is still very much a focus on law enforcement and prosecution, rather than prevention and protection. Despite the policy leading to some arrests evidence suggests there are still failures by the police in ensuring protection for victim(s) following arrest, particularly, as is the norm if not remanded, when perpetrators would only be held in police custody for up to 24 hours—with any further detention dependent on evidence being gathered in order to charge and/or remand perpetrators into custody. Crucially, sometimes fatally, there is evidence of 'cautions' being used instead of arrest, with higher rates of use in domestic cases compared to other instances of violent crime (Refuge 2014). Additionally, confusion about the implementation of the policy, especially when perpetrators made counter-allegations — leading to the arrest of women as victims, which in fact was three times more likely (*Ibid*).

Also, concern exists surrounding the amount of time it can take for a case to reach trial where the suspect has pleaded not guilty. There can be repeated court hearings each of which causes further anxiety and added trauma to the victim via defence statements, seeking to sully victims' names and often further incidents of violence or harassment. The timescale between arrest and trial can be a difficult one, and has often been highlighted as the time when there have been missed opportunities to provide continued support and protection for women, mothers and their children. Protection during this vulnerable time is key to effective policing in relation to domestic abuse.

▌▌ Pause for Thought

What is your view on Positive Action — Do you think choices should be taken away from women? Do you think if police use Positive Action in relation to domestic abuse, they have a bigger responsibility to protect the 'victim'? — How can police more effectively protect and prevent such abuse? — How could services link together to offer more protection? — Read the 2014 HMIC report 'Everyone's Business' — should cuts to services place people at risk? — Do they?

Independent Police Complaints Commission (IPCC) reports provide evidence of where police have 'missed opportunities to safeguard' and protect mothers and victims of domestic violence, cases like Jeanette Goodwin, Maria Stubbings, Christine Chambers and her daughter Shania, Rachel Slack and her baby son Auden to mention but a few. However it is not only following police positive action that women are at their most vulnerable — equally it can be when a mother has reached the point where she has felt able to extricate herself from the relationship—and her abuser is 'losing control.' Very often it is not only failings in one service where 'missed opportunities' to safeguard, protect and prevent further harm or death occur, as will be additionally discussed in the Courts chapter (*Chapter 5*) and can be illustrated by the arguably avoidable death of Jane Clough.

Jane Clough: A 26-year-old nurse and mother of a nine-month-old baby girl murdered in July 2010

Jane, whose case is also be referred to in the Courts chapter (*Chapter 5*), was murdered by her ex-partner in cold blood in the car park of the hospital where she worked as a nurse. She was stabbed 71 times and had her throat slit. Jane had 'predicted' her own death, stating in her diary that she was certain her ex-partner would 'kill her if she ever found the courage to leave.' At the time of her death her ex-partner was on bail for previous assault and several counts of rape against Jane. Her ex had initially been remanded into custody but was released on appeal by a Crown Court judge (this will be discussed further in the Courts chapter (*Chapter 5*)). His release on bail was vehemently opposed by the police and the Crown Prosecution Service. Her killer, Johnathan Vass stated he had killed her in 'retribution' for her being prepared to give evidence against him with regard to the rape allegations.

Policing Domestic Abuse as an Officer

Police officers are meant to be 'tough', resilient and able to deal with anything—and as the approved mental health practitioner (AMHP) highlights in her chapter—honest self-reflection and self-awareness and reflexivity is an important part of working with people—especially when working with people may have challenging outcomes. Of course the most challenging of circumstances are for those whose lived experience is one of control, physical and/or sexual violence and emotional abuse or control. That is emphatically re-iterated. But as with prison officers who undertake sex offender training courses (SOTP) working closely with paedophiles and listening to stories of horrendous abuse day-in-day-out, or the AMHP who described her honest frustration working with personality disordered individuals—for police officers working within a domestic abuse unit can also be challenging and stressful. In my experience many domestic abuse unit officers describe living with depression and use unhealthy coping strategies. There is no doubt that dealing with statements, seeing injuries and witnessing crimes where vicious behaviour has been committed by perpetrators—who should arguably be closest and kindest to their victim—takes its toll. My current role is my most emotionally challenging to date. It can be as frustrating as it is rewarding. For every domestic violence survivor supported to escape the cycle of violence, there are another two or three women who have not yet found a way to overcome the barriers described earlier and to leave. As officers we understand generally this is through being terrified of the consequences, a previous bad experience of the criminal justice system or being dependant on their abuser financially or as a result of drugs or alcohol addiction—but in all honesty that doesn't always stop the feelings of frustration, helplessness and despair—for the women, mothers and their child(ren) and a society in which this occurs—not for us but for them. Key to working effectively, and crucially, continuing to work effectively as domestic abuse unit officers is ironically having the same opportunities of freedom and 'emotional safety' (obviously in a lesser but nevertheless similar fashion) as victims—to be able to secure supportive non-judgemental supervision—without feeling like we are failing. This is key in supporting officers to effectively support others thus facilitating protection and prevention by allowing the best opportunities to provide that 'emotional safety' in turn for women and mothers—however many times it takes. However it has to be said that in challenging times with cuts to services—ours and the important third sector partnership agencies that support us, fewer officers, challenging timeframes and targets, there are real concerns about the ability to deliver the kind of supportive proactive and preventative service that is the ideal—and instead we end up delivering, hopefully still an effective service, but very much a reactive one.

Reactive only services can have devastating consequences such as situations highlighted earlier—where women and mothers whose lived experience has been long-term abuse. Where for complex reasons any intervention or support may have proved insufficient or failed. Resulting in women, often mothers, protecting their children, who will 'snap'-finding themselves in a situation where having been victims they are now facing custodial sentences as perpetrators for a serious offence—as their *first* offence. Many women once they have reach this point have described the 'necessity' to do 'real damage' in order to avoid repercussions—i.e. to seriously injure or kill to avoid being killed—or to avoid their children being harmed (think back to Isad).

When Policing Makes a Difference

Enid: A 26-year-old white female and the mother of Polly aged six

This vignette is drawn from Enid's victim impact statement for the court.

My name is Enid, I am a mum, well I used to be—now I'm just trying to be a mum again…I was in a relationship with John for eight months—it sounds a ridiculously short period of time for my life to fall apart but that's all it was. When I met John I'd just come out a relationship with Polly's dad. It wasn't a bad relationship really but he had an affair with my best friend. My dad said it was because I'm boring—but my mum said that's rubbish he was just a pig. When I think of it now I find it hard to explain how I didn't leave—it wasn't even like he waited months to hit me—he didn't—he hit me in the first week. Blacked both my eyes and knocked me out. I just didn't leave the house for a while and didn't see any one till the bruises faded. Which I think John liked. But he was so sorry and attentive and apologetic, I believed him when he said he would never hit me again. Then bit-by-bit he just really took me apart—he would nit-pick and tell me I was crap at keeping the house clean, that I was a rubbish mum to Polly and that Polly would be better off with her dad because I was so thick. Then he started to hit me regularly and it was almost like I didn't notice, in fact sometimes—and this sounds sick—I was glad to be hit—because waiting to be hit was worse. I would just get used to all the 'rules' to avoid getting hit and do everything the right way, spread his butter right, wear the right clothes, not talk when the news was on, all of it—then he'd change the 'rules' on a whim and I'd get hit anyway. I felt hopeless and stupid. Polly's dad told social services because Polly saw what happened, he never hit her—well she hadn't broke his rules. Social services said I had to leave him because I wasn't 'demonstrating the ability to protect her' but he said he would kill us both if I left him, and I truly believed he would—so I let Polly go to her dad's so the social wouldn't come again as they wound him up too, they didn't come back once Polly was at her dad's. I almost didn't notice she'd gone I was so numb—but then I must have because I used to go and sit in her room and cry. I was in there when he got me that last time—he said I'd been seeing another man—I hadn't even left the house for weeks, it was stupid. But he hit me, with Polly's scooter—I was bleeding and barely conscious and he dragged me in the kitchen. I had no idea what for. As we got into the kitchen he told me that 'this is the day you stop lying or die'. I told him I hadn't lied and that I loved him. This just seemed to make it worse. He lit the burners on the stove and told me he was going to cause an explosion to make my death look like an accident. By this time I was terrified and crying uncontrollably. I don't know how it happened but I ended-up on the floor crouched over. John was pacing around the kitchen muttering like a mad man. He put a frying pan on the stove and poured some olive oil into it. I remember thinking it was strange that he wanted to cook something but I didn't say anything. After a while the pan began smoking as the oil was burning, I begged him not to burn the place down but he just kept telling me not to even look at him.

After a while he took the pan off the stove and walked over to me. He said, 'Don't make me do this, tell me the truth.' I couldn't even speak I was so upset and scared. He carried on shouting for a bit, then just stood staring at me for ages, I don't know how long. Without warning he then swung the pan at me causing hot oil inside to splash all over my neck and chest. I was in immediate pain and began screaming louder than I thought possible. I've never felt pain like it. John shouted 'shut up' over-and-over and then knelt down beside me. I thought this was the bit where he usually apologises and gets upset, instead he pulled a tea towel out of the laundry pile and began pushing it into my mouth. He was pulling my mouth open to try and force the tea towel down. It was making me retch. While he was doing this he was squeezing my neck with his other hand, I could feel it was wet but didn't know if it was blood or burst blisters from the burns. I had spots in front of my eyes and I wet myself while this was happening; I was so scared. I thought I was going to die. At some point the phone rang, John stood up straightaway and ran to answer, shouting about it probably being one of the men I was having sex with. While he was out of the room I dragged myself to the back door, got up and ran out. I ran down the alleyway and straight into the road. Someone, I don't even know who it was, pulled over and let me into their car. I was still crying hysterically and couldn't speak but they just took me straight to hospital where I stayed for five days.

It took over a week for the police to find John, during that time he constantly texted me telling me he was coming back to finish the job and that he would kill my mum as well as he knew I'd gone there. I was and still am terrified even though he is currently in prison. I don't think I'll ever feel safe from him. I didn't want to press charges at all, but the police said they would anyway, court was awful, heart-breaking—for my mum too hearing it all, she felt like she should have seen it—but I hid it all. The police were amazing and they were really supportive to me. I dealt with the same officer all the time—I'd met her when she came to the hospital and she was who I spoke to all the time, she was the only one I could tell the details too—it was too much for anyone else, even the victim support woman, although she was brilliant too. Between them that officer and the victim support woman got me through. The police said he'd been prosecuted before for other women, that's what made me give evidence, I had no idea about any of this and I don't want him to ever hurt anyone again. Because of him I lost my daughter, nearly lost all of my family and friends and any self-confidence/self-esteem I ever had. The police have said when he's out there will be licence conditions, he'll have to stay away from me and maybe this town and I can have a panic alarm and they will keep me informed. I never thought anything like this could happen to someone like me, I'm from a nice home with a nice family—although my dad did always used to say I'd make anyone want to smack me but he didn't mean it. I'm going to go to college now, getting my life back—the victim support women said it's important for me to get out there and not let him take my life. So I'm trying. I don't want to be on my own forever, but I know it will be hard to trust but I'll try.

▌▌ Pause for Thought

How did you feel reading about Enid — How do you think Enid felt living it? Can you see any clues as to how/why, clues how John was able to exert control over Enid? Domestic abuse covers the breadth of class/culture/gender and age — do you think it could happen to you? — If so why? If not why? — How can society increase individuals 'protective factors' to prevent abusers succeeding in controlling and abusive behaviour? — What can/should society do to reduce the chances of people growing-up to abuse? — Which is most important? What did you think of Enid's statement saying she could only tell the police officer details 'as they could take it'? Can they? How can officers be supported to manage their own responses to other people's trauma? Would it be easy to ask for support? — If not why not? — What would make it easier? What do you think the future holds for Enid and Polly?

Policing Partnerships and Protecting Mothers

The Home Affairs Committee (2008) report revealed the costs of domestic violence reached £25.3 billion in 2005-6, and recommended a national strategy to include prevention, education and intervention, along with better protection for victims. However, the report also acknowledged funding cuts were impacting on police resources and voluntary and third sector specialist supportive services and that this was affecting the ability to adhere to guidelines. Since then there have been further significant cuts to resources and funding and the police are undergoing systematic review — review that will change the face of policing as we know it (see the link to the 2014 Reform report, 'The Police Mission in the Twenty-First Century' in the *Student Online Resource Bank* in the *Appendix* to this book).

As a result of several highly visible cases in which police were seen to have at best 'under-performed' and 'under-protected' and at worst failed — leading to deaths in 2013 — the Home Secretary commissioned a report into policing and domestic abuse. 'Everyone's Business' published in 2014 found:

> 'In too many forces there are weaknesses in the service provided to victims; some of these are serious and this means that victims are put at unnecessary risk. Many forces need to take action now.
>
> Domestic abuse is a priority on paper but, in the majority of forces, not in practice.' (HMIC 2014:6)

A crucial part of improving the response to domestic abuse in relation to policing is to ensure police embrace partnership working. Often of key significance in assisting people to withdraw from violent situations is access to support services which may include housing, financial, psychological, practical and childcare support — together with enabling women to feel a sense of 'emotional safety', opportunity and obviously physical safety. The Home Office circular, updated in 2000, to chief constables required that the police ensure they protect victims and children from further abuse, treat domestic abuse as seriously as other forms of violence, anticipate the risks of reconciliation between victims and their perpetrators and properly record and monitor such cases. This meant the police service needed to be aware of refuges and other statutory or voluntary agencies who could help, as well as ensuring they were building a robust case for the CPS and courts. Examples of voluntary groups who help women as victims of domestic abuse include national charities such as Women's Aid, offering refuge and other support services, and smaller scale charities such as My Sister's Place, based in Middlesbrough, who offer a one-stop-shop for women aged 16 or over who have experienced or are experiencing domestic violence' (My Sister's Place website, 2015). A core focus is to work in partnership with others to achieve this and make communities safer, whilst advocating for change to better protect women, mothers and children. A key part of this is local knowledge of local support — particularly in relation to diverse or hard to reach communities. Working visibly, proactively — building knowledge together

111

and listening to the issues and barriers women, mothers and children may need to overcome—will assist individual forces and officers to better understand the complexities of domestic abuse and its impact.

The impact of domestic abuse for mothers and their child(ren) in terms of long-lasting psychological trauma and emotional and psychological damage needs to be better understood. There are recommendations to expand the definitions of post-traumatic stress disorder to include those experiencing domestic abuse (Jordan 2013; Refuge 2014), in order to allow victims to use a diagnosis of psychiatric injury to bring cases to court, under the Offences Against the Person Act 1861. This would also assist women in terms of securing additional support and is key to recognising the value of a trauma-informed practice model as a way of working with women who have survived domestic abuse. Not only is this an important by way of response, but also by way of prevention it will enable women to feel empowered and in control in relation to future choices for them and their child(ren).

The 2014 HMIC report highlights the importance of independent domestic violence advisors (IDVAs) and multi-agency risk assessments conferences (MARACS) in relation to having as full and in-depth understanding of domestic abuse situations where risk of harm exists:

> '[A]t the heart of MARAC is the working assumption that no single agency or individual can see the complete picture of the life of the victim—but that all may have insights that are crucial to their safety.' (2014: HMIC)

However what is often forgotten is that the person with perhaps the most 'insight', but often with the least heard 'voice' is that of the person experiencing the abuse. Their voice needs to be at the centre of the policing of women and mothers in relation to domestic abuse. In the words of one of the victims interviewed for the HMIC report when asked what she wanted from police, she said that she wanted to:

> '... be heard. Listen to what I'm saying to you—don't just write it down. Take on board what I'm telling you.'

CHAPTER 5

Mothers in the Dock
A Critical Reflection of Women, Mothers and the Courts

Lucy Baldwin and Leila Mezoughi

'Poverty is the mother of crime.' (Marcus Aurelius)

This chapter aims to present illustration and understanding of women, specifically mothers, in relation to the law and their court experiences. It contains a brief historical perspective of the court and its 'relationship' with women, which has mirrored through time wider societal attitudes to women and mothers—particularly those who are 'deviant' or break the law. The judiciary's historical relationship with women and mothers is of particular significance not *only* because the 'laws of the land' generally reflect the position of women in society but because courts, after the police, are the 'gatekeepers' in relation to how women and mothers are responded to when they break the law—quite simply 'what comes next'. The judiciary therefore, in relation to experience and decision-making processes, has a significant and profound impact on mothers and their children. This will be explored in the context of judicial attitudes, processes and sentencing decisions relating to women and mothers.

The perspectives of women and mothers in relation to courts are explored via case studies and vignettes. The former are either from the public domain and referenced accordingly or based on reflections from practice of the authors. The reader is asked to critically reflect on 'practice'-related issues and the feelings and experiences of women, question the judicial system and its decisions and to explore opportunities and/or the need for positive change.

Historical Context and a Legacy of Assumptions

As also stated in the Prison chapter (*Chapter 6*), reflection regarding the position of women and mothers in the CJS is incomplete if one doesn't cast an eye backwards to explore a telling legacy. Zedner (1991) explores the origins of penological and criminological attention in relation to women and mothers, agreeing Smart's (1976) work *Women, Crime and Criminology* heralds the start of formal feminist criminological study: however she suggests interest in *The Female Offender* can be traced back to even before Lombrosso's work of the afore mentioned title in 1895 (*Ibid*). Zedner (1991) writes that women comprised a much higher percentage of the prison population in Victorian times than now, but suggests rather than this being a result of women and mothers being more 'criminal' in tendency, this was at least in part as a result of being labelled and criminalised by courts; largely because they were acting outside of their supposed 'moral duty' and feminine respectability (*Ibid*). Mid-to-late 19th-century perception of women and mothers was somewhat paradoxical, aligned to either end of an extreme—women were either 'seen' as (as they were 'meant' to be) innocent, restrained and pure and yet also 'feared' to be capable of being deceitful, cunning, deviant and immoral. Women as mothers were viewed as somehow 'responsible' for the moral health and wellbeing, not only of themselves but of their children, families and ergo wider society:

> 'Female crime has a much worse effect on the morals of the young, and is therefore a more powerfully depraving character than crimes of men [...] the influence and example of the mother are all powerful; and corruption if it be there, exists in the source and must taint the stream.' (Symons 1849:25)

As Zedner (1991) highlights, citing Hill (1864: 134), much is revealed about the attitude of the judicial response to women and mothers at the time:

> 'The conduct of the female sex more deeply affects the wellbeing of the community—A bad woman inflicts more moral injury to society than a bad man.'

Women, especially mothers, were seen as the major source of corruption and juvenile delinquency—mothers offending with their children (begging for example) were seen as acting both against 'nature' and against 'righteousness and femininity.' Prostitution, a 'crime' for which many women found themselves before the courts, was seen as an act which 'led' men away from virtue, 'robbing' them not only of money but of good character. Visiting prostitutes was seen as the 'fault' of the woman or mother for being 'available' rather than any men paying for sex—hence the origins of the rather anomalous position of a law which criminalised women for soliciting or exchanging sex for monetary gain—yet didn't criminalise men for their rôle in the 'exchange.' This unequal situation shockingly prevailed until the Sexual offences Act 1985 when 'persistent kerb crawling' became an offence—and not really until April 2010 when the caveat of 'persistent' was removed.

‖ Pause for Thought

The Policing and Crime Act 2009 removed the term 'common prostitute' from the law—What are the connotations of such a term?—Has that description had an impact on perceptions of women and their sexuality? In the 18th/19th-century prostitution was most often associated with poverty—has anything changed?—How is prostitution viewed?—Do you think it should be legalised?—Would this offer women more or less 'protection'?—Is prostitution automatically incompatible with 'good' mothering?—Do you have a 'professional' and a 'personal' response?

Prostitution is often associated with coercion as well as poverty—but there is a counter argument that it is also a valid and occupational choice—MacKinnon (2005) however states: 'If prostitution is a free choice, why are the women with the fewest choices the ones most often found doing it?' What is your view on this?

The 'moralising' response to women law breakers was palpable, males were seen as 'sinners' but women, and as we have seen especially mothers, were seen as depraved, deviant, wanton and dangerous. Depravity and shamelessness were labels associated with offences that would not in any court be classed as 'serious', such as pick-pocketing, alcoholism, soliciting — being indicative of immoral lifestyle choices, and therefore 'perverse'. Mary Carpenter made clear she saw women law-breakers as a 'moral menace', despite her being a 'sympathetic prison philanthropist' and supportive of prison reform — even from a philanthropic position her view indicates the attitudes of the time:

> 'The very susceptibility and tenderness of women's nature render her more completely diseased in her whole nature when this is perverted to evil; and when a woman is enlisted on the side of evil, she is far more dangerous to society than the other sex.' (1864b: 1:31-32)

Throughout the 18th and early 19th-centuries women and mothers as law breakers were most often seen as 'bad' and/or morally-lacking as described above, in the latter half of the 19th-century the growing influence of psychiatry and biological factors added to the 'understanding' of women as criminals, and wherever women were not seen as 'bad' they were seen as 'mad'. The Mental Health chapter (*Chapter 2*) explores the historical perspective of women and psychiatry and the Prison chapter (*Chapter 6*) alludes to the 'acceptance' the historical (or hysterical!) fear of the perceived destabilising effect on society of 'mad' or 'bad' women. Thus resulting in penal policies (and therefore sentencing patterns) that assume women law breakers are generally 'disturbed' or 'inadequate' (Zedner 1991). The lasting influence of such beliefs it has been suggested is that women who break the law are seen as 'doubly deviant' (Heidensohn 1981; Gelsthorpe 2004). In a similar way to mental health issues for women not being 'left at the prison gate' (a point made elsewhere in this book), indeed perceptions of women and mothers were not left out of the passing of laws or outside of the courtroom; consequently leaving a legacy that influenced not only developments in legislation and policy but also moral judgements, sentencing decisions and patterns (Haidt 2012; Canton 2015).

Attitudes from wider society are often reflected in its 'organizations' — as highlighted by Macpherson (1999) in his observation that the police were 'institutionally racist'. This phrase is often misunderstood — 'institutional' racism or sexism is often by its very definition 'invisible' due to its uncon-sciousness. To spend time as 'individuals' defending one's position in an 'I am not a racist/sexist person' — is reductionist and a perfect demon-stration of failure to recognise the historical legacy of outdated cultural values and norms from colonialist and overtly patriarchal values that no longer have a place in contemporary society (not accepting they ever did as a 'truth'). We are all to some extent products of our environment and without proactive thought direction we can find ourselves thinking and feeling unconsciously driven thoughts — constructions of mother-hood are a perfect example of this — we all hold a view of the qualities of good and bad mothering and similarly we have ideas (even ideals) around what men 'should' be like and what women 'should' be like and where they 'sit' or 'fit' in society. Jurors do not leave these pre concep-tions outside in the lobby either.

To illustrate the principle — an exercise set my students

Close your eyes and imagine the scenery, the characters and the people in what follows. Visualise in your mind's-eye a scenario where a young nurse is experiencing sexual harassment in the workplace from a senior consultant — the scenario continues with the nurse speaking to a line manager who doesn't support the nurse's claim and is dismissive of any talk of a legal claim. The nurse then speaks with another manager who is supportive — they seek legal representation and visit a lawyer who takes the case — the case is heard before a judge ... and so on ... (Poetic licence is taken with the process!). (The point being, at no point either here or during the exercise in class do I mention the gender, race or sexuality of the nurse or in fact any of the 'rôles').

I then ask a classroom of students what they 'pictured'. Nine times out of ten the young nurse is female, the sexual harassment is heterosexual, the consultant generally male, the first manager is male, the second is female, the lawyer and the judge male — and all are usually white. Despite the fact I teach in a city with a diverse population and where my classroom population is equally diverse — the answers are consistently the same — every year. In unpicking this, I encourage students to think about the unconscious messages about gender, class, race, sexuality or disability that are perpetuated by media, books, rôle models, religion and society in general, thus illustrating institutionalised 'isms'. This is exactly why things as simple as children's books need to be truly representative of an equal, fair and diverse society — children's books depicting two mummies, two daddies or single parents as a 'family', or images of male nurses and female judges, or positive dual heritage and racially representative rôle models and disabled (visibly and invisibly) people — isn't being overly sensitive or evidence of political correctness 'gone mad' — it genuinely isn't — it is a depiction of a world where fairness, equality and importantly, visibility, matter.

Macpherson (1999) also made the point that in order to effectively police diverse communities the police had to have a diverse representation themselves. This argument is valid across all organizations but never more so than in those with power — the courts being an obvious example.

However the judiciary and the courts are arguably *not* representative of contemporary society in relation to ethnicity, class or gender, as is primitively, perhaps, but pertinently illustrated by the nurse/court vignette above. The government has stated there is a commitment to improving judicial diversity and in 2013 the Judicial Diversity Taskforce published a report highlighting the need for this work to continue. Nick Fluck, the president of the Law Society stated in the report:

'I wholeheartedly believe in the need for our judges to reflect the communities which they serve. I support the Law Society's efforts to improve judicial diversity and the chances for solicitors to be appointed as judges in our courts and tribunals. I am committed to keeping judicial diversity as a priority for the Law Society in the year that I am the president. I shall take every opportunity to encourage good quality applicants from within the profession and to publicise to solicitors the value and rewards of serving society as a judge.' (2013:7)

There is no doubt that diversity remains a contemporary issue for the judiciary and there is a recognition that the longstanding inequality cannot persist—however, as its stands, less than 25 per cent of the judiciary is female and less than six per cent from black, Asian or ethnic minorities—with both female gender and ethnicity becoming less visible in correlation with higher rank and status. Why does this matter?—Quite simply as Baroness Hale states, 'Diverse courts are better courts' (Baroness Hale became Britain's first ever woman Supreme Court judge after joining the existing all male Law Lords in 2004).

Pause for Thought

Do you think courts ought to be more representative of society?—Why? What about 'attitudes' of the jury—Do you think jurors are ever a 'blank slate'?—What are the implications of this?—How might it feel as a female 'victim' of longstanding domestic abuse to be in a courtroom with mostly 'powerful' men? What do you think of the idea of gendered courts? Have you been in a courtroom?—What does it/might it feel like?—If we think about perceptions and 'wearing' of labels and legacies—does it feel like a place where everyone is 'equal'...? Think about class as well as gender? What does this add to the mix? Are there class barriers to certain professions?—Why/Why not?

There are many barriers in relation to access to justice, indeed the courtroom and criminal process itself can feel inaccessible or intimidating to defendants, vulnerable witnesses particularly—not only in relation to gender, ethnicity and class but also to disability—imagine being deaf or blind—or physically disabled either as a witness, a defendant or indeed a legal professional. Flynn (2015) suggests that access to justice for people with disabilities is a challenge, and despite being legislated for courts in the UK are still falling short of a service that is anywhere near equal in any part of the CJS in actual fact. This will be further discussed in the closing chapter. '

Media, Mothers and Court

This chapter has illustrated how 'the general public' and indeed court practitioners are influenced by cultural norms and values—representations of which are of course reflected in the media. Hough and Roberts (2011) found that the media play a part in the public perception that sentences are overly lenient, a perception often directed particularly towards women (Morris 1987; Hedderman and Gelsthorpe 1997) and that the judiciary is 'far removed' from most of society. They suggest that 'the public' are generally lauded to be 'crying out' for more punitive sentences meaning increased use of custody—however what they also found was that when given accurate information and background information about an offender then the public are much less likely to call for more punitive responses, i.e. custodial sentences. Hough also suggests that the general public often only have an awareness of either prison or probation and so do not make 'informed choices' when asked for an opinion. Similarly, in lay discussions around gender specific sentencing, often the response is 'women should be treated the same as men'—'If you do the crime you do the time' being a favourite. However, again when presented with more facts and detail Hough and Roberts (2013) found the public tend to review their opinion.

If only at least in part, it is from the media that a large number of the 'public' form their view of 'criminals', stereotypes, images and associated attributes creeping like smoke, inconspicuously permeating minds and creating images of 'truth' and 'facts'—whilst littering news reports with emotive and damaging terms that in reality can present a 'distorted' but newsworthy truth (Jewkes 2011; Marsh and Melville 2009).

Sally Clark: Convicted of killing her two baby sons a year apart. Christopher 12 weeks, Harry eight weeks.

In court the prosecution used 'expert witnesses' (later discredited) who mistakenly suggested that 'cot death' or sudden infant death syndrome has no relationship with family history. In addition the prosecution focused its argument on the appearance, personal characteristics and attributes and working life of Sally. The media—who largely reported the prosecution side, commented on her 'short, harsh' hairstyle, her supposed lack of emotion—the fact she was an 'ambitious solicitor with a nanny'—who had 'worried about getting her pre-pregnancy figure back' and didn't look how 'one would expect a grieving mother to look.' In short the media presented Sally as someone who was as far from the 'maternal ideal' as could be—and therefore on that basis alone she 'must be guilty.' Sally Clark was indeed found guilty and sentenced to prison. Her family including her husband fought for her release and this eventually happened after a second appeal—three years later—and only following the release of 'vital information' withheld by the prosecution at the time of her first trial. Withheld despite the prosecution having a duty to reveal this evidence (called 'exculpatory evidence': evidence to support the innocence of the accused) even if not requested to do so. (Her second son had in fact died of a bacterial infection). Tragically, Sally was forever changed by her experience and died only four years following her release of alcohol poisoning at the age of 43.

Pause for Thought

Are you influenced by media reports?—Have you ever looked at a picture of a women in the press and thought 'She "looks" guilty'? Why do you think the same image of Myra Hyndley was used over-and-over for decades even though others were available? What is your view on 'double deviancy' and its impact in the contemporary courtroom?

It is important to note that in reporting court business, journalists are sometimes restricted in terms of legalities and criminal procedural requirements—particularly during the chronological development of a trial. In the English judicial system a trial is opened by the prosecutor—thus the 'headlines' of cases 'set the scene' for a 'trial by media' also. Goc (2007) suggests that this at the will of the media, reinforces the position of the prosecution and reduces the position of the defence. Ericson (1997) and Fulton (2005) suggest this effectively means the media can reshape the facts or 'imaginatively construct them to fit' a certain frame or angle that without being explicit can reflect and retell well-known tropes associated with bad, evil or neglectful women and mothers.

> ## ▌▌ **Pause for Thought**
>
> Think about how Madeline McCann's mother, Kate and her 'maternalness' (or apparent lack of it) was presented in the media — What was she being judged on? — Maxine Carr is called by the press 'one of the most reviled women in the UK' — she was not implicated in the deaths of Holly Wells and Jessica Chapman in 2002 — she gave their killer, her boyfriend an alibi, was sentenced to custody and released after serving 21 months — yet she is one of only four people granted anonymity for life in the UK (the other three are Mary Bell, Robert Thompson and Jon Venables (who all killed a child) — Do you think she should have served a custodial sentence? — Do you think she ought to have the anonymity? Why? — Why do you think she was given a 'new' identity when many other women who commit serious offences aren't? — Which 'trial' will have the most impact on her life, the one in court or the one in the media?

Pryce (2013), Gerry (2015) and Baldwin (2015d) have discussed the 'traumatising effect' of court. Giving evidence and being further exposed in the media can trigger post-traumatic stress symptom or re-traumatise a vulnerable person further. High profile cases can attract unwelcome and unnecessary speculation and intrusion, even with regard to facts that may have nothing at all to do with a particular case. Fear of giving evidence in court and living through the exposure and the trauma of facing abusers is a significant factor in why so many rapes and so much domestic abuse goes unreported and the rape conviction rate is so appallingly low (Rape Crisis 2015). Women and mothers already traumatised by an event cannot always make the most 'robust' witnesses and when cross-examined may crumble, alternatively if they are strong and 'together' then like Sally Clark it is questioned whether they are having the 'right' emotional response. In the case of mothers, sometimes despite the most horrendous abuse, the mothers will want to spare their 'children' even adult children (who may be present in court) the details of the abuse. I spoke with one woman who told me she hadn't realised the detail of her statement would be given in court in full and she knew her son was there (he was an adult) and she was just unable to speak on the stand — which the prosecutor took as her having made it all up. Had this woman taken advantage of the Witness Support Service offered at the court this situation may have been avoided or at least sensitively managed — but she was fearful and reluctant to speak to anyone 'professional'. The CPS has a well-resources online support library for witnesses and victims — but not everyone can or will access online or be directed to this. Another woman I worked with told me she used to have a recurring dream that she was in court naked and everyone was 'judging' her body as a measure of her truth — one doesn't have to be Freud to make the connection about how court felt to her.

▌▌ Pause for Thought

Is enough thought given to court support for vulnerable witnesses or the traumatising effect of giving evidence or being a witness in distressing cases? How can mothers be enabled to balance the divided loyalties they may feel giving evidence against their child's parent?

Felicity Gerry QC (2015) raises a valid point that court staff and jurors too suffer secondary trauma as a result of what they see and hear in court and read in court papers — but there is nothing 'built'-in by way of support as perhaps there might be for the emergency services — What could be done to recognise and address further 'trauma 'in the CJS?...

Look up the new Advocacy Toolkits championed by Felicity Gerry and the Advocates Gateway.

Women, Mothers and the Law

In addressing how the law responds to mothers it is perhaps important to affirm the point that women in general have had an at best uneasy, at worst completely unequal relationship with 'the law'. The Police chapter (*Chapter 4*) makes reference to some aspects of the law that have assisted and supported patriarchal views of male superiority and ownership over women — but unfortunately there is a great deal more evidence on which to draw (not the least of which is the UK's shockingly low conviction rate for rape — seven per cent. Re-visiting history would reveal laws and legislation relating to women's position as the 'possession' of firstly her father, then of her husband (hence the term to 'give away' in marriage ceremonies). It would also reveal laws preventing women from divorcing their husbands (but not men from divorcing women). In addition gender restrictive laws relating to women's rights to own property, to have access to education, to vote, to equal pay, the right to decide what happens to her own body—even the right to physical, emotional and sexual safety—unbelievably prior to 1994 a man could not be charged with rape if the victim was his wife (because of common law conjugal rights). Men fighting for continued freedom and emancipation in the 'great wars' was seen as 'heroic', whereas women fighting for emancipation and equality has often been viewed by society—but also crucially by the judiciary—as deviant and 'criminal' resulting in women and mothers being imprisoned—essentially for fighting for a range of 'rights' their male counterparts were able to take for granted.

‖ Pause for Thought

The Bourne Ruling. The Offences Against the Person Act 1861 made it illegal and punishable by life imprisonment to procure an abortion or as a mother to have an abortion under any circumstances—this was amended by the Infant Life Preservation Act in 1929 which permitted abortion only in situations of 'good faith for the sole purpose of preserving the life of the mother' (England and Wales only). Death from 'backstreet abortions' was relatively commonplace as were prosecutions related to abortions. In 1938 a 14-year-old-girl was gang raped by five soldiers and became pregnant as a result. An eminent gynaecologist Mr Aleck Bourne carried out an illegal abortion—as a result of which he was prosecuted. At his trial at the Central Criminal Court (Old Bailey) the judge directed the jury to acquit Dr Bourne, following a successful defence on the grounds that the definition of 'preserving the life of the mother' could be more broadly interpreted than meaning 'imminent death'—and could include such severe mental distress that the mother's life might be 'in danger.' The case set a precedent and between then and the Abortion Act 1967 women were 'allowed' to terminate pregnancies if they were able to convince two doctors that their 'life would be in danger if the pregnancy continued' (i.e. they would be suicidal) *R v. Bourne* 3 All ER 615 [1938].

Following the 1967 Act, abortion is still closely regulated and requires the signature of two doctors to confirm a fixed set of criteria exist. Feminist pressure groups feel that abortion with the exception of the cut-off point of 24 weeks ought not to be in the statute at all. However it is important to remember that both abortion and sterilisation remain illegal to women in many countries (and in Northern Ireland brutally strict conditions apply) and in others sterilisation is only permitted for married women with the 'permission' of the husband (As indeed used to be the case in England and Wales). Irish and Northern Irish women and girls are 'forced' to travel to England to have abortions — and can be sentenced to 14 years' imprisonment if convicted of having an abortion or taking substances to cause an abortion. There are several cases currently being assessed for appeal relating to one mother who brought her 15-year-old daughter to the UK for an abortion — another mother to be who had a termination because her baby had not developed a brain, but she had to travel to the UK to have an abortion alone rather than one at home with family support — in Northern Ireland she would have been forced to give birth to the baby and allow it to die (which was inevitable). Should women be criminalised for having abortions? — If you were a juror with a particular view one way or the other — would you ask to be excused? — Should you? — Or is your view as valid as anyone else's, whatever it is? What then in cases of mothers guilty of other crimes? — What would you find 'too difficult' — if anything?

The Police chapter (*Chapter 4*) highlights aspects of the law and its relationship over time to women and mothers concerning domestic abuse — so this chapter will avoid repetition. However the tragic death of Jane Clough also highlighted in that chapter warrants a place here too.

Jane Clough: A 26-year-old nurse and mother to a baby girl. Murdered July 2010

Jane courageously ended a violent relationship with the father of her child—She did so to 'protect her daughter' and despite previously being too afraid to report him she finally did after he raped her when her daughter was six-weeks-old and in the same room—he was charged with assault and nine rapes against her—some committed whilst she was pregnant. Johnathan Vass, her ex-partner, a paramedic, was arrested and remanded in custody. Jane who, having not only left him but also reported him, was prepared to give evidence against him 'predicted' that if he could get to her he would kill her, writing such in her diary—and police also felt she was at risk and sought remand. Vass appealed against his remand, and despite vehement opposition from the police and the Crown Prosecution Service (CPS), to Jane and the family's disbelief, the Crown Court judge ignored the warnings and ordered his release on bail. There was no right of appeal as the decision had been made in the Crown Court and not the magistrates' court. Terrified, Jane rarely left the house. Eventually after six months, although remaining scared and continuing to write her fears in her diary, Jane eventually returned to work as a nurse—Vass brutally killed her in the hospital car park as she returned to her car. Her family felt the Crown Court judge had failed Jane—but then were to feel failed again by an additional judge who eventually sentenced Vass to life imprisonment—but ordered the rapes to lie on file. Jane's family fought tirelessly for Jane's voice to be heard because as her father said, 'So far as we are concerned, he is not being treated as a sexual offender. But the fact is that Jane paid for the right to have those charges with her life.'

Jane's family succeeded not only in changing the guidance in relation to charges 'lying on file'—which would the Director of Public Prosecutions (DPP) stated, 'Now become the exception rather than the rule'—they also succeeded in changing the law in relation to a right of appeal. In July 2012, royal assent was given to a change in the law meaning appeal against Crown Court decisions would be possible—bringing them in line with magistrates' decisions. Her father said, 'Jane would be alive if he hadn't been granted bail.'

Pause for Thought

Why do think it was that magistrates' decisions could be challenged by appeal but those of Crown Court judges couldn't be? — What are the messages 'behind' this? What is your perception of the legal profession and professionals? — What is this based on? — Do these kind of feelings affect how mothers might 'feel' in court settings?

Attitudes to women *per se* compound the views and responses to mothers in court, particularly when we add into the mix expectations and constructions of motherhood and how that can shape courtroom decisions and processes. These idealised reflections on motherhood together with the expectations and qualities associated with it are very often revealed in court reporting (see later in the chapter) and in sentencing remarks and decisions as previously mentioned in *Chapter 1* (Minson 2014; Baldwin 2015a and c).

One such case is that of Ursula Nevin, a 24-year-old mother of two children under five — sentenced to five months in custody for receiving one pair of shorts stolen during the 2011 Manchester riots. Ursula had no previous convictions, and at no point is there any suggestion that she was involved in the original theft of the shorts or even attended the riots — she simply accepted a single item of clothing from her lodger. Whilst this may have been misguided as a decision, is there any way this amounts to an offence 'so serious' as to warrant custody. In his sentencing remarks the judge said to her:

'The first reaction [as a mother] you would expect someone to have is get that stuff out of my house — I have two children that I am responsible for [...] you would expect decent people to speak up and say, not that is wrong [...]. You are a rôle model to your sons yet you decided to have a look and keep something for yourself' (*R v Nevin* 2011)

So was Ms Nevin judged on the seriousness of her offence? — Or because she was not apparently a 'perfect' mother? (Baldwin 2015a and c), certainly the fact she was a mother to a one-year-old and a five-year-old was not considered by the original judge sufficient reason for a community disposal. Ms Nevin was thankfully released upon appeal when a more sympathetic if not benevolent judge told her, 'You must have felt you were [...] trapped in a circle of hell, I am sure the courts will not be troubled by you again. Leave now and look after your children' (Epstein 2012).

In her research, Sharpe (2015) recounts a sentencing decision that is almost unbelievable, Ellen, mother of one, was given six months in prison on the day she was due to give birth. Sharpe (*Ibid*) describes how this caused Ellen to collapse in the dock screaming. She had previously been sent to prison five times for breaching an original probation order — the repeat further custodial sentences perhaps demonstrating the sentencers' 'frustration' as described by Hedderman and Gunby (see later in the chapter); additionally highlighting that prison hadn't proved effective. The Community chapter (*Chapter 9*) highlights how perhaps earlier holistic intervention may have provided an alternative to custody, potentially preventing repeated prison sentences and separation form her oldest child — via addressing the complex needs of Ellen, who had a strained relationship with her mother, a baby at 17-years-of-age and a violent partner who had hurt her so badly she was hospitalised several times during her pregnancy.

When a young mother is living her life in chaos then breach has to be something that has the potential to occur — unless the 'causes' of the chaos are addressed — repeated court decisions to send her to custody cannot be in her best interests or that of her existing child. Under Transforming Rehabilitation (TR) women serving even short sentences will now be subject to 12 months supervision — which although this is being presented as a positive move, is a cause for great concern that it will simply 'create opportunities' for breach and therefore increase the chances of women becoming revolving door prisoners — possibly for an offence that in the first instance is likely to have not even warranted a custodial sentence. Unless provision exists to address women's complex needs and their very different pathways into offending and courts are willing (or, as my proposal would have them, directed) to use them, then TR will prove to be a ticking time-bomb for women and for mothers — and therefore in the longer-term for the children of mothers sent repeatedly to prison for breach.

Factors Influencing Sentencing Decisions and the Impact of those Decisions on Mothers and their Children

'Women…"Rather Like Difficult Men"…' (Priestley 1999; 70)

Interestingly, although there have often been calls for 'improvements' to the male prison estate (Prison Reform Trust 2014; Howard league 2014) it is less common to see calls for the 'abolition' of prison for men or emphasis on the harm sentencing men to custody can 'do' to male prisoners than is evident in the research and writing in relation to women, mothers and prison — despite the fact that evidence suggests the male prison population is also a 'vulnerable population' in terms of mental health, previous experience of abuse, being in care, etc. — and also despite the fact that 71 per cent of men are in prison for non-violent offences (Prison Reform Trust 2014).

Whilst male prisoners are not the focus of this text the authors would not wish to ignore them completely or fail to present the view that prison for 'many' is often not the 'best' option and, even more rarely, should be considered as the *only* option (Halliday Report 2001). In relation to 'separating' the issue of women and mothers in the CJS from men, Priestley in his work regarding the world of Victorian criminal justice, makes the point that there was an 'absence' of specific policy in relation to women — there was an awareness that women and women's needs were 'different' to men's, but there appeared to be a hands-in-the-air approach as to how to 'deal' with them. As Davie (2010) puts it there was the interminable 'problem' of what to do with women who break the law. How best should the courts 'deal' with 'them'? Robinson (1862:45) writes in *A Prison Matron, Life in a Female Prison* especially when:

'There is not one man to match the worst inmates of our female prisons. There are some women — so wholly and entirely bad that the chaplains give up in despair [...] There are some women less easy to tame than the creatures of the jungle and one is almost sceptical of believing that there was ever an innocent child or a better life belonging to them.'

Hedderman and Gunby (2013) in their research found sentencers who seemed to share this 'What else can we do with them?' attitude — particularly magistrates — and in the case of sentencing women and mothers, it is mainly magistrates, that feel that women have 'exhausted the options' or continued to offend whatever the previous disposals. Understanding sentencing patterns in England and Wales requires an unpicking of the complex set of factors influencing decision-making. Including understanding women's and mothers' pathways into offending and their offending characteristics.

The majority of women sentenced to custody by the courts are not violent offenders (86 per cent), the majority are mothers (66 per cent of children under 18 — many more of children over 18). The Prison Reform Trust (2014) states a further 40 per cent of women are sentenced for theft or handling stolen goods, many of the rest for benefit-related offences, offences related to prostitution and offences under the Education Act and 'failure' to ensure school attendance (Baldwin 2015a and 1). Yet, despite the low level offending and the number of women that are mothers, especially single mothers — the courts are continuing to sentence mothers to prison. Various chapters in this book highlight the astronomical rise of the female prison population in the last 20 years (doubling since 1995). However, significantly, there is no correlating rise in females or mothers actually *offending* — only in the numbers of women and mothers *sentenced* to custody (Gelsthorpe and Morris 2002; Deakin and Spencer 2003; Hedderman 2004). Sentencing to custody has prevailed despite there being a wealth of evidence-based research and economically reasoned arguments supporting alternatives to custody (Reed 2014; Corston 2007).

The Ministry of Justice (2012) report 'A Distinct Approach' outlines some costs of sending a woman to prison. A basic female prison place is costed at nearly £56,500—although this can increase dramatically depending on a woman's individual and complex needs—for example a women on 'close supervision' to prevent suicide or self-harm will 'cost' more in terms of staff hours (we are unable to cost the 'harm' to the women themselves in monetary value—if we could perhaps it would be 'easier' to fight for change!) However, it may not be possible to objectively 'measure' individual harm and distress but a small observable 'snapshot' over 12 months at only *one* prison revealed 2,771 incidents of self-harm—for one woman, 93 occasions in one month, also revealing a significant number of staff restraints/interventions in that period were undertaken to remove ligatures (Sandler and Coles 2008)—perhaps some indicator of the 'cost' to individuals and incidentally staff forced to manage situations and levels of distress they have little training for? Alternatively, a community order will cost somewhere in the region of £2,800, a holistic intervention from a community-based women's resource centre—which would address complex needs and offer additional support—£1,360 per annum (MOJ 2012).

There is a substantial body of evidence and research from practitioners, academics, activists and women and mothers themselves making it clear that prison for women does 'not work' culminating in the Corston report (2007). Corston suggests in fact being sentenced to custody can increase the re-offending rate for women and further 'harm' women, especially mothers additionally irreversibly damaging relationships with children and families. The 2014 Bromley Briefings suggest that, 'If alternatives to prison were to achieve an additional reduction of just six per cent in offending by women, the estate would recoup the investment required to achieve this in just one year' (Prison Reform Trust 2014: 4).

There is a wealth of evidence from a plethora of researchers about the impact of harm on mothers and children (we will come back to this) as a result of custodial sentences—and indeed evidenced research to support claims that prison does little or nothing positive in relation to desistance (APPG 2015; Prison Reform Trust 2014). Hough and Roberts (1999) and Hough *et al* (1913) found one feature affecting the increased use of custodial sentences was an 'apparent':

'... political desire to respond to public dissatisfaction with sentencing [which] has been an important factor shaping recent penal policy [and therefore sentencing decisions] both in Britain and abroad.' (1999; 1; 1:13)

Although, as previously mentioned, when given more detail, this 'need' to assuage the public is reduced as they would generally make different decisions. 'Detail' such as the overwhelming reality that when a father is sent to prison, a partner or a family member will care for his children and they will remain in the family home (that is not to suggest they are unaffected). However, when a mother goes to prison, only five per cent of children remain in their own home, only nine per cent are cared for by their fathers and 14 per cent of the 20,000 children affected every year by maternal incarceration go directly into the care of a local authority (Prison Reform Trust 2014; Reed 2013; Baldwin 2015a and 1).

What is more, many women sentenced to very short sentences, even if only on remand for weeks rather than months—which is not uncommon (Epstein 2012; APPG 2015) will lose their home as well as their children—making it difficult often impossible for her children to be returned to her care. Reed (2014) in her paper 'Orphans of Justice' highlights the additional 'costs' of imprisoning mothers economically for society and psychologically for mothers and children. Reed (*Ibid*) found that the cost per child of being in the care of the local authority can, depending on level of need and response to the trauma of maternal incarceration, range from around £60,000 per year to an astronomical sum in excess of £500,000 per year if the child has complex psychological needs and offending behaviour. Various studies have found that children of incarcerated parents, especially mothers are at least three times more likely endure mental health issues, offending or anti-social behavioural issues, and more likely to find themselves in the CJS in the future—either as a victim or an offender (Caddle and Crisp 1997; Murray and Farrington 2008; Greene, Haney and Hutado 2000).

So despite this wealth of almost universally accepted evidence (rare in itself!) from eminent, knowledgeable professionals, activists and campaigners from across a broad spectrum of practice backgrounds, all informed by research spanning a period of over 30 years, the existence of many sensible and comprehensive reports about what should/could change and representations from women and mothers themselves about what would 'work' for them—why are sentencers still deferring to custody when other options exist? The short answer is because they can. There are of course additional factors that come into play, lack of appreciation of the complexities of and pathways into offending for women—and not least as Epstein (2012) suggests because sentencers are 'failing' (choosing?) not to take into account guidelines which suggests, nay actually require, them to undertake the 'balancing exercise' related to Article 8 of the Human Rights Act (1998) in conjunction with the European Convention.

When a court sentences mothers with dependent children, 'rights of the child' under Article 8 are engaged as imprisonment, by definition, 'forcibly separates the mother and child, depriving the child of parental care.' Following a case involving two young mothers in 2001, Lord Phillips, then Master of the Rolls, made it clear what is required:

> 'It goes without saying that since 2nd October 2000 sentencing courts have been public authorities within the meaning of section 6 of the Human Rights Act. If the passing of a custodial sentence involves the separation of a mother from her very young child (or, indeed, from any of her children) the sentencing court is bound to carry out the balancing exercise before deciding that the seriousness of the offence justifies the separation of mother and child. If the court does not have sufficient information about the likely consequences of the compulsory separation, it must, in compliance with its obligations under section 6(1) ask for more...' ([2001] EWCA Civ 1151)

Accordingly, sentencers must: (1) acquire information about dependent children: and (2) balance the Article 8 rights of the child against the seriousness of the mother's offence. (Epstein 2012)

It is not that sentencers ignore completely the presence of dependants, indeed the Sentencing Council regards sole or primary care for dependant relatives 'as something that ought to be given mitigating consideration.' However, mitigation in relation to the offender and their sentencing outcome is very different to real consideration of the welfare of dependent children, or of the devastating long-term and short-term implication of the incarceration of mothers (Baldwin 2015a and 1; Epstein 2012).

Judges and magistrates however retain the right to 'discretion' and indeed apply exactly that. In her study (*Ibid*) Epstein found in all 75 cases included in it that there was 'no evidence of any specific consideration of Article 8 rights of the child', additionally that any reference to the welfare of any dependent children was at best 'inconsistent'. Minson (2014) discussed similar results in relation to inconsistency and discretion in her Howard League paper 'Mitigating Motherhood', although she found some sentencers did consider the children and reduce the length of the custodial sentence imposed. However, the point is that disruption and damage occurs with a sentence of any length, and the ideal outcome would arguably not be *shorter* custodial sentences, but *fewer* custodial sentences (Baldwin 2015a).

Over-use of remands in custody (as opposed to the release of women on bail whilst they are on remand) is a very real issue affecting women and mothers in the CJS. Between 1995-2005, there was a 105 per cent increase of the female custodial remand population compared to a 24 per cent increase in the male population. The APPG (2015) found:

> 'Rates of pre-trial remand for women are high. Approximately 40 per cent of women who enter prison in any one year are unconvicted, with 3,754 remanded in the 12 months ending June 2014. Few of these women go on to be convicted or receive a custodial sentence with 71 per cent of those remanded in the magistrates' courts and 41 per cent of those remanded by the Crown Courts not receiving a prison sentence.' (Howard League 2015; APPG 2015)

The APPG (2015); Marougka (2012); Minson (2014) and others have expressed concern at the 'use' of remand. From the research it is evident that remand is often employed, as arguably are custodial sentences in circumstances where risk of harm is low but risk of re-offending may be high and a mother's life may be 'chaotic', meaning the court will be concerned about her 'ability' to comply with court orders and may even feel that because of her chaos children will not be effected as they are "cared for by extended family often anyway" (Marougka 2012). However this response, whether it is due to a lack of resources or a lack of understanding of complexities of offending behaviour creates an almost tautological situation particularly if the mother is offending to support a substance addiction. O'Malley (2013) puts forward the view that prison can for some be a 'safe haven' a time to reflect on the chaos of their lives and an opportunity to withdraw from substances in a supportive and secure environment. This may very well be true but arguably also reveals much about the accessibility and availability of services and support on the 'outside.

Prison cannot and should not ever be an option considered by sentencers as a means of accessing services, arguably especially in the case of mothers. The gaps in service provision need to be filled — not ways found around them. The Midwife chapter (*Chapter 8*) and the Psychotherapist chapter (*Chapter 7*) talk of mothers almost wanting to be in prison to access care and freedom from worry and stress — as they did in Victorian times as mentioned in the Prison chapter (*Chapter 6*) — it is a sad indictment of the failings of society when anyone would prefer prison to freedom.

Tragically, a period on remand or short sentence (which the majority of mothers serve) is often 'long enough' for women and mothers to lose their homes and their children to the care system. Once children have been taken into care, very often it can take months or years for mothers and children to be re-united — compounded by their lack of housing.

'There is no provision of family housing on release for mothers that [do not have] custody of their children. This issue causes a Catch 22 situation because without suitable family accommodation it is much more difficult for the mothers to regain custody of their children.' (Re-Unite 2015).

Once a mother has lost her home and her children to care, it is perhaps not difficult to imagine how that might make her more vulnerable to re-offending, particularly if her offending is related to substance misuse — and so the cycle begins again — for mothers and for children.

Abbi: A 24-year-old mother of three children, Jayden seven, Petra four and Archie one

Jayden has physical and learning difficulties. Abbi has been 'in trouble' on-an-off since she was 15 when she began sniffing gas at school—'to impress Jayden's dad'. He was a 'runner' for a local gang, a 'well-respected, longstanding gang member' with a reputation for being unpredictable and aggressive. Family suspected he was physically abusive to Abbi but she hadn't ever confirmed this. Jayden's dad was stabbed and killed in front of her by a rival gang member when he was 19 and Abbi was 17 and pregnant with Jayden. Abbi gave evidence at the trial of his killers, which she found traumatic and was regarded by some in her community as a 'grass'. She continued to use gas and also began using other drugs whilst she was pregnant. Abbi struggled to cope and despite being pregnant her substance misuse escalated as she 'used' to 'forget stuff'. Petra and Archie were both the result of one-night stands and Abbi had no contact with either father. Abbi's lifestyle had led to social services becoming involved and her children were placed on the 'At-risk' Register—She was notoriously difficult to engage and would often miss appointments, but her children and her had a close bond and were physically well cared for. Jayden often stayed with Abbi's mum—who was supportive but despairing. Abbi had several convictions for shoplifting, mainly for stealing coffee and meat—which she would sell to fund her substance misuse—She was very strict about not using her benefit money for drugs as that was 'for the kids'—but continued to shoplift. Abbi had amassed cautions, fines and directions to stay away from certain local shops—which she breached regularly. She failed to appear in court following her latest breach and a warrant was issued for her arrest. She was remanded into custody. Her mother unable to take all three children, Jayden, Petra and Archie were taken into temporary foster care.

Abbi phoned her mum on reception into custody, said her transfer from the court to prison was 'terrifying', she was scared someone would 'know she was a grass' and was petrified she would be killed like Jayden's dad, she pleaded with her mum to 'get her babies back.' Abbi sobbed down the phone telling her mum she would kill herself if she had to stay there.

> ▌▌ **Pause for Thought**
>
> What do you think should/will happen to Abbi? Should the sentencers consider her personal circumstances as well as her children? — Or is it the rôle of the court to simply 'uphold' the law? — If Abbi is sentenced to prison — how do you think this will play out? — And if she isn't? — In considering other chapters, where/how can you see other potential positive interventions? — Think of those chapters — How should Abbi be 'managed' whilst on remand? What are the 'risk' factors?

Over the Threshold — 'So Serious'?

The Halliday Report, the Howard League (2014), Prison Reform Trust (2014), Hough and Roberts (2011) all reinforce the principle that 'punishment' and its form must be proportionate, and in relation to custody, particularly, ought to be over the threshold of the bar of 'so serious' as to only warrant custody and additionally be balanced against the end goals for 'society' together with the 'cost' to the individual (Baldwin 2015a:179:12:337). Perhaps it could be argued a further significant factor that can be applied to sentencing women and mothers, as is supported by Hedderman and Gundy (2013), is the fact that despite sentencers insisting there is a mindfulness of imposing a custodial sentence only when an offence is 'so serious' in reality. Eighty-five per cent of women in prison are incarcerated for non-violent offences. If in reality mothers were only imprisoned for offences that are 'so serious' then why are mothers imprisoned for failing to ensure unruly teenagers are attending school? (*Given what we 'know' about the complexities and family issues often surrounding school non-attendance — how anyone can think that punishing a family further — creating hardship and tension by imprisoning very often single mothers is something that I genuinely believe is at least ill-advised at best ridiculous*). Think also of Ursula Nevin highlighted earlier in this chapter and more recently the case of Syndi Baker, a pregnant mother who also had a ten-month old baby. 'Her crime? Writing love letters, albeit from a position of trust, but for writing love letters' and nothing more (Baldwin 2015a: 179: 10; 197).

Who, if anyone at all, benefits from prison sentences of this type? Does the punishment/use of custody really fit the crime? Not only is the answer to this question mostly, 'No', it also invites questions such as: what is punishment, how do we define it? Is it only and at its best custody? What is the purpose of punishment? In relation to the increasing prison population for women and mothers lies sentencers' lack of understanding and willingness to recognise the need to address the complexities of women's pathways into offending, together with lack of acceptance and understanding of the comparable impact on mothers and children when mothers appear before the courts. Hedderman and Gunby (2013) found that knowledge of the excellent community resources and indeed knowledge of the futility and ineffectiveness of custodial sentences for women was still not enough to stop magistrates from continuing to send women to prison for non-serious offences.

Magistrates sentence four fifths of women in the CJS so it is primarily they who can and should be part of the solution to address an unacceptable situation. Furthermore, I would suggest that magistrates should not just be 'encouraged' to change in relation to sentencing practice—but be 'required' to change. Sentencers truly must adopt the approach of sentencing women to custody *only* when the offence is 'so serious' as to warrant it—and in the case of mothers and carers passing a custodial sentence *only following*, and more importantly *only after demonstrating* the 'balancing exercise' has been undertaken and completed. Until this is done the female prison population will remain essentially unchanged. Positive change for women, for mothers and their children—and indeed society as a whole—must come. It is hoped that this chapter has illustrated that at least courts need to be at the 'vanguard of change' (Baldwin 2015a) whilst working in partnership with the knowledge, expertise and experience of those who understand the complexities of women and offending and the impact on mothers and children when their 'voice' of experience is not heard.

CHAPTER 6

Mothering from Prison
Understanding Mothers and Grandmothers, a Prison Perspective

Lucy Baldwin

'How Can They be "Caring When They Have the Keys"?' (Ursula)

Introduction

This chapter provides further insight into life for women in the criminal justice system (CJS), specifically mothers sentenced to custody. It contains a brief historical context of women and prison, with reflection on how this relates to women's position in wider society. Statistics are presented and discussed and aspects of the rôle and responses of prison staff explored, although the focus is firmly on the *mother* in prison, the emotions, experiences and challenges she faces whilst incarcerated, rather than a detailed discussion of the rôles of prison officers and other prison staff.

This is not a chapter about offending behaviour programmes or what is available for mothers to 'do' in a prison — obviously of great importance too, and can. Regrettably, this chapter can only 'scratch the surface' of the complexities in relation to mothers in prison. There is no doubt there is some evidence of positive changes in relation to prison for women (outside of the argument whether the majority ought to be there at all). Motivation and justification to challenge inadequate and oppressive regimes, to provide a more compassionate and holistic response to women who break the law is evidenced throughout this book (for example in the Midwife chapter (*Chapter 8*), Psychotherapist chapter (*Chapter 7*) and Courts chapter (*Chapter 5*)s). Additionally, there are numerous examples of positive and engaging 'work' being undertaken in prison like that of excellent organizations like Coaching Inside and Out (CIAO) and Re–Unite, but importantly for this chapter itself here is the opportunity to remind ourselves of what it can *feel* like to *be* a mother and/or a grand-mother in prison. To that end, it is illustrated by a case studies, vignettes and illustrations presenting mothers and examples of some of the issues they face whilst incarcerated.

Vignettes include 'Nina' whose experience is presented in the form of her first letter to her daughter from prison. All of the women's stories here are based on an amalgamation of women and women's stories the author has 'heard' throughout years of practice, reflection and experience. Nina's story was chosen for discussion because she is as typical as she is untypical of a mother in prison. We know that many, if not most women arrive there having survived challenging, abusive, disadvan-taged and difficult lives (Carlen and Worrall 2004; Devlin 1998; Morris 1987) — something highlighted and discussed extensively throughout the book. However, there are also many mothers and grandmothers who come to prison having led more 'ordinary' lives — furthermore grandmothers are often invisible in the relevant literature and so it was felt important to give them a voice. The quote at the start of this chapter comes from an interview with Ursula, who was interviewed during research for the book, a mother of five who had spent four years in prison and whose grandchildren were born whilst she was serving her sentence. Her quote is illustrative of the challenge in establishing open, honest, trusting, empathic and supportive relationships when 'power' is at its core — unfortunately, and I felt really sad about this, in her experience she did not feel that any prison staff she came across had demonstrated 'care'. In fact she said:

'Care, what care — who cares about prisoners, the public don't care what happens to prisoners, how can they [the officers] be caring when they have the keys. Nobody cares.' (Ursula 2015).

Perhaps this is more understandable when we remember that prison isn't a place where people 'trust easily'. Particularly those who have expe-rienced a lifetime of breaches of trust. In fact Ursula goes on to say:

'I came from a broken personal life, a world where it was dangerous to trust anyone. I didn't come to prison as a person who trusted.'

The chapter is written very much with an appreciation that simply 'understanding' and 'responding' to women who are already in prison is not and nor should it be the starting point; the actual starting point is challenging the inequalities and injustices existing in wider society that have a direct influence on how and why women come to prison in the first instance. The best case scenario would be a fair and just society where injustice, poverty and food banks don't exist—where prison is used sparingly—and, wherever it is used, it is used humanely and respectfully—where women and mothers are imprisoned rarely and *only* when they pose a serious risk of harm to others and when children are rarely if ever born to mothers who are behind bars (Baldwin 2015f). However whilst ever politicians and policy-makers take time to catch-up with this view, it remains important to strive to work positively, effectively, respectfully and compassionately with all those who are incarcerated.

The chapter encourages the reader to reflect critically around practice issues relating to mothers in custody by using 'Pauses for Thought' alongside the case studies. These thought spaces are designed to encourage readers/practitioners to place themselves in what may for some feel like an unimaginable position—but nevertheless to try; in addition they serve to raise pertinent questions for consideration and discussion together with encouraging additional reflection from a prison practitioner perspective. Furthermore, they may invite the reader to reflect on how culture and diversity issues may provide additional challenges, for mothers themselves and practitioners in relation to meeting their needs—thereby encouraging the reader to think of how and why any obstacles to quality of service and positive experiences can be overcome. The chapter *does not* focus heavily on women's 'pathways into offending' as that is discussed more fully in chapters such as the Courts chapter (*Chapter 5*) and the Community Supervision chapter (*Chapter 9*)—although Nina's story does provide an opportunity for critical reflection of the complex set of circumstances and factors that led an 'ordinary' woman to break the law.

Historical Perspective

Looking at the historical perspective in relation to women and criminal and social justice is a fascinating journey on which to embark and reflect. In tracing the origins of punishment, penal developments and prison reform for women it is impossible not to acknowledge the powerful influence of both religion and patriarchy—to not include or acknowledge the significance of their influence, legacy and relevance to current practice would render such discussion incomplete.

Without delving too deeply, even a whistle-stop tour through history reveals much about how girls, women, mothers and grandmothers in the CJS have been perceived and responded to—and significantly how that response has reflected women's position in wider society (Zedner 1995). Historically, theological and anthropological reflections relating to women and 'deviant' behaviour are littered with reference to women as being 'less than' or subordinate to men. Such beliefs have had a long-lasting influence on how women and ergo mothers who were also criminals or 'deviants' (like the biblical Eve perhaps?) have been responded to throughout history, even before the inception of the CJS (Carlen and Worrall 2004; Smart 1976 *et al*).

As a result of the abolition of 'transportation' (the enforced migration of convicts to the colonies) which saw the majority of convicted women who fell afoul of the law shipped to another country, there followed an enforced 'period of reflection' (Davie 2010:39) on the 'problem of what to do with female prisoners.' This was compounded by the accepted idealised stereotype that women were indeed the 'weaker sex'—and therefore 'unsuitable' for hard labour—which was much the norm in relation to dealing with male convicts of the time.

Early prison reformers such and John Howard (after whom the Howard League for penal reform is named) in the late-18th-century and Jeremy Bentham and Elizabeth Fry in the early-19th-century were very much influenced by religion. Although all of them held a fundamental humanitarian belief that physical prison conditions ought to be improved for every prisoner, for women their emphasis was heavily influenced by religion as well as patriarchy, believing that 'lost souls' and 'fallen angels' could find their way 'back to femininity', 'virtue' and civilised society.

Toward the end of the 19th and in the early part of the 20th-century attention focused on female criminality and was informed by ever-increasing concern and a biological perspective not least,

> '... because in their rôle as mothers, they were identified as the biological source of crime and degeneracy.' (Zedner 1991;14:308)

What followed, famously described by Lombrosso in *The Female Offender* (1895) was the start of an increasingly biological and medicalised model of thinking in relation to women law-breakers, which amazingly prevailed and influenced penal policy until as late as the mid-20th-century (with the re-rôling of HM Prison Holloway as a psychiatric unit and the proposed (though later scrapped) model for all female prisons (see Rock 1996).

Our whistle-stop tour of the historical position of women and mothers in the CJS unfortunately concludes in a place not dissimilar enough to where it began, i.e. where women's needs in the prison estate are still 'subsumed by men's', where a system designed largely by men for men prevails and where the complexities related to female law breaking are not accommodated (Carlen 2002; Corston 2007; Bastick and Townhead 2008).

Pause for Thought

What are your initial thoughts about prison for women? — Do you think there ought to be gendered approaches to imprisonment? — Does treating someone fairly necessarily mean treating them the same?

Facts, Figures and Context for Mothers and Prison

> 'I woke up in the early hours of the morning and it was still there [the worry about my daughter] — the first thing that came into my head. I had pictures of my little girl in the cell. Before I knew what I was doing I was slitting my wrists.' (Carlen: 'Sharon' 1988:100)

This quote is almost 28-years-old, one would hope things would be very different in 2015. But are they? Since 1995, the female prison population has more than doubled. In 1995, 2,000 women and 6,000 children were affected by maternal incarceration. The Prison Reform Trust suggest that this figure is now closer to 12,000 women with 20,000 children affected annually by it. Unfortunately many mothers are still being incarcerated—so tragically the above quote has not become outdated, redundant nor would it be unfamiliar to today's prison experience for women and mothers. Women account for 52 per cent of the overall UK national incidents of self-harm in prison despite only making up five per cent of the prison population (Corston 2011). Whilst this is blatantly an unacceptable and undesirable statistic it is perhaps 'understandable' when viewed with the additional context that the female prison population is one that is already vulnerable. Particularly when we remember that 46 per cent of women in prison have previously attempted suicide at some point in their lives (Prison Reform Trust 2014). We know from research and from other chapters too that women in prison are already a 'vulnerable population'—because many, indeed most come to prison having experienced abuse, trauma, disadvantage and victimisation in one form or another at some point in their lives (Carlen 2002; Carlen and Worrall 2004; Corston 2007 and others).

Pause for Thought

What responsibility does this place on prison officers—who have little by way of mental health training?—How 'safe' or 'unsafe' might this make vulnerable women feel? Is this 'fair' on either party?—What could be different?

Most of the female prison population are mothers, 66 per cent are mothers of children under 18—removing the under 18 caveat, the number of mothers in prison rises significantly and whilst no accurate figure exists it seems reasonable to suggest that this figure would be closer to 80 per cent if not higher. It is perhaps not difficult to appreciate how challenging it is for mothers to be dealing with the 'fallout from pain-filled lives' on top of issues associated with and surrounding motherhood and imprisonment (Baldwin 2015c and 2). As highlighted in the opening chapter:

> '...for many women the experience of prison is made worse because they are anxious all of the time about their children's wellbeing—or even their whereabout.' (Corston 2007.3.25:33)

'Mothering' from prison is a common feature of a female prisoner's life, facilitating successful and positive mothering from prison can be a key factor in not only maintaining positive mother/child relationships but is also in a mother 'managing her time' whilst maintaining her mother status and identity (Enos 2001). Many women will phone their children daily in order to maintain a role within the family—Indeed Corston (2007) talks of women 'running homes' from prison (33: 3.25), mothers will swap 'canteen' for phonecards, going without treats or sometimes essentials in order to have credit on their precious phonecards (Baldwin 2015c) so they can speak to their children.

Baroness Hale suggests that for many women in in prison:

> ' .. they still define themselves and are defined by others by their rôle in the family. It is an important component in our sense of self-identity and self-esteem. To become a prisoner is almost by definition to become a bad mother.' (Corston 2007; 2:2.17)

Ursula: Mother of five sentenced to eight years in prison

> 'One day when I phoned home my middle daughter came on the phone sobbing, absolutely sobbing—you know those big breathy sobs like when you can't catch your breath—I was terrified and was like... "Oh darling what's the matter tell me what's wrong" ...my daughter went on to tell me that her leotard wasn't clean and she needed it for a gymnastics competition—there was no soap powder in the house and daddy didn't know what to do... I told her to check if there was shampoo in the house to wash it with or to pop next door and ask to borrow a cup of powder...

My daughter went off the phone relatively happy and purposeful, but me?...God I came off that phone so upset...it was such a small thing but it broke me, I felt so ...Well I felt so much — angry with myself, angry with him and just — well just powerless — hopeless — disconnected — it was just awful — I went quiet for a while after that. I think that's when it hit me you know ...when I "knew" I was a bad mother — once I knew I wasn't a good mother, nothing else about me made sense'.

> ▌▌ **Pause for Thought**
>
> Officers might not always know that something like this occurred and may respond to a situation at 'face value' — How might Ursula react to officers asking her to comply with a 'rule' or come to an offending behaviour group immediately after this phone call — and how might that be perceived? How could Ursula's withdrawal manifest itself — or be construed by officers? — What would help Ursula and other mothers in situations such as this? What would help the children?

Sandra Enos (2001) in her text *Mothering From the Inside* talks of the challenge for mothers to retain and maintain an identity of 'good mother' in an environment presenting challenges to that claim — often the successful assignation of rôles is related to activities associated with that rôle — a firefighter will put out fires, a police officer patrols and makes arrests — similarly a mother 'mothers'. Therefore Enos (*Ibid*) suggests that the retained identity of 'good mother' is partially challenged because the lack of the ability to undertake 'daily care' and regular 'duties' associated with the rôle and identity of a good mother. Additionally, like Corston, Enos in her research found that:

> 'The very fact of imprisonment threatened claims to good motherhood, because the women had committed offences that led to the separation from children in the first place.' (Enos 2001:102)

Mothers who for whatever reason cannot maintain involvement and a mothering rôle from prison, as Ursula so eloquently and poignantly describes, often feel powerless, angry, frustrated and depressed—which Kesteven (2002) highlights 'can lead to breaches of prison discipline, suicide and/or self-harm.' In addition to managing mothering from a distance, mothering-related emotions and being separated from their children most mothers are doing so on top of dealing with numerous additional challenges (Baldwin 2015f and c). The Prison Reform Trust (2014) suggest over half of women in custody have experienced some form of domestic abuse, 49 per cent suffer from anxiety and/or depression and 46 per cent had made at least one attempt at suicide prior to being sent to prison. Research has repeatedly confirmed that narratives of the lives of many women in custody hold lived experiences in relation to abusive childhoods, abusive relationships, mental health issues, victimisation, inequality and discrimination. Perhaps when considered in this light the aforementioned seemingly very high statistic related to self-harm is easier to understand?

Pause for Thought

Is this different for male prisoners?—Do you think prison will feel the same to both?—If not, why not?—What could be done to assist women in the management of these feelings? How and why do men and women manage their emotions differently—how does/might prison accommodate that difference? Should it try?

What then of the mothers themselves? Are our prisons full of violent abusive women, imprisoned for serious offences rendering them a risk to the public and whose children would be 'better off without them'? No they are not, quite the contrary in fact and as the Courts chapter (*Chapter 5*) explores more fully, 81 per cent of women in custody are jailed for non-violent offences (Prison Reform Trust 2014)—the majority being for theft/handling, financially motivated or breach of community penalties (*Ibid*). Over half of women and therefore mothers in prison are jailed for offences deemed not 'serious enough' as to warrant a sentence any longer than six months—so will often serve less, only weeks. Yet in that short space of time many will lose their homes and their children.

For 85 per cent of mothers in jail, prison is the first time they have been separated from their children for any significant period of time, only five per cent of children of mothers in prison will remain in their own homes, 14 per cent will go directly into the care of the local authority. When a father goes to prison, overwhelmingly (just under half) they leave their children in the care of a partner or the child's mother, however when a mother goes to prison only nine per cent of those mothers are leaving children in the care of their fathers (Corston 2007). For prison staff working with parents in prison this fact can have a significant influence and impact on how parents 'manage' their sentences.

However, Rowe (2011) reminds us of the importance of not treating or regarding women—even mothers—in prison as one homogenous group—suggesting mothers ought not to be 'reduced in terms of social identity,' neither in expectation, assumption or rôles (Jones 1993; Bosworth 1999). It is important to recognise that not all women in prison are mothers and not all mothers will feel the same during a custodial sentence, indeed some will 'act-out' their emotions and/or disengage, others will repress all emotion and focus intently on achieving sentence plan targets in order to 'do their time' and leave prison in as uneventful a manner as possible. Others still will adopt an approach somewhere in between, varied at different points in their sentence—for example during periods of celebration or rituals when family might traditionally be together, birthdays, weddings, funerals—all of the 'normal' occurrences in a person's life—from most of which they will be excluded. Some may see prison as an opportunity and a sanctuary (O'Malley 2014) others will be devastated and lost.

Prison Officers and Relationships
Working as prison staff with mothers can be both a challenging and rewarding task—and obviously there are good and bad prison officers as there are in all prison rôles—indeed all rôles in society. Often, as has been described in other chapters and in indeed other literature (Rich 1995; Enos 2001), the identification with the 'mother' role, particularly *between* mothers, in many circumstances transcends other identities of self, and women as mothers can unite even in apparently disconnected

situations. I recall when my youngest son was on active service as a soldier, I was in a doctor's waiting room and a news flash came on about a soldier's death in my sons regiment— my heart was in my mouth— even though rationality tells you, 'They would have called.' I had tears in my eyes for the whole bulletin— a women I had never met, would probably never meet again, looked at me, patted my hand and said simply 'me too' —with the same tears in her eyes. At that moment we were just two mothers who understood the emotions in the other. This could just as easily have occurred when I was in a women's prison and I think would have played out exactly the same— regardless of whether one of us was staff and one a prisoner.

Crawley (2004) talks about prison as an 'emotional arena' and a space where there is an interplay of emotions and emotional management between prisoners and staff. Working as a mother with mothers in prison I found it impossible not to empathise with mothers in pain because of separation from their children and felt it important to convey that without collusion or judgement, but compassion and human kindness— none of those responses ought to be at odds with what Crawley (*Ibid*) refers to as the 'feeling rules' between prison staff and prisoners.

❚❚ Pause for Thought

If you are a mother do you think you would identify with mothers in prison? — What are the dangers of over-identification or 'collusion'?— Would this depend on what the mother 'had done'?— What about mothers in prison for harming their children, would you feel the same? — Why?— Has the word 'deserving' featured in your thoughts — or would it in conversations with those outside of your profession? — What are the implications of this thought process? If a mother asks you to post a letter to her children 'to avoid the prison stamp' will you? If yes, why? — If no, why not? — How could this be seen from a security perspective?

Many professional rôles working with mothers in the CJS are more fleeting than others, prison staff, particularly prison officers may have 'relationships' with prisoners that are months or years long (especially during longer sentences); additionally through periods that are likely to include 'personal traumas, difficulties and disappointments during their sentence' (Crawley 2004: 6:4:414).

Crawley (2004) found differences in the way male and female officers interacted with prisoners, but stated both observed the 'feeling rules', i.e. an agreed code almost of what emotions are 'ok' and 'not ok' to express—and to what extent. She suggests that how officers *feel* about their work and about prisoners has 'significant implications, not only for the routine practices of prisons (and hence the nature and quality of imprisonment itself)' (*Ibid*: 6:4:414-417).

Where does this leave the role of a prison staff member, for example a prison officer—what is their primary rôle? Arguably, it is one of many hats, at different times, often at different times in one day prison officers may feel like a prison chaplain, a social worker, a custodian, a nurse, a psychologist and even a parent. There is no more a 'typical officer' as there is a 'typical prisoner', as perhaps is illustrated by Nina (below). Babs, a 56-year-old mother of three, grandmother of two who served three years for benefits-related offences illustrates Crawley's point about the connection between officer relationships and the 'quality of imprisonment' and told me—without a trace of irony:

> 'Prison officers are just like humans really!—there's good and bad ones like there is in any job—but if you get a bad bus driver it might only spoil your journey—but if you get a bad screw—well, it can affect everything about your world for months or years—they can have so much power over you and everything you can or can't do in prison'.

Liebling and Coyle (2008) suggest that although it has become almost cliché to state it, nevertheless prison relationships between staff and those in custody are 'at the heart of the prison' and prisoners themselves have described them as the difference between making prison 'bearable and unbearable'. For that reason alone it is important to listen to the voices of both—in order that 'good' relationships are established and maintained and 'good' practice repeated; less effective practice examined in order that lessons are learned, and poor relationships avoided. Perhaps given that one half of the relationship doesn't have their own 'voice' and relatively little power—then it is all the more important to listen harder to those.

However, one might ask whether it in fact reasonable to ask for the involved parties to present a completely unbiased reflection on what is essentially an unequal relationship? From either the perspective of the 'prisoner' who is locked-up or the officer—who is of course an 'agent of the state' turning the key. Arguably both are influenced in terms of perception and experience by their rôle and therefore their position of power—or powerlessness. That is not to minimise in anyway the negative experiences many have reported in relation to prison staff, but equally there are examples of positive experiences and prison officer testimonies that suggest that, although officers recognise the inequality of the relationship and the ultimate power this gives them, it remains important to them to treat 'prisoners' as 'human beings' and with dignity and respect. There have long been calls to further develop prison officer training (Liebling and Coyle 2008). Crawley (2004) specifically advocates a graduate only entry and professional qualification route—as opposed to the existing eight weeks basic training followed by a probationary period—which is the current route—and for officers to complete a more extensive training period than is currently required. I would further suggest that working from a trauma-informed perspective is something which needs to be incorporated into prison officer training—which will serve to both minimise additional harm for prisoners together with promoting resilience, understanding and skilfulness in officers.

As with any group—there may be factors that each 'group' has in common with another but perhaps one of the key factors in relation to successful prison relationships is fundamentally being respectful, mindful, non-judgemental, kind and where possible flexible in relation to individual circumstances; perhaps looking 'behind' the face of prisoner or prison officer and seeing one human being doing the best they can in circumstances that can be challenging—in what is essentially a fundamentally unnatural and to some extent controlled environment.

Prison — At What Cost?

Obviously children under the age of 18 may need their mothers more than those over 18 and therefore deemed 'adult', that much is perhaps obvious — but do we think that incarcerating a mother, possibly a grandmother too — will have little or no impact on a family? Do we stop needing our mothers once we reach the age of 18? Indeed not. Hence one of the reasons for choosing Nina as a case study in this chapter, is to illustrate that mothering and the emotional pull of 'children' of any age has an impact on the majority of women serving a prison sentence.

That said it is worth examining the facts and figures surrounding the impact of maternal incarceration, on children too. As well as only five per cent staying in their own homes, children of imprisoned mothers are three times more likely to suffer from mental health, anti-social or behavioural issues, and are more likely to become offenders/victims as adults — and more so as children of imprisoned mothers than of imprisoned fathers (Prison Reform Trust 2012). The focus of this book is on mothers, to attempt to explore the experiential and emotional impact of maternal incarceration on children within the confines of this chapter would be to do both a disservice. The fallout for children is vast and requires detailed consideration, discussion and developments in its own right, e.g. the continuing the work of Barnados, Women's Breakout, Children of Prisoners Europe (COPE). However a small glimpse of the experience of maternal imprisonment for a child through the lens of a mother can be illustrated by Ursula's experiences.

Ursula continued

'I was thankful that I was going to be able to speak with my daughter on her birthday and although feeling sad and separate I put on my 'mummy mask' and made the call to my daughter — I managed to get hold of her just before her party — but was surprised to hear her sounding flat and sad — I asked her what was the matter and her innocent question nearly broke my heart. She said, 'Mummy I don't know where to say that you are?'... In her bewildered voice — she went on — 'Last year's party I said to my friends you were at work, Christmas I said to my friends you were at work — but

I can't say you are at work again today can I?—No-one is alllwaaaays at work are they'. I hung up after offering her some excuse—I can't remember what—I was so heartbroken.

I went back to my cell and cried my eyes out. No way would I cry in front of anyone—not the officers and not the other women really—you have to be tough and to be honest they are all going through the same thing anyway—so why would you then burden them with your stuff too?'

‖ Pause for Thought

How do women manage this, how do children manage this? Barnados' (I-Hop) work with children who have a parent in prison, as do Children of Prisoners Europe (COPE)—see www.notmycrimestillmysentence. org…How would you cope as a parent reading this?—What would your children be like if you 'went away' for months, or years?—Would you want them to visit? How would this make you feel?

Nina's story

Nina's story is told via a copy of letter written by her, a 47-year-old-mother, to Charlotte, her 23-year-old daughter—on her reception into custody following her sentence for fraud/theft relating to charity donations collected by her. Nina was sentenced to ten months in custody.

Charlotte,

How can I even begin to say sorry—I don't even know where to start. I know by now you will know where I am and what I have done.

You will know that everything you thought about me as a mother was wrong, everything I taught you about being a good, honest , decent person—you must feel was a lie. It wasn't, you are a good and decent person—and I'm so proud of you—it's me that isn't good or decent anymore and I'm so sorry Charlotte. So sorry.

I am so sorry not to have told you this was all going on, I feel even worse that I haven't prepared you for me being locked-up, let alone told you I had been arrested. It's been such an awful few months keeping this from you—the moment I was arrested all I could see was you, how this will affect you. I know you will think, 'Well why couldn't she think like that before and not do this'... I know you will feel let down and betrayed and all of the things I would feel in your shoes—ashamed I expect too—I know it will have been in the paper by now and I know that will mortify you.

But honestly, believe me when I tell you this Charlotte, I could not feel worse than I do right now—I don't know how to live with myself for what I know you must be going through.

I wanted to try to explain to you what happened and how it happened because on paper it looks so bad. I know the papers will be saying, 'Grandmother stole charity money'...And I know that's exactly what it is really. Charlotte, I'm so sorry. I'm not making excuses but I want to explain. When your dad died and your brother left home I think I just fell apart a bit. All I have ever been since I was 18 is a wife and a mother—and suddenly it felt like I was neither. I'm not saying that to make you or anyone else feel sorry for me—I don't mean it that way—I just felt empty—like I had no purpose.

You have your Wayne to look after you and I know you visit as much as you can, our Jenny has James and well me—after you girls left I think I just poured more love into George and your dad. I know you all think George was spoilt and I did too much for him, but truth is I liked it—what else was I going to do? Remember our house growing-up love—it was madness wasn't it?—you all at home—arguing and fighting—playing and mess-making—I loved it all—even when you all brought four mates home and announced there and then they would be all sleeping over!!!!—Yeah I shouted and moaned and huffed and puffed about food and feeding 'the five thousand' but honestly? Honestly Charlie I loved it—the house lived and breathed kids—I loved the fussing and looking after you all... I even loved the mess in a funny sort of way...(I know I bet you never thought you would hear me say that!)

When you girls left—it was just your dad, me and George—it felt so quiet so still, too tidy—George was always out with his mates, I know he's a good boy and never took advantage—but he was out a lot—but he always paid his board on time—I know you girls thought I didn't charge him enough—but he helped in other ways love—he'd bring home the meat or puddings—he did his bit love. He helped me a lot with money really. When your dad was still working the house was literally empty for hours with just me waiting for the phone to ring hoping it would be you or our Jenny ringing to chat—or I'd ring you. I know you have busy lives love—and I always seemed to ring at the wrong time—but I missed you girls so much—I hated being on my own—I couldn't handle not doing something—or maybe not being needed—I don't know—anyway that's why I went to work in the charity shop—and I loved it .

I loved being around people doing things to help—I suppose you could say, what is it you lot say, I got a buzz from it—yes I was buzzin!…I enjoyed working there, enjoyed working with people. I was just getting to a happy place again when our Jen rang to say her and James had been approved to emigrate…I still can't think about that day without filling-up. I felt awful, selfish and mean-spirited but I was so upset—where had I gone wrong as a mum that she was going to live in another country!!! Now she has a baby—I have a grandbaby—I haven't even seen—I ache to hold that baby so much I can't tell you—how was I ever going to have the money to get to bloody New Zealand—I don't even know where it is let alone have the money to go. Yes they Skype on that laptop thing but it's not the same—that baby is my flesh and blood too. I haven't kissed him or smelled his neck or changed his nappy. It breaks my heart.

Then when George left home to go and live with that Marie—well that nearly finished me off—all my babies—gone—none of you needing me…I know this sounds selfish and I'm so sorry I'm just trying to explain why I did what I did…George and Marie, I know they are happy and need their own lives and space and I'm happy for you all I really am—that you have partners who love you…but then you all didn't need me and I just felt useless, hopeless, dead inside—nothing made me happy anymore—not my soaps. Not even the shop much ... but I had your dad.

Me and your dad had been together since we were 14, he loved me and I loved him—despite the shouting and nagging we knew we had each other and we looked after each other—your dad even suggested we get a dog when George left 'cos he knew I was upset—and you know he hates dogs ... But he knew I missed looking after something—he just knew.

When he had that heart attack a month after George left I thought I would die too, of a broken heart. You read of it in the papers don't you—it happens and I thought it would happen to me. I think a bit of me even wanted it to happen to me.

Now I really was on my own, George and Marie living so far away, I was terrified you would move further away too—then when you told me you were pregnant that made that fear even bigger. I was so excited. I was going to be a proper granny. We decided I'd be Nanny and Wayne's mum would be Grandma. But I was too scared to be happy—what if you went—I felt like I'd lost everyone and I didn't want to lose you or the new baby too—I know Wayne's family are from down South, I didn't want you to move away as well. I thought if I bought you and Wayne loads and bought loads for the baby coming then you would depend on me and not move.

It sounds so selfish when I write it like this doesn't it but when you said that day—when I bought you the baby clothes and the baby bath and things , you said, 'Oh mum whatever would we do without you?'...I just felt like I had a purpose again. But without your dad's wages and George's board I had nothing but benefits and no chance of a job at my age with no skills or qualifications to my name. All I've ever done is be a mum—who would give me a job?

At first I just 'borrowed' a bit from the till at the shop if I knew I was seeing you so I could buy a little baby present—then I'd put it back when I got my benefits and no one seemed to notice—so I did it more often—and then one week I didn't put it back and no one noticed so I just took a bit every week so I could get you and the baby something every week.

I couldn't believe it when they charged me and said it had all added up to just over £500—Five hundred quid love—Isn't that terrible? It didn't feel that much when I thought I was just taking a bit here and a bit there—and I know you won't even want to use the baby stuff I got you now—knowing it was all bought with stolen money—it was all for nothing. Worse than anything—I will miss my grandbaby coming—I won't be—can't be with you like a mother should be when her baby has a baby…All its life when the baby grows up that child will say, 'Nanny, Do you remember when I was born?'…and I will always know I was in prison for that. I can't see this baby until its months old—I'm so ashamed, I don't know how I'm going to cope with the guilt of not being there for you, the thought of you having your first baby without your mum. It's not right.

How will you cope—? what if you learn to cope so well you don't even want or need me when I get out—I have let you down so much—I can't even begin to think of what you must be going through right now—it must have been such a shock—your good old reliable mum arrested, sentenced and in prison and you knew nothing of it until Auntie Val would have come and told you like I asked if I got jail at court today—not that either of us thought for a minute I would really.

I don't even know how quick you will get this letter from in here so I know you'll have questions after questions and now you have the burden of telling our George and Jenny…They did say I could have rang you from here tonight—but I couldn't. I couldn't face talking to you without you at least having something from me to explain a bit about what I've done and why. I know we've been close you and me since you were little—I told you all your life not to keep secrets and I have kept this from you—please don't hate me Charlie. I didn't tell you 'cos I wanted to protect you—I suppose a bit as well because I'm ashamed and didn't want you to know. I didn't want you to be ashamed of your mum.

I went guilty straightaway so quick really—but I was hoping for a community order, then I would never have had to tell you—I packed a bag anyway so I do have some bits so don't worry—The judge said it was worse what I did because it was from a charity shop—he said I was stealing from people who already don't have much. Oh Charlie I was so ashamed—I'm glad you weren't there to hear him say those things about me—It felt like he was speaking about someone else—a common criminal—not me—I'm just a mum from …, not a criminal. Except I am now aren't I…I can't even be a mum because I'm in here.

I love you Charlie and I'm sorry I've let you down. I don't want you to come to this place—not even when the baby comes—I don't want my baby to see the inside of a dirty prison so please don't come.

But please write if you can find it in your heart to forgive me and be there for me when I get out? Auntie Val will bring messages if you don't want to write and she will sort the other stuff out so you don't have to worry. Please know that I love you with all my heart and am just—well I'm just sorry.

Look after that precious baby MY precious baby.

Love always

MUM

▌▌ Pause for Thought

How might Nina be presenting herself in prison? —What will be important to look out for? What is important on 'reception' into prison? —What do you take from this letter about Nina's perception of herself and her life experiences? How do you think Nina will react if her children disengage with her? Do you recognise her 'pathway into offending'?

What if Nina couldn't read or write? Or was deaf and in a prison without adapted phones? What are your thoughts about Nina and her letter?

What will a custodial sentence 'achieve' in relation to Nina — was it the 'right 'sentence? — Was it the most effective sentence? If you were her personal officer how would you/could you use this positively with Nina? — What are the risks of Nina re-offending? — If an accurate risk assessment/pre-sentence report has been done do you think it would have recommended a custodial sentence (Sentencers can ignore 'recommendations')? — What alternative to custody may have been 'better'? — Given that she would be low risk of harm, low risk of offending? — Was 12 months of supervision costing between £2-3,000 for the year following a custodial sentence costing between approx. £40,000 to 50,000 per annum cost effective? — Do you think community payback would have /should have been considered? Why do you think it wasn't?

Mothers and Visits

'Visits or no visits, my pain, their pain, whichever you decide, there's still pain, I've done two lots of time now and I still don't know if it's best to let them come or not.' (Farrah, a mother of three aged six, nine and eleven)

Children, visits and prison can be a contentious and emotional issue (the Midwife chapter (*Chapter 8*) concerning pregnant mothers explores very young children 'living' 'in prison) and one which can divide opinion in scholars, prison officers and indeed mothers in prison too. I have heard officers say — both between themselves and to mothers — 'I wouldn't let my child visit a prison — let them be searched, no way.' Mothers themselves are often torn between missing their children and allowing them to come to the prison — many describe a desire to not want their children to ever visit a prison and think it's 'normal', and indeed many prison staff are divided and uncertain on this; in a discussion with prison staff where the pros and cons of children visiting was being debated an initially opposing staff member diluted their initial 'instinctive no' viewpoint':

'…but then anyone who has ever been inside a visits room in a women's prison will see children happy as Larry — children, especially the under-fives—all from different backgrounds, running around often playing with each other like it is a giant playground—all completely unfazed. It's the older ones who seem to struggle more, from about eight to nine to teenagers—they often find the visits boring, forced (like in a hospital visit kind of way), embarrassing and difficult, you can see them visibly struggling. I don't know what's best' (Prison staff member 2015).

We know that many mothers in prison have pre-existing mental health issues and many more develop whilst a woman is in custody (Prison Reform Trust 2014)—understandable perhaps when facing the challenges of prison and lack of contact from their children and families—partly due to the distance and partly because some women choose to insist their children do not visit them in prison. O'Malley (2013) in her doctoral research finds many women, particularly those on shorter sentences took the decision not to allow their children to visit, suggesting that although they missed their children dearly some mothers chose this 'protective mechanism' over-and-above their own maternal need to see and hold their child. Furthermore O'Malley (*Ibid*) suggests that not all women will actually admit to having children or be honest about where they are to their children because of their own guilt and shame or desire to 'protect their child's innocence' and in such circumstances visits are therefore not a consideration.

Jaqueline: Mum to Nelly four and Nancy six months

'[I]t breaks my heart , it really does, my four-year-old is frightened of the dogs and had nightmares after the first time she came—so I don't let her come no more—she did nothing wrong—she's a baby—why would I bring her up telling her people can't touch her—and let officers touch her and search her and check her sister's nappy too—it's not right—I can't bear to think of it so I told my sister not to bring them any more—I think she was relieved to be honest.'

║║ Pause for Thought

Imagine being a child of four and visiting a prison — What must that feel like? How can prisons help facilitate family contact? Would you make the same decision as Jaqueline — what might the impact of that be? (See the work of I-Hop, Barnados and Re-Unite).

Vicky Pryce in the *Foreword* to this book reminds us powerfully that even when children do visit prison, this can serve to be a more painful reminder of the physical separation from their children which can and does become unbearable for some mothers and grandmothers in custody. Mothers have described the separation, particularly when it is the first significant period of time away from their child as like a 'physical, deep pain that envelops you.' One client who was engaged with the coaching support, Coaching In and Out (CIAO), facilitated by HM Prison Styal 'equated the ten days she had been without her daughter to a drug addict going cold turkey,' bearing not only her own pain but as a mother her daughters pain too — and on missing her daughter's birthday said she felt, 'I'm not serving this sentence. My family is' (McGregor 2015;40-41).

O'Malley (2013) suggests not all mothers in prison will have positive relationships with their children even before prison, perhaps due to chaotic lives and addictions — and may in fact already have lost their children to care — for some such mothers prison can offer an opportunity for reflection, motivation and positive change (*Ibid*).

Hoever, notwithstanding how emotionally challenging and physically difficult visits may be for mothers in prison and their children, research consistently shows that contact with children and visits are an important part, not only of maintaining a relationship and a bond, but also in terms of the mothers' desistance form further offending (Prison Reform Trust 2014; Barnados 2014) — it is vital that visits reflect individual circumstances and must be balanced against the best interests for the child too (O'Malley 2014).

Fourteen per cent of the female prison population are foreign nationals (Prison Reform Trust 2014) and for these mothers anxiety and maintaining contact and relationship with children and families is more complex. Not only is contact difficult or impossible — but many women face deportation on release—and for some that is despite having years of residence behind them, friends family in the UK, even children born there.

Yana: A young looking mother of three, aged three, five and 18 months

Yana is 22-years-old but very young looking. She was forced to traffic drugs into the UK from her native Nigeria. She was convicted of carrying 41 packages of cocaine in her stomach. The drugs had a street value of £40,000. Despite explaining to the judge that she was forced to traffic the drugs by a drug gang that had, allegedly, already beaten her husband so badly he could no longer work—for refusing to be a mule. They had then 'stolen' her youngest child—telling her they would only return the child once she had successfully carried the drugs—Yana was sentenced to eight years. She did not speak any English and although a translator was provided for her at her trial, she understood little of what was happening around her during it. She was isolated and depressed on the wings and had no contact with her family or children, unsure for months into her sentence that they even knew where she was. Yana was reluctant to engage with her sentence plan because she didn't understand what was required of her and was restricted in her ability to engage because of the language barrier. On hearing music from a room in her prison location, she followed the sound and found a music therapy group singing and dancing a Nigerian lullaby—only one of the other women was Nigerian but had chosen the Nigerian music from a selection the therapist had brought. Yana was brought to tears by the sound of music from her home with words she understood—slowly she began to interact, with the music therapist only, eventually engaging with her fellow Nigerian on the wing—who did speak English. Yana was able to communicate finally and so was able to gradually share her story and secure appropriate support to help her understand what would happen to her.

Although Yana's depression lifted her struggle and fears were far from over as she faced immediate deportation on release into the grip of the drug gang she feared would kill her for failing to deliver the drugs. Her youngest child was still 'missing', she was applying for asylum, however the process is long and drawn-out with potentially decisions about her case not being made until her last few days in custody. Her personal officer has made sure that she has contact with the Hibiscus initiative—an organization that works positively with women in the criminal justice system, both in the community and in custody. Hibiscus provide essential welfare and advocacy support assisting women to overcome the language barrier, understand the processes they are engaged in and assist in relation to welfare and contact issues regarding their children. Yana's personal officer was a significant help to her and even learnt a few words of Nigerian—not so much that she could have a conversation—but sufficient to greet her in her own language—something Yana greatly appreciated and valued. The officer was key in securing translators to attend sentence planning, resisting the prison suggestions to use her English speaking Nigerian prison colleague—insisting Yana had the same right to confidentiality as anyone else.

‖ Pause for Thought

How must it feel to be in an alien environment, in another country when you don't share language or cultural norms with anyone around you? What would you feel most? You see other mothers having visits, photographs of their children and sharing stories of motherhood and shared experiences—and you don't even know if your children are alive or dead or will remember you on your release?—What is your rôle here?—What can you do to make a difference? Do you think the officer was 'right' to learn a few words of Nigerian or was it unprofessional/inappropriate?

The Hibiscus project works with women like Yana, the Welfare and Advocacy Project works positively and supportively with foreign national women in the CJS and prisons. The service offers emotional and practical support. Historically, its client base were women like Yana in prison for drugs-related offences, however increasingly the women and mothers they work with are in the CJS as a result of benefit fraud, document and/or employment offences—some related to illegal activities such as cannabis farming (many of whom display clear signs of having been victims of trafficking). An independent review of the project in 2013 concluded:

'Hibiscus is unique in its service provision and it is entirely probable that if. they did not exist, their services would have to be developed in order for the government and prisons to meet standards of human rights for prisoners as well as meet the needs of a particularly vulnerable group of women.' (Hibiscus Annual Report 2013:10)

Concluding Thoughts, Proposals and Best Hopes

Although there is evidence of ongoing positive change in relation to reducing the female prison population and the number of mothers sent to prison (and in this regard the CJS generally) (PRT 2014; Howard league 2014) there is still much left to be achieved. Systemic change is possible, as evidenced by the 'new and bold' approach to women and criminal justice being adopted by Scotland (see Community chapter (*Chapter 9*) for further discussion). It is clear that it is in everyone's best interests that short sentences are avoided and alternatives to custody are explored as a requirement (see closing chapter for further discussion). Needing to be 'heard' is not unique to foreign national women and mothers in custody. Listening to the 'voice' of women and mothers in prison is vital in the journey towards positive change. It is hoped that system-wide positive change will result in fewer and fewer women going to prison at all.

With the reduction in the welfarist nature of probation work together with the increased demands of a growing prison population and challenging staff ratios, arguably there is a 'welfare gap' in prison (and arguably even across the entire CJS) perhaps leaving room for a specific rôle that will alleviate some of the responsibility from officers, but provide advocacy and support for mothers—importantly also being a link person between 'inside' and 'outside' agencies, particularly those relating to mothers and children and especially where social services are already involved—or involved as a direct result of a sentence—again something probation used to be involved more heavily in than is its current remit. O'Malley (2013) suggests (and I concur) that this gap could potentially be filled by a prison-based social worker. This is something that will be re-visited in the closing chapter.

There is no do doubt that examples of excellence and a plethora of wonderful examples of interventions and initiatives within prisons like the aforementioned Coaching Inside and Out (CIAO), Women in Prison (WIP), Re-Unite and HMP Peterbrough's First Day Out project together with some improvements for services for mothers and babies. Yet we still have a system full of inconsistencies that McIvor (2004) suggests that by virtue of their comparative size means prison culture and provision is dominated by the needs of men. Chesney-Lind and Pasko (2004) also suggest their 'numbers' render them subsumed—however I would counter that view with the suggestion that, as is being demonstrated in Scotland, the 'small' (though still too large!) number of women in prison actually affords more opportunities for creative, innovative supportive holistic and therefore effective interventions to take place.

Women, mothers and grandmothers quite simply have different, complex needs and responses to them should reflect this (Hollin and Palmer 2006; Corston 2007; Scraton and Moore 2005). As highlighted in *Chapter 1*, trauma-informed models of working need to be more present in work with women in prison and in the wider CJS. Given previous discussion surrounding issues of power and authority, arguably 'outside' specially trained staff may be better placed to undertake this work—rather than adding it the already vast list of rôles prison officers are required to undertake (no disrespect intended towards prison officers at all).

The women in this chapter are as typical as they are unique, however feelings of loss, shame, bewilderment and devastation—whatever age women are when they enter prison, are often amongst the many feelings and emotions that are shared, frequently as a result of the lived experiences of past trauma. Working through this from a position of 'emotional safety' will be further discussed in the closing chapter.

Prison may or may not always feel like a safe place for women—but for sure it shouldn't ever feel like a place that inflicts more 'harm'. Managing simple things with understanding and flexibility may mean the difference between past traumatic experiences being triggered or not, searches for example, 'minimising and eliminating further harm' wherever possible should be considered as essential, to both mothers and children. Sometimes this can be achieved by relatively simple things—such as in-cell telephones, something which already exists in some male prisons in the UK—when we 'know' the significance and importance of continued 'mothering' from prison why has this not been considered for the female estate? Additionally, smaller 'custodial units' could be modelled on a 'whole establishment' basis as a 'therapeutic' regime—similar to HM Prison Grendon (a men's prison). Grendon's regime is unique and dates progressively from the 1960s (although it has in modern times been partly replicated at HM Prison Dovegate and on some other prison units), as the therapeutic programme is the core work of the whole establishment. It was originally opened as an experimental psychiatric prison to provide treatment for prisoners with anti-social personality disorders, under the direction of a medical superintendent.

In more recent years it has been brought more in line with the rest of the male prison estate and has for many years been run by a Prison Service governor. It continue to operate a ground-breaking regime in its therapeutic care of offenders.

> 'Grendon aims to help prisoners develop more positive relationships, to change how they relate to others and to reduce their risk of re-offending.' (*Inside Time* 2014)

Arguably this model of working would lend itself well to working with women in the aforementioned smaller units for women and mothers—but specifically designed for their complex needs.

This chapter has highlighted the need for positive change in relation to women and mothers in the CJS. Specific proposals are further discussed in the closing chapter—however it is clear that as well as reducing the number of women and mothers in prison there needs to be a more considered approach to working with them focusing on protection and early intervention and prevention of criminalisation in the first place.

> 'The criminal justice system fails catastrophically when women end up in prison.' (APPG 2015:6)

CHAPTER 7

A Psychodynamic Understanding of Mothers and Babies in Prison

Pamela Stewart

'As mothers we are the windows through which our children first see the world. Let us be conscious of the view.' (Anon)

This chapter explores one aspect the unique rôle of a prison psycho-therapist working in a women's prison. It is intended to facilitate an understanding not only of my rôle in this particular aspect of prison life but also of the women with whom I engage and who engage with me. I hope it will provide insight into the challenges many of the women face who come to prison, challenges they faced long before prison and possibly which they will face long after they leave. Women I work with show me the very extremes of human feeling and failing—I see extremes in vulnerability and extremes in strength over adversity. What I hope you see reading this chapter is the 'importance of compassion, honesty, responsibility, nurturing and human kindness—for all of us but maybe especially for those whose own start in life was not perhaps quite as it should be' (Baldwin 2015c and d).

The chapter highlighted the resilience of the human spirit in case stud-ies—based on women I have worked with during my time as a prison psychotherapist and which are used to assist understanding of the lived experience of some of the mothers in custody. It does not ask the reader to draw any conclusions on the 'rightness' or 'wrongness' of imposing custodial sentences on women or mothers—it simply describes what can happen as a result—and through the 'Pauses for Thought' encour-ages the reader to think critically and reflectively about the mothers in the chapter and what would produce the best outcomes for them and their children.

I am grateful to my own children for making me a mother and dedicate this chapter to all the mothers and children I have worked with for nearly 20 years. Without their openness and generosity this work would not be possible.

Statistics from the Prison Reform Trust provide a context in which to consider female offending: 70 per cent of female sentenced prisoners have two or more mental health disorders and 30 per cent a previous psychiatric admission before coming to prison. Sixty-three per cent of female sentenced prisoners have a neurotic disorder, over three times the level of the general population. Fifty-seven per cent of female prisoners have a personality disorder (2014) and 46 per cent have made a previous attempt at suicide. These dry statistics demonstrate the close relationship between mental distress and offending or perhaps more accurately between mental distress chaotic lives and poor choices. Psychoanalysis provides a lens through which to view the stories behind these statistics.

From a psychoanalytic perspective, the relationship between mother and baby is regarded as central to individual development. For this particular chapter in *Mothering Justice* it is fitting to spend time thinking about the experience of mothers who are in prison with their babies. Working with both the baby and the mother provides an opportunity to see how an incarcerated mother directly relates to her child and also to reflect on the way in which the mother may have been cared for as a baby herself. Many women in prison (indeed many men in prison) have lived through disadvantage, poverty, inequality and challenged childhoods. Over a quarter of the adult prison population have been in the care of the local authority and over 40 per cent of the prison population of under 21s (Ministry of Justice 2012). Over a quarter of girls leaving care will be pregnant or have a child (*Ibid*).

'The most terrible poverty is loneliness, and the feeling of being unloved.' Mother Theresa.

▮▮ Pause for Thought

If you have spent your life in 'care' or in-and-out of foster homes—do you think you would be fully 'equipped' to deal with life, responsibility and choices?—In what ways might you be vulnerable? What do we learn from our parents?—What are we 'meant' to learn?—What are the implications for us if we don't?—What similarities might prison have to 'care'?

Born Inside

My own involvement with mothers and babies began in HM Prison Holloway in 1996, when I started a project for the mothers in prison which I named 'Born Inside' (funded since 2011 by the International Montessori Association). I am supported in the running of both groups by a trained Montessori early years specialist and National Childbirth Trust teacher, Beverley Maragh.

It soon became clear that in order to gain a deeper, richer understanding of a mother's experience, it would be useful to run an additional group for pregnant women, many of whom, but not all, might get a place on one of the now six Mother and Baby Units (MBUs) in the country (In 2012 the MBU closed at Holloway, reducing the total number of places for a mother and her baby to 70). As a result of the Holloway closure, the Montessori Born Inside project now offers two separate therapy groups for mothers and babies at HM Prison Bronzefield. Operated by Sodexo Justice Services, Bronzefield is located near Heathrow, approximately a two hour journey from central London, making this a more difficult prison to reach for many families compared with Holloway. However this is not an unusual situation for families of women in prison—the average distance a women is located away from her family whilst in prison is 60 miles—with many over 100 miles away (Prison Reform Trust 2014).

In both groups, the psychoanalytical importance of the mother-baby bond forms the central focus. In the MBU group, both mother and baby are physically present in the room with Beverley and myself. As the therapy progresses, other family members enter into the story as the mother recounts her own experience as a child, and talks of additional children she may be separated from due to her imprisonment, often far from her own home. Over time, and through the reliability and non-judgemental nature of the therapist, the mother may come to connect aspects of how she herself was mothered with her own offending behaviour.

> ## ▐▌ Pause for Thought
>
> For mothers who do not have their children with them in prison — think of the logistics and the expense for children visiting their mothers there. Sixty-six per cent of women in prison are mothers of children under 18 — How might this impact on children's experience of the mother/child relationship and the subsequent consequences for their mental well-being? Do you think children 'should' visit prisons? How might mothers feel about their children visiting?

To give some context to the psychodynamic understanding of the Born Inside project, I will first outline certain of the theoretical foundations of forensic psychotherapy. Next I will introduce you to one of the mothers with whom I have worked. Finally, I will consider what can happen to women in prison who have their babies removed and adopted.

There are many aspects to mothering and to being a mother in prison. My view will be through the perspective of my psychotherapy training and experience, although I appreciate there are many ways of looking at this topic. Indeed, the more perspectives we have on this material, the richer our work becomes.

The Rôle of the Forensic Psychotherapist as Informed by Psychoanalytical Theory

The forensic psychotherapist sees the crime as a symptom of something in the perpetrator, as well as being terrible for the victim. Both victim and perpetrator must be kept in mind by the therapist. Often a result of impulsiveness, the crime usually occurs when the woman is in a highly emotional state, which affects her ability to think and to process her actions. This non-thinking state is described by psychoanalysts Anthony Bateman and Peter Fonagy (Bateman and Fonagy 2004) as a 'failure to mentalise.' Overwhelmed by emotion, the woman, often under the influence of drugs or alcohol, or under great stress, acts mindlessly. A failure to mentalise — to connect her feelings with her behaviour — is not put forward here as a defence for the mother's actions. Rather, it helps us to understand the dynamics of her thinking and how it has brought her into contact with the criminal justice system (CJS).

Forensic psychotherapy pays attention to the unconscious — to the feelings that we have but keep well away from our conscious mind. Freud developed a theory of the unconscious, which remains important in contemporary thought. No-one is completely rational all of the time. We all have moments when we make bad decisions, and we can all feel strong, destructive emotions. Growing-up, a baby whose caregiver is able to manage the baby's emotions provides the child with the experience of what British psychoanalyst Donald Winnicott (1967) termed 'holding'. The mother is able to hold the baby's emotions in her own mind and make sense of them for the baby. Instead of seeing the crying baby as being naughty, the 'good enough' mother (another term developed by Winnicott) is able to think about why the baby is crying and to do her best to resolve the distress. This mother does not have to be perfect but she does need to be curious about her baby's experiences and to enquire emotionally into the feelings that underlie the child's behaviour. In contrast, a harsh, critical, judging mother is not curious about her baby according to Winnicot and may, because of her own childhood experiences, be dismissive of the baby's attempts at communication. Rejection of or violence towards the child can be the outcome. It is perhaps worth reiterating there are additional more complex factors that may have relevance here and altogether different theoretical perspectives — but this chapter is singularly concerned with psychoanalytical theory and explanation.

The therapist aims to provide an emotional experience for the mother and baby, where the mother feels sufficiently 'held' in mind that she is able to think about her baby as a person with feelings. Serious problems arise when the mother is unable to do this. Mothers with very distorted thinking may view the baby as a persecutor — out to get them. Forensic psychotherapy is indebted to the findings of Dr Estella Wellden in her seminal work on perverse motherhood, *Mother, Madonna, Whore: The Idealisation and Denigration of Motherhood* (2000). Obviously there are a range of factors which may distort a women's thinking in relation to her child and these may include mental illness (post-puerperal psychosis, schizophrenia and post-natal depression for example), or mind altering substance or even partner coercion — however the focus here is on the mother's ability to 'recognise' and meet the needs of her child. Further research into child sexual abuse committed by women and mothers is a current concern for psychotherapists as more female paedophiles enter the CJS (Gannon and Cortoni 2010).

▌▌ Pause for Thought

Would you find it more challenging to work with female perpetrators of sexual abuse than males? — And with mother perpetrators more so? — If so, why? — How would you 'wear' your views as a professional? — What protective factors would you need to undertake this work as a practitioner? Could you? How and why might other prisoners react to female sex offenders in prison? — What is your view on this?

The rôle of the forensic psychotherapist is not to judge the woman. The court has already done that. The therapist's role is to be what Winnicott (above) termed a 'good enough parent'; through the development of the therapeutic relationship, the therapist aims to help the woman understand her own mind so that she is better able to think about her actions instead of acting out her feelings. What we are about is turning thoughtless acts into actless thoughts. This approach helps the baby to develop. A deep understanding of our own experience and a curiosity about why we do things protect us all from making bad judgements and committing impulsive acts. History does not have to repeat itself. Through early interventions with mothers, the experience between the baby and the mother can be different. To be very clear, the therapist aims to challenge the woman's past behaviour patterns so that she can 'change' and not repeat the patterns of her early childhood experiences. The traumatised mother may 'remember almost nothing, but she is repeating the past in the present, and the repetition — dreadful to watch — has caught a baby in its morbid path' (Fraiberg: 1980:55).

None of us is born a blank sheet. Neuroscience shows that the baby's brain arrives partly but not completely formed. How the baby develops will depend a great deal on the relationships he or she encounters. Contemporary psychoanalysis places great emphasis on early relationships because it is within these that we learn to relate to others and to ourselves. When the early years are marked by neglect, the child does not develop well physically, emotionally or cognitively. Poor pre-natal care, poverty, being a witness to domestic violence (48 per cent of women in prison) and particularly living through emotional or sexual abuse (53 per cent) greatly hinder healthy development (National Offender Management Service—Offender Equalities Annual Report 2013/14). As Sue Gerhardt makes clear in her book *Why Love Matters: How Affection Shapes a Baby's Brain* (2004) there are negative outcomes for babies whose mothering was disrupted or regarded as what Winnicot would term 'not good enough.' Learning to think about one's own experience requires a caregiver (the 'good enough mother') who is able to understand and encourage her child. The experience of a distracted, depressed, sometimes addicted mother limits early development. The brain scans of neglected children show far less development than those of a child meeting his or her milestones. If a mother has experienced such neglect as a child, this can seriously compromise her capacity to mother her own child.

I am not attacking mothers who struggle; such mothers need understanding and support. However, I am highly critical of a society that fails to support them. Mental distress and illness is closely linked to adverse childhood experiences. Over half of the women who enter prison have serious mental issues (as we can see from the statistics quoted above), and prison can offer an opportunity to work with such mothers in therapy; mothers who might not come within a million miles of therapeutic provision in the community.

Pause for Thought

Corston (2007) talks about the view that simply going to prison can make a women self-identify as a 'bad mother'—how might that feel? What impact might this have on a mother's ability or motivation to parent, either from prison or on release? — Especially if her own experience of being parented was lacking? What pressure and expectations are there on women to be 'good mothers' and for it to come 'naturally'? — What do you think about this expectation? Is it the same for fathers? — If not why not? And where do these expectations come from?

As an experienced practitioner with many years under my belt I have unfortunately born witness to cycles and patterns repeating themselves in families — although not inevitable by any means, evidence does lend itself to an argument that destructive behaviour and damaged lifestyles can have an intergenerational legacy and impact.

It is not uncommon to hear mothers talking about visiting their own mothers in prison, or having fathers and other relatives behind bars. Having a parent in prison is a disaster for children, often destroying the family unit and forcing children into care. Only five per cent of children whose mother is imprisoned remain in their own home, with 14 per cent going directly into the care of the local authority (Prison Reform Trust 2014). The National Offender Management Service 2013/2014 estimates that one in four female offenders have themselves been though the care system. No matter how much we might like to cheer ourselves up by reassuring thoughts of childhood resilience, the prison population is full of people from greatly damaged childhoods, and it is from such damage that the 'child' can, even without intention, simply by default 'damage' others. In the pregnancy group, we have worked with women who experienced up to 56 foster placements growing-up. Many women, and therefore their children too are failed by the system and then punished for that failure. The stories recounted by the mothers are evidence of this. There is so much more to the stories than women just being 'bad' or 'mad'.

To give life to these ideas, the following is a brief case history of a mother who first came to the pregnancy group and what followed on from that.

Case study: Claire and Tilly — Their journey from the pregnancy group to release

Claire appeared in the pregnancy group looking very tired and bedraggled in a prison-issue grey tracksuit. She kept her eyes firmly on the ground, and I noticed she held a folder tightly in her hand. Later she told me she had brought the folder in case she was given any information about the group. I had the feeling that Claire was desperate about something and was clinging to the folder for dear life. I wondered what she was looking for and what the group could offer her. Surrounding her was an air of unease and desperation. As she took her place at the table where the group gather weekly for tea and fruit, the other women looked unwelcomingly in her direction. What were they picking-up? Did they know her? Did her air of desperation resonate with them or make them anxious?

> ## Pause for Thought
>
> It is worth reflecting for a moment that if all of these questions were running through my mind — what must have been running through Claire's? — Perhaps she was thinking, 'Will they accept me, do I have to speak — I am scared?'

I introduced Claire to the group and the group to her by saying that this was a weekly confidential group for any pregnant women who wished to attend, emphasising the need to keep what we spoke about within the confines of the group.

One of the mothers chimed in with the standard, 'What is said in here stays in here.' I added that the group was an opportunity for the mothers to explore what having a baby means to them, and also to consider the impact of being pregnant and giving birth while in custody. Another mother added chirpily, 'It also means we can get together like normal mums who just want to spend time together and think about having a baby' (It is interesting how important this brief piece of normalcy was to mothers in the group — where they could be 'just mothers' and that rôle transcended any

175

other 'label', especially prisoner). She smiled and the other women nodded in agreement. No matter how tough the women act on the outside, all of them, in my experience, suffer a deep sense of shame about being pregnant in prison.

▌▌ Pause for Thought

Expectations of motherhood — not just by society as an abstract concept — but by women of women. What is the source of their 'shame'? Groups in prison are difficult to run for many reasons. One of the problems is that many of the women find it extremely unsettling being in a group situation, due to the negative experiences of violence in their families of origin. Just being able to be in a room and talk with others is often a new experience that can seem very threatening at first. And yet, who amongst us has not felt that stomach-clenching anxiety on entering a room full of people, be it a classroom, a staff group or even a party? Another problem arises from the fact that, as the women all live together, they can abuse the information from the groups and reveal intimate and personal details told to them in confidence. As emphasised elsewhere in this book, prison isn't a place where people 'trust' easily. Particularly those who have experienced a lifetime of breaches of that trust. (Baldwin 2015d).

Direct questions are usually best avoided. Although I never ask outright what the women are in prison for, I do ask them if they would like to say if this is their first pregnancy.

On asking Claire this question, colour seemed to drain from her already pale and anxious face. I was about to say that she did not have to answer if she did not want to share this information, when she whispered that this was her eighth pregnancy and her ninth expected baby, adding in an even quieter voice that one of her twins had died before the delivery. Of her own accord she added that all of these children had been taken by social services for adoption. The other women looked shocked but remained silent as I thanked her for being so open. The other question I ask is if they will still be in custody when the baby is born and if so will the mother apply for a place on the Mother and Baby Unit (MBU), which has space for ten mothers and eleven babies at any one time. Claire nodded silently at this, appearing as if she was already at the end of a very long road.

> Think about the Child Protection Social Work chapter (*Chapter 3*) here — think of the competing priorities of need and the old adage that the best predictor of future behaviour is past behaviour (Munro 2008) — What must Claire have been feeling like? — Why do you think she 'kept on getting pregnant'?

One of the other young women, 19-year-old Ruby, a glamorous and highly made-up first-time Mum, said that she was glad she would not be in prison when her baby was born and spoke at length about what she would be doing with her baby in the community. Ruby spoke about all the things she was planning to buy and the time she would spend going out with her friends for coffee. This struck me as rather insensitive because Claire would still be in prison when she gave birth. In addition, the question of getting a place on the MBU is always one of great uncertainty for the pregnant women as it requires a very detailed report from social services about the mother.

Clearly, a mother whose eight babies have all been removed by local authorities is not in a strong position to be allowed to keep her baby in prison. This seemed too personal to pursue in the group because Claire would be very much aware of how slim her chances were. Claire held herself with quiet dignity and I was impressed by her honesty in the group and what felt like her determination to try to keep her yet-to-be-born child. I cannot imagine the amount of courage it took for her to remain present and composed when faced with so much anxiety and uncertainty.

The chances of obtaining a place on the MBU felt to me to be so slim that I did a lot of work with Claire between the groups. Offering her individual psychotherapy, to which she readily agreed. Claire told me about the years of sexual abuse she had endured in her family from a very early age. She had also been physically abused by her uncle, who liked to tie her to a chair and pop balloons near her left ear until eventually she became deaf. As often happens, the abused child grows up to be the abused partner, and indeed Claire spoke of very violent partners and the amount of brutality she had suffered from them — which had in turn been influential in social services decision-making in relation to taking her children. There were concerns about Claire's 'ability to protect' her children — however once each child was taken support services to enable Claire to move away from violent and dependant relationships would be withdrawn — as the concerns regarding the safety of the child would be redundant. The loss of each child produced in Claire a need to replace the loss to heal her pain and so on the cycle went.

❘❘ Pause for Thought

Does this example bring to life the difficulties presented in the Social Work chapter (which deals with child protection) (*Chapter 3*)? — What needs to change? — How could this situation have been different for Claire and her children? How do you feel about Claire's situation?

With the individual therapy as a support, Claire became much more vocal in the group, and her increasing capacity to speak for herself was a pleasure to see. She joined in when the other pregnant women talked about what it would mean to them to be a good mother and what good mothering would look like.

I explained about the 'good enough mother', and they liked the idea that there is no such thing as a perfect mother and that the most important person to a baby is its mother. We were able to talk about how much the baby already knows and recognises about the mother from birth. The women enjoyed knowing this and said that this made them feel 'special to someone.' Claire was able to say that she wanted to love and care for her baby and did not think that being a good mother meant buying lots of equipment and clothes for the baby. This is always a hot topic as many of the women equate being a good mother with material provision. What we are exploring in the group is the importance of the mother as the first person the baby will get to know, and how critical this first relationship is for the baby's emotional, physical and cognitive development.

Many mothers appear disbelieving at this point and I explore with them what their own mothers were like: had they felt safe, loved and emotionally cared for and protected? The answer in prison pregnancy groups is usually no. This leads on to being able to encourage the women to speak about what it really means to them to feel connected to their child and to be able to understand how their baby is feeling. Together we speak about how the baby's emotions, as do our own, underpin behaviour, and question whether a baby can actually be naughty. We talk about what makes a 'good' baby and how the baby can make us feel.

▌▌ Pause for Thought

Are you struck by the similarities between this group of women and any other 'ordinary' group of women on the 'outside'? — What does this tell us? — What relevance has resilience? — What assists and what hinders it? — What were the key 'elements' that enabled these mothers to speak freely to one another in these sessions? What do you think makes a good enough mother? — What are the conflicts for child protection services?

During these sessions, Claire listened and sometimes joined in but I could see how she worried about the future. Having lost so many children it is not hard to imagine how terrified she was about also eventually losing this child too.

> After a great deal of support from the staff on the MBU, reports to social services and therapeutic input, Claire was allowed a cell on the unit. This permission took a lot of time and this meant that during the pregnancy She was under enormous strain.

I have thought about the impact of this stress on her subsequent struggles to bond and feed Tilly, which showed up later in the mother and baby therapy group — although perhaps on reflection I can see Claire may additionally have been too frightened to become attached to her daughter and even afraid to love her in case she followed the others into care.

> After Tilly was born, Claire attended the weekly mother and baby group. However, she remained uncomfortable with the other mothers and struggled to stay in the room, often thinking of reasons to leave. This indicated how difficult she found being with other people, which makes complete sense considering her history. She was terrified of being judged not 'good enough'. Tilly was a small baby who struggled to feed. Claire put this down to the formula not being right but I sensed there was more to this. To me she was clearly struggling to bond with her baby and to feel safe enough to relax. In the group we would speak about ways of holding and soothing the baby, and Claire was able to use the encouragement from the other mothers. Claire's abusive father died when the baby was a few weeks old and the prison allowed her and Tilly to attend the funeral, which seemed to give her some sense of closure. Although the charity Prisoner's Families was willing to provide a grant to enable Claire's mother to visit, she never did keep the appointments made for the meetings.

This made me think about Claire's own experience of being mothered, and what it was like for her growing-up without a mother to protect her and take an interest in her emotional and physical welfare.

❙❙ Pause for Thought

Revisit for a moment the quote 'The most terrible poverty is loneliness, and the feeling of being unloved' together with the one at the head of this chapter, 'As Mothers we are the windows through which our children first see the world. Let us be conscious of the view' — This chapter has talked about the legacy and pattern from inadequate mothering — How might Claire be feeling — as a 'child' rather than as a mother? — How might that impact on her ability to 'mother' Tilly? What needs to happen for children to avoid repeating patterns?

As Claire's sentence neared its end, the MBU staff worked hard to find her supported accommodation. She had made good use of the structure and safety of the unit, and both she and Tilly were making progress in their relationship. Over the three months, Claire opened up to discussions and was more able to make use of suggestions rather than to experience them as criticisms. As in the initial pregnancy group, the other women did not warm to her but they accepted her and tried to be friendly. This was a new experience for Claire and she seemed more able to remain in the group and talk and chat to Tilly when feeding her. This increased Tilly's capacity to feed and gave Claire more confidence in herself as a mother, which we could comment on and encourage — one wonders if she had not had access to this positive feedback and support what then might the consequences have been for her self-confidence and her ability to parent Tilly?

Fairy-tale endings are rare in life and even rarer in prison. However, Claire demonstrated her own resilience in asking for help and attending the groups and her individual psychotherapy. The prison helped Claire move on to a safe environment where the progress she had made as a mother in prison could continue, illustrating that strange paradox that, for some vulnerable women, the place they learn to feel safe for the first time is in custody. There is a growing need for provision for mothers who are not as fortunate as Claire, who do not get to keep their babies and secure a place on the MBU — indeed most MBUs run well under capacity most of the time as many applications are refused (see the prison Midwife chapter (*Chapter 8*)). Increasingly, we are seeing women in the pregnancy group who will have their babies removed from the delivery room. Removal at birth can be due to many factors, primarily the history of other children being removed because of the mother's drug or alcohol problems, or the nature of her conviction — and as we have seen from the Social Work chapter (which deals with child protection) (*Chapter 3*) due to risk averse policy decisions that are 'nervous' of giving mothers like Claire a chance or real opportunity to change. One mother with a serious history of addiction and violence tied her baby's dummy to her belt and said that she used the dummy at night to keep herself from crying. Often such bereaved mothers seek to fill the emptiness caused by a baby's removal by subsequent pregnancies. One such mother was Maddy.

Maddy: A 'persistent offender' who struggled to retain information'

Maddy—a women labelled a 'persistent offender' with a criminal record that stretched back to her teens—attended the weekly pregnancy group, where she reflected on her time in care as a young girl and the sexual and physical abuse she had experienced. She struggled to retain information and I wondered if she had a learning difficulty. However, she showed up regularly every week, and always spoke about how hard she was trying to keep this baby and her hopes for the future.

Maddy did not have a home and lived in a tent when she was not in prison. Her problems with alcohol had contributed to her violently attacking a homeless person, which was the reason for her current period in prison. Despite everyone's best efforts, the Mother and Baby Board, with social services, did not think she would be able to care for her child. Consequently, the baby, a little girl named Jenna, was removed hours after birth.

At least in Maddy's case she was able to hold and briefly breastfeed her daughter. Women who are in prison for sexually abusing children are not allowed to touch the babies before they are removed. Much more work needs to be done to support women whose babies are removed to stop the pattern of multiple subsequent pregnancy. Sadly, Maddy left prison, not only without her baby, but also without any form of birth control or medication. All of us who worked with her expect to see her back in prison, pregnant again within a short time as history repeats itself.

> ### ▌▌ Pause for Thought
>
> Do you think the decision to remove Maddy's baby was the right one? — What do you think would be best for Maddy's child? — Long-term foster care with a view to re uniting mother and child, or open

or closed adoption? (Open adoption is with contact; closed is without contact until the child reaches 18 and can make its own choices).

Pregnancy and birth are highly emotional times when many mothers feel deeply-motivated to change bad patterns of behaviour in order to look after and care for their baby. Women in prison are some of the most vulnerable people in society. Being inside offers these women the opportunity to receive psychological care that is often not available to them in the community. By respecting the prisoner's experience, the therapist can help redress the negative patterns of relating and help the mother achieve a different relationship with her baby to the one she herself experienced as a child.

Conclusion

Since the Born Inside groups are about encouraging the women to speak for themselves and to reflect on their own experience of becoming mothers in prison, the last word should go to the mothers. One, a young (19-year-old) first-time mother, wrote in her own words:

'The groups have been really helpful to myself and other inmates. I have benefitted immensely from attending both groups. They have been beyond supportive to myself and others and I believe that this support is required. I started in the pregnancy group at Bronzefield as a first time mother. The group helped knowledge me on my pregnancy and what was due to come as becoming a mother. I could raise concerns and get help and advice and ease the stress. The support and help was really positive on me and I believe on others. They are open-minded. It is comfortable to speak in confidence about any issues.'

Another mother wrote:

'We could sit together and feel like ordinary mums talking about our babies.'

CHAPTER 8

A Pregnant Pause
Expecting in the Prison Estate

Laura Abbott

Introduction

This chapter presents an insight into the reality of giving birth in prison. It first gives a brief historical context of maternity care in the female prison estate with reference to women and their position in society on a wider societal level. Facts and figures surrounding women, pregnancy and prison are presented and the rôle of the midwife explored; the chapter then gives itself over to its main focus—which is to describe the processes and challenges faced by women and girls giving birth whilst incarcerated in our current system. It is illustrated via case studies presented in a variety of formats, including a birth plan. These facilitate understanding and are representative of and based on women we work with via maternity services throughout the prison estate. There is no 'typical' case as each mother, each birth, each child and the circumstances he or she is born into are unique—however as with most professions there are issues we see time-and-time-again. Whilst this is tragic in the sense that it means cycles are not being broken—it does mean that we as practitioners can continue to learn and develop the most effective and reflective ways possible in which to work positively with mothers in custody.

The chapter is written from the perspective that whilst ever pregnant women are being sent to prison there needs to be a positive, compassionate, egalitarian and professional responses to pregnant women and girls. However, there is a wider debate to be heard about mothers and sentencing which will be reflected on later in the book, raising questions about whether babies should ever be born to women whilst they are in custody.

When babies are being born to women in custody midwives have a statutory duty of care, governed by the Nursing and Midwifery Council Midwives' Rules and Code of Practice (NMC 2012 and NMC 2015). In the UK all women have the right to high quality maternity care whatever their circumstances. However, there is an appreciation that mothers-to-be in prison face additional and specific challenges which this chapter highlights and discusses. Throughout the history of women in prison there have been many positive changes resulting from shining a spotlight on practice that is poor, lacking or simply requiring change; midwives have often been instrumental in that change by challenging conditions and demanding 'better' treatment.

In 1995, during the first day of his inspection of HM Prison Holloway a midwife stated to Sir David Ramsbotham, then Chief inspector of Prisons:

'I have never seen anything so inhuman as the way they treat women at Holloway' (Ramsbottom 2003:1)

This statement together with other conversations with women and staff informing him of the routine shackling of women during labour and birth resulted in Sir David's now legendary walk-out on the second day of that inspection, refusing to resume it until changes were made (Ramsbottom 2003). This courageous step, Sir David's drive and the subsequent publicity heralded by women's champions such as the late childbirth sociologist, Sheila Kitzinger who, following this high profile publicity, inspired a group of North London ante-natal teachers and consequently led to Birth Companions, supporting pregnant prisoners during pregnancy, childbirth and post-natally in prison, formed in 1996 with Sheila as honorary president.

Thankfully, things have significantly moved on and HM Prisons Holloway, Bronzefield and Styal are now at the vanguard of positive change for mothers in custody — supported and informed by midwives and a number of charitable organizations such as Birth Companions, Women in Prison, Re–Unite and the National Childbirth Trust. Thankfully, giving birth in shackles or 'behind bars' is now most often in the past (mothers are 'taken out' to local hospitals to actually give birth) and Mother and Baby Units (MBUs) in prison have received positive reports from inspections and women who have benefitted from their services.

The Royal College of Midwives (RCM) position paper for childbearing prisoner's states:

> 'Midwives should ensure that the dignity of every prisoner who is pregnant or in labour is preserved, regardless of her situation, or the way in which care is delivered. It is the midwife's responsibility to ask for restraints to be removed during consultations and all examinations including those of an intimate nature and during birth.' RCM (2008:2)

This was updated slightly in 2014 and then included additional reference to 'transfers between areas' and stating that any 'restraint' of pregnant women should only be used where there has been an assessed risk, and that risk is to herself, her unborn baby or to others (RCM 2014: 2).

The 'Pauses for Thought' in this chapter encourage readers/practitioners to place themselves in what may feel like an unthinkable position—but nevertheless to try. They asks the reader to reflect on how culture and diversity issues may provide additional challenges for mothers themselves and for staff working with them in relation to meeting their needs—encouraging the reader to think of how and why any obstacles to quality of service and experiences can be overcome. Overall, the chapter hopes to provide insight into the reality of pregnancy in prison with positive reflections and guidance to assist effective and reflective practice. Wherever it happens, birth is an event and experience women will remember for the rest of their lives—and whatever the circumstances it ought to be an experience that is as positive as it is possible to be.

Historical Perspective: Maternity and Prison

The first purpose-built prison for women is understood to have been in 1645 in Holland (Zedner 1998). Historically, women law breakers were held within male prisons where they were employed as cleaners, cooks or weavers. Prior to single sex prisons, women were often without any supervision, particularly at night and sexual assaults by staff were commonplace, resulting in many becoming pregnant whilst imprisoned (Craig 2009). That all women were prostitutes was a common assumption regarding female prisoners (Zedner 1998).

Gender, or even pregnancy, did not prevent women from being punished or imprisoned, with the exception of capital punishment (usually by hanging). Callahan (2013) reported that women may have used their femininity, particularly in 'pleading their bellies' to prove pregnancy and therefore avoid it. However in the late 18th and early 19th-centuries pregnancy provided no guarantees of mercy for women lawbreakers who would sometimes pay to have their abdomen filled with fluid to make them look pregnant, however this rarely worked and in extreme cases not only were women sentenced to hang but also subjected to anatomisation (dissection) in Surgeon's Hall (Callahan 2013). For those women who became pregnant whilst incarcerated—either via prostitution whilst inside prison or who were exploited by male prison guards and inmates—inhumane ways to exert control on women were used with reports that punishments such as 'strapping', 'handcuffing', 'solitary confinement' and the separation of women from their babies were often employed as means of punishment (Craig 2009).

British reformists such as Elizabeth Fry were instrumental in the implementation of prison reform in the 1800s as well as segregating prisoners by gender (Zedner 1988). Fry advocated the employment of female wardens for the women prisoners not only for protection but to act as 'rôle models'. This was addressed earlier in the USA following the death of a pregnant mother during childbirth following 'a flogging'(Craig 2009). It was the 1870s when this was addressed in the UK, although interestingly there remains a significant gender imbalance of prison staff with only 28 per cent of officers being female (Hanson 2008). Gender discrimination was a common theme historically and conditions and attitudes to women reflected the view of wider society of the time (Carlen and Worrall 2004).

Children went to prison alongside their mothers and, prior to prison reform policy in 1823, babies born to mothers in prison stayed with them for the remainder of their sentences (Zedner 1998). Craig (2009) reported that illegitimate children translated to the 'crime of bastardy' where children and their mothers were imprisoned. The separation of women from their babies was often used as punishment alongside other inhumane ways to enforce control such as branding and strapping (*Ibid*). In the poverty ridden early-19th-century, it is reported women would sometimes commit a petty crime whilst pregnant to ensure imprisonment where they would be safe and sheltered, receive food and care. Although overcrowding and mistreatment was common it was reported that some women did view prison as a refuge (Craig 2009). Unwell or alcoholic pregnant women viewed prison life as having access to medical care during pregnancy and in the post-natal period with their new-born babies (Zedner 1998). It is tragic and telling that examples of women saying the very same things can be found in the 21st-century (Baldwin 2015c and f).

Mothers, Pregnancy and Prison

There are approximately 4,000 women who are incarcerated at any one time in the UK (Ministry of Justice 2015). The majority are already mothers, 66 per cent being mothers of children under the age of 18. Many of the remainder are mothers and grandmothers of over 18s or classed as childbearing women. Many women enter the prison system already pregnant and this is often only made apparent to them when they have initial health checks (Corston 2007). Although there are no official figures recording the number of custodial births, the joint NSPCC/Barnados' report 'All Babies Count' (2014), estimates that around a 100 babies are born whilst their mothers are in prison every year (Prison Service Order 4800:297.08 states that 120 babies are estimated to be born to mothers in prison each year). Countless women in prison are victims and survivors themselves, often pregnant from violent partners, many have suffered previous sexual abuse and rape, and many are women who self-harm or misuse substances (Corston 2007; North 2006; Gullberg, 2013). The majority of women in prison have mental health issues (Social Exclusion Unit 2002), which can have significance when working with woman who are pregnant in prison—a situation that is by definition stressful and something which may exacerbate pre-existing mental health issues. Women giving birth during a custodial sentence are a high risk group in terms of developing post-natal depression and therefore, often, subsequent attachment issues.

Following an agreement based on formal contact between HM Prison Service (HMPS) and the National Health Service (NHS) in 2000, prisons were required to provide the 'same level of care and access to services' as those in the wider community (North 2006). This should mean that ante-natal and post-natal care for women in prison is equal to that of pregnant women in the community. However in her report for the Maternity Alliance, North (*Ibid*) found that maternity services were lacking and inconsistent across the prison estate. It remains the case that charitable, third sector organizations and pressure groups continue to shout louder than government policy-makers for better services for pregnant women in custody. North (2006) found HMPS was failing to consistently record statistics relating to pregnancy and childbirth, including the number of births, still births, miscarriage and baby weight. This is despite guidelines clearly requesting all of the above and more in Prison Service Order (PSO) 4801 relating to Mother and Baby Units first issued in 2000; latterly cancelled and replaced by Prison Service Instruction (PSI) 54-2011 (see the *Student Online Resource Bank* in the *Appendix* to this book) which provides guidance for MBUs and the wider prison population who might be pregnant but not allocated an MBU place. However, in their report commissioned by the NSPCC and Barnados, Galloway et al (2014) suggest that this guidance is not consistently followed.

▌▌ Pause for Thought

How might it feel to be pregnant in prison? — What are your initial thoughts about sentencing pregnant women to custody? Think of Ellie, the teenage mum mentioned in *Chapter 1* sentenced on her due date for five pounds' worth of shoplifting — Do you think this was 'just'?

Midwives in a Prison Setting

The International Confederation of Midwives (ICM) (2011) defined a midwife as an accountable, responsible professional who works in:

'…partnership with women to give support, care and advice during pregnancy, labour and the postpartum period, conducting births and providing care for the newborn'.

This includes:

'... preventative measures, health counselling, education and preparation for parenthood practising in a variety of settings including hospital, home and the community.' (ICM 2011:12)

The Nursing and Midwifery Council (NMC) is the governing body outlining standards, codes of conduct and statutory responsibilities for practice in the UK. Midwives are the lead health care professional for childbearing women (Marshall and Raynor 2014). Examples of excellence in prison midwifery care can be found in Haringey; an award-winning team of midwives work to support mothers in prison. The Royal College of Midwives (RCM) (2014) position statement suggests that all women who are pregnant in prison should receive high quality continuity of care from a midwife. Marshall and Raynor (2014) suggest 'disadvantaged groups' are hardest to access and yet most in need of high quality maternity care. Ironically, when women are in prison, they may have greater access to midwifery services than on the 'outside', where, in particular, disadvantaged groups and vulnerable women are less likely to access maternity services.

Continuity of care is important for all pregnant women (Hodnett *et al*, 2011). Abbott (2014) advocates the view that this has particular importance for mothers in custody, suggesting it is the 'gold standard' for women and this is highlighted via the case study 'Yasemine' (below). Working positively with mothers in prison can be an opportunity for them to get to know and trust their midwives, potentially helping to start the process of addressing any complex health needs. Pregnant women in the community should be able to speak to a midwife 24/7 about any concerns via call systems and are encouraged to telephone in case of concerns (such as reduced baby movements, bleeding, unusual itching) which may indicate a need for assessment. Women in prison do have access to 24-hour healthcare but there is not necessarily a trained midwife on duty and means relying on a third person. There are some excellent practices. For instance, Birth Companions report that Holloway Prison has a 24-hour phone line direct to a labour ward where a woman can call if she has any concerns and the midwife can then make a decision for referral or not. However, there are variations and no specific standard set.

Pause for Thought

Who do most people call if they have pregnancy related worries? — How might it feel to have restricted access to professional and personal support when pregnant?

Could there be an option for a specially trained pregnancy 'listener' who could give peer support? This could be a prisoner who has herself given birth as an inmate and thus provide unique listening and practical support, especially to those women who are new to prison.

Our rôle as professionals is to deliver care in a non-judgemental way. The evidence suggests that stigma and being judgemental can negatively impact upon health behaviours and capacity for change. We need to be mindful of our own prejudices and of the shame a woman may already be feeling and not negate her further.

Pause for Thought

How are midwives seen by mothers? — Is it as 'agents of the state' who might be part of taking her child? Or the friendly face of child-related services? — Is this different for women with previous involvement with child protection/protective services or women in prison? — How do we build trust? — What is important?

Ante-natal Care in Prison

The Nursing and Midwifery Order (2001), Article 45 states that unless in an emergency only a registered medical practitioner or registered midwife can attend a woman in childbirth (obviously notwithstanding family or the birth companion). Most women in prison are classified as having high-risk pregnancies due to their previous and underlying health issues. Midwives providing midwifery care for women are usually part of a community midwifery team or sometimes a complex health midwifery team. Midwives will often hold a clinic in the prison once or twice a week. However, midwives in the hospital units or ante-natal clinics may have limited contact or knowledge of caring for a pregnant woman in prison. It can be especially hard to know how to care for a woman who may be on 'bed watch' as a midwife may feel unable to ask a prison officer to leave the room being unaware of prison protocols (during intimate examinations for example). Midwives may be unaware of the fact that such protocol means that prison officers are required to accompany her, rather than the woman being dangerous which can be an easy assumption to make. Greater training during midwifery programmes would help dispel fears.

Ante-natal classes are provided for women in the community. However, there is no standard provision or guidance for the NHS to provide classes in prison. It is understood that many women entering the criminal justice system have complex health needs (Galloway *et al*, 2014). Prison can sometimes offer refuge, shelter, food and a place of safety for women just as it did over 100 years ago. Many women may come into prison already malnourished due to drugs and alcohol addiction and therefore adequate nutrition should be essential and is something that would be addressed by ante-natal and post-natal pregnancy care — arguably more effectively for this group of women than perhaps it may have been done in the community. This is something that Galloway *et al* (*Ibid*) call for to be put in place by statute and included in the Birth Charter (see later in this chapter) which together with greater dissemination of knowledge will ensure that midwives have defined expertise and knowledge of how to care for a pregnant woman in prison in labour and post-natally.

Case Study I: Yasemine

Yasemine was 17-years-old when she had her first son, Ryan. As a child, she was abused sexually by her violent step-father and spent a number of years in foster care until she was allowed to move back in with her mother (who had since left her partner). She was permanently excluded from school at the age of 15 and spent much of her time with a group of young men who would provide her with skunk, marijuana and vodka in return for sex. Sometimes Yasemine was so drunk she did not know which of the men she had had sex with or how many. She does not know who the father of her son is. When she was pregnant she was housed, with her mother, in a different town. The group of men she was hanging around with have since been arrested for being part of a paedophile ring taking advantage of young underage girls from a local care home.

Yasemine paid little attention to her health and avoided going to see her midwife. She subsequently went into labour at 34 weeks pregnant. Ryan was cared for in the special care baby unit for six weeks. Yasemine had a difficult labour and the midwives reported her regressing as if she were a young child. However, she bonded well with her son and felt very protective of him, especially as he was so tiny. With support through the complex social needs midwife, the health visiting team and social services, Yasemine was able to take her new son home with her mum.

She was a dedicated mother but struggled with post-natal depression when Ryan was six-months-old. This led her to resume drinking and having sex for money, often leaving Ryan with her mother. She would often steal from shops to sell goods for cash but was caught stealing jewellery when Ryan was 18-months-old. She found out she was pregnant again whilst in custody. She was sentenced to ten months' imprisonment at 28 weeks pregnant and held on the first night wing for two nights and then on a wing where she shared a room with four other women one of whom told her she was 'disgraceful and should be ashamed' of being in prison whilst pregnant.

Pregnancy, especially a first pregnancy can be an emotional and challenging time for many mothers, but prison brings with it an added set of fears and anxieties that many on the outside take for granted. Writing a birth plan is an important part of ante-natal care and a very useful tool for both midwives and mothers as a means of addressing fears and anxieties about pregnancy and birth. In this context, this is best illustrated by Yasmine herself. She was asked to write her 'birth plan' which for a prison mother can be incredibly simple in comparison to that of some woman in the community, where often the smallest of things are taken for granted as 'standard' (e.g. choice over who is in the room). Often every 'additional' detail can be discussed, from the position of giving birth, who cuts the cord, who and how many will be allowed to visit, through to background music—in prison this plan is often much more basic. Yasemine's plan is best illustrated by sharing it sharing it alongside her thoughts as entered in her birth plan diary.

My Birth Plan—By Yasemine

I saw my midwife today. I am 32 weeks pregnant. She said I should write a birth plan. The things I want in labour, a list of my choices. So here goes:

I want all the drugs going. Everything, I want to feel numb. How can I get away with that one? How on earth will I survive a drugs test when I get back if I take drugs in labour? I have heard they stay in your system for weeks. Who will believe me? I will just go without. Last time was so painful and I had horrible flashbacks to when I was little. I don't want anyone to touch me.

I want my Mum. I want my Mum to be with me, to hold my hand. That is not going to happen though is it? My Mum is looking after my two-year-old and is still so angry with me. She will never get there in time and has to take two buses and a train just to get here and who will look after my boy? His birth was quick so I doubt she will get there. I don't want to be on my own but who else is there to come down? Who would look after my boy if she could make it anyway?

I want nobody to judge me. I know what they are all thinking. I get those looks off them all when I am cuffed for my scans and in the ante-natal department. I feel so humiliated. I feel so paranoid. I know I am bad but I would never hurt anyone. They look at me like I am dangerous or some-thing. Some Officers are good and take the cuffs off just outside the clinic but others leave them on. It is so embarrassing. I know I have done wrong. There is not a second that goes by in here that I am not reminded of what

I have done. I am judging myself and don't want those looks when I go to have my baby. I just want to feel normal and be treated like I am normal. I hope the midwife I get is nice to me. I feel bad enough about myself already. I am scared as to how bad the shame makes me feel but cutting while I'm pregnant feels wrong—but it's hard not to, it's normally how I cope but they will see the scars on my legs when I'm having the baby—and if there's new ones they might think I'm mental and take my baby forever.

I want my baby cleaned up before they put it on me. I don't want them to put my baby on me all slimy and wet. It just does not feel right. I do want to breastfeed this time I think. The midwife who comes into the prison has told me about the health benefits for my baby. It did feel wrong last time and makes me remember horrible things but I do want to give it a go although not in front of the officers, but they won't leave to let me try on my own so I don't know really. I do know it is best for the baby, the midwives tell me that all the time but I am scared of feeling horrible about my baby, I'm scared it will feel unnatural and I'll be rubbish at it.

I want photographs of my baby. If they take him away from me I am scared I will forget what he looks like. I need to have some pictures up in my cell. What if they take him straight away? I don't think I could live with that, without knowing my baby. What if I don't get a place on the MBU? What if the board doesn't sit in time? When will I know if I get a place and where will it be? Will Mum be able to bring Ryan to see me? Will Ryan hate me for having another baby? Maybe I should try not to love him in case they take him?

I want not to feel scared. I am not scared of the pain but I am scared of who will be with me. I don't want a male PO on bed watch. I don't want a man staring at me when I give birth. It's creepy, but I know I won't have a choice.

I want to get to the hospital in time. What if they don't unlock me in time? What if I have the baby on my own? What if something happens to the baby? What if they don't believe that I'm in labour? I am so stressed! I am so worried that I will give birth in my cell. I don't want my baby to be born in prison. I don't want HMP on his birth certificate.

The End. I hope that's what she wanted—I don't want to look stupid.

Pause for Thought

How might Yasemine feel about going into labour? How might she feel about being alone in labour? How might a prison officer attending help Yasemine in labour if she has no family support? What if she didn't speak English, how might that feel? Would she even apply for the Mother and Baby Unit (MBU) — would her application be considered in the same way?

At 36 weeks pregnant, Yasemine found out she had a space on the MBU in a prison two hours away. She was transferred by prison van at 39 weeks pregnant to the MBU where she was able to have her own room and prepare for the new baby.

Factors Affecting a 'Positive Pregnancy'

There are many factors that affect how 'positive' the pregnancy experience is for any woman, but for women pregnant in prison their significance can be exaggerated. Prison is a particularly stressful environment for pregnant mothers (Marshall 2010; Corston 2007; Price 2005; Abbott 2014). In pregnancy we know that stress increases levels of cortisol in the body, which crosses the placenta and may impact upon the health of the foetus (Gerhardt 2004). Therefore, it could be argued that it is the rôle of those working with the pregnant woman in custody to be mindful of this impact and it can be disputed as to whether prison is somewhere we should be sending any pregnant woman. Link and Phelan (2001) specifically state that inequalities of stigmatisation can have negative consequences for mothers and ergo their children. In prison, a woman is always visible and has nowhere to hide or be private and these characteristics are something that Laing (1990) suggests can enhance self-consciousness, shame, embarrassment and anxiety amongst those already highly stressed. Marshall (2010) reports that, alongside fear, many women feel specific shame and guilt when incarcerated whilst pregnant. Whilst the prison environment is likely to be stressful, care can be taken not to exacerbate a woman's anxiety and stress, it is important for prison staff to engage positively, compassionately and supportively. Given some of the challenges to positive prison staff/prisoner relationships, particularly around the issues of power and control — as highlighted in the Prison chapter (*Chapter 6*) sometimes it is perhaps important to expand and continue utilising support from outside agencies such as Birth Companions; striving to work to the current guidelines in the PSI 2011 — particularly until a specific PSO for pregnancy is agreed. Birth Companions report that women often feel great shame when handcuffed attending a clinic outside of the prison (Birth Companions 2013), even when the cuffs are taken off just prior to entering the hospital.

Murphy and Rosenbaum (1999) describe the impact of stigma and stereotyping on pregnant women and girls who may misuse substances, earn money via prostitution or have histories of drug abuse. Sharpe (2015) reiterates the impact of shame and stigma on women and girls in the CJS and further suggests that the impact of negative labelling can last for many years, affect parenting, self-esteem and self-worth and motivation in relation to desistance. Key to working positively with pregnant women and girls in the CJS is adopting a non-judgemental approach, and supportive positive relationships using supportive and positive language (Mason *et al*, 2001, Murphy and Rosenbaum 1999).

Case Study 2: Jemma

Jemma had seen many different men come in and out of her Mum's life and, at the age of 12, one of mum's boyfriends began sexually abusing her. Her personality changed from being a subdued and timid girl to becoming angry and aggressive, lashing out at her mum and siblings. Jemma started smoking and drinking and was often brought home drunk by friends or the police. At 13 she started truanting from school and when she was 14 was permanently excluded for hitting a teacher. At 15, Jemma ran away from home and moved into a squat after meeting a man who said he would help her find work as a model. She became addicted to drugs and, by the time she was 17, she had a £200 a day heroin habit—the only way to fund her habit was to steal and prostitute herself. At 19-years-old, Jemma was arrested and charged with robbery and possession of class-A drugs and given an 18 month prison sentence. On the first night wing of the prison, Jemma was asked if she might be pregnant. She had no idea. A test showed she was. Jemma reported that things said to her included, 'Another junkie having a baby for the state'—'How can you look after a baby when you can't look after yourself?' and 'You will be a shit mum, you're a junkie.'

▌▌ Pause for Thought

How must it feel to Jemma hearing this?—To listen to these comments what might it do to her self-worth?—How do you feel if you see a heavily pregnant women smoking?—How would you feel about a pregnant mum using drugs? What is important in how practitioners engage with Jemma?—If 'personal' you and 'professional' you have conflicting view-points, how will you address this?

We have seen throughout this book that women in prison are a 'vulnerable population' (Baldwin 2015c), arguably pregnant women and girls in prison are more vulnerable than most. Psychiatric illness is a leading cause of indirect maternal death in the UK and as was tragically illustrated by cases such as Charlotte Bevan in the opening chapter (Centre for Maternal and Child Enquiries 2011). It is understood that pregnant women in prison are more likely to suffer from mental illness or mental distress, making sensitive care and comprehensive psychological assessment essential for all pregnant women there. This is important for the woman's health but also the future health of her unborn baby, whether or not separation is going to occur (Gerhardt 2004). Harne and Riley (2013) looked at the impact of prison on mothers' mental health. Unsurprisingly, it was found that, during pregnancy, especially if unsupported emotionally, a woman's poor mental health will be exacerbated. In turn, this may lead to further complexities post-release. 'Unconditional' emotional support from charities such as Birth Companions and projects such as Born Inside during pregnancy and birth enable a woman who is in prison to feel 'normal' (Marshall 2010). Munroe *et al* (2012) suggest that improved pregnancy outcomes are more likely should a comprehensive assessment be undertaken for all pregnant women with a pre-existing mental health diagnosis, arguing this is especially important in prison where the likelihood of mental health problems is increasingly likely. Both the Royal College of Midwives (RCM) (2012) and Royal College of Obstetrics and Gynaecology (RCOG) (2011) suggest that women who may have serious mental health issues or potential for mental illness should have coordinated and specialist care. Forty-six per cent of women in prison have attempted suicide at some time in their lives and many use self-harm as a 'coping strategy'. The National Society for the Prevention of Cruelty to Children (NSPCC) (2011) suggests the importance not only of appropriate assessment but that health care professionals are given the 'tools' in order to identify issues and plan care. A coordinated multi-disciplinary approach should therefore ensure women in need have regular mental health assessments by a midwife and health care providers. Obviously this will require ongoing training in order to identify and support those women at-risk.

Emotional support from experienced psychotherapists such as Pamela Stewart, founder of the Born Inside project provide unconditional support for pregnant women and women with their babies and help with the transition to parenthood whether being separated from their baby or not. Pamela works alongside a Montessori teacher, both of whom have demonstrated over many years of how babies and new mothers can thrive with this kind of approach which encourages attachment and bonding in a non-judgemental way. Shame, guilt and isolation are common feelings that are reported by a pregnant woman in prison. Projects such as Born Inside and the ante-natal and post-natal groups that Birth Companions provide can positively impact upon the psychological health of new mothers and provide an environment that encourages parenting strategies which can be transferred post-release. The female prison population, by the very nature of its demographics, may have lower self-efficacy than women on the outside. The setting of the prison estate means that women are deprived of a basic level of control and could have reduced self-esteem which may impact upon their 'social cognition' (Connor and Norman, 2005) thus reducing the chance of behaviour change. Being in prison and having a loss of control may also lead to a crisis point and therefore impact upon stress levels and make keeping mentally well a struggle.

Conversely, the prison setting may be the first time a woman with these characteristics has had a safe place to shelter, has organized meal-times and bedtimes, access to healthcare and better nutrition. Therefore, it could be argued that self-efficacy may be increased for some and also may affect motivation for a change in behaviour as discussed by Norman *et al* (2005). Indeed prison may be a place where stress is temporarily reduced, especially if a woman is in a violent relationship or has been a victim of sexual exploitation. However, the uncertainty, fear of what will happen when released impacts upon a woman and her anticipation whatever her circumstances on the outside and anxiety levels may therefore be high.

There obviously are particular anxieties around giving birth, especially for women remanded whilst pregnant—Birth Companions report that those on remand worry about whether they will still be in prison for the birth. One of the greatest concerns for pregnant prisoners reported by Birth Companions is caused by not knowing whether they will get a place on an MBU.

Pause for Thought

Think about how it feels waiting for a space—not knowing if you will be able to keep your baby with you. If you are refused a place your baby will definitely 'go outside'—What must it feel like to be pregnant knowing you may lose your child hours after birth?—At least for a time? How can we help?

Mother and Baby Units

There are eight mother and baby units (MBUs) in the UK. Six in England, two in Scotland and none in Wales (Galloway *et al*, 2014). MBUs are separate units that remain within a prison meaning that a woman who is in prison, and allocated a space, can keep her baby with her for until he or she is 18-months-old. However it is important to note that out of a population of approximately 4,000 women, 66 per cent of whom are mothers of children under 18, only 64 of those women at any one time will have her baby or babies with her—there are 70 spaces for babies allowing for three sets of twins at any one time in the female prison estate (Prison Reform Trust). A pregnant woman has to apply for a place on an MBU and this can be an anxious time for her, waiting to see if she has one. Marshall (2010) reports that this wait can be incredibly distressing for the woman, especially not knowing whether she will be separated from her baby or not.

The rejection level for MBUs in England is high, in the year running up to February 2012, 246 women applied for a space but only 116 were agreed. In the same period in Scotland only three women applied for a space and all were agreed. In England in 2011, 2012 and 2013, MBUs were under–occupied by just under or just over 50 per cent (36/76, 49/76 and 50/76). Scotland and Northern Ireland have significantly fewer pregnant women in custody—something returned to later. Wales does not have a female prison or an MBU so it is difficult to get accurate figures for Welsh mothers.

Some women may have only recently given birth when sentenced to custody—meaning their babies will stay outside whilst an MBU place is applied for. This period of separation can be particularly painful whilst a mother waits to see if she has a place with her baby. Female prisons are often some distance from relatives and a woman's existing children. For some women there is a 'Sophie's choice' about whether to stay near her existing children 'outside' and so have visits or choose to apply for an MBU space to be with her baby—but meaning visits from her older children are reduced or unlikely due to the distance involved. Mothers who do have a baby on the MBU normally still have to return to 'work' when the baby is six-weeks-old. Mothers who are not allocated a space are separated from their babies within hours of birth (usually no more than six hours) and returned to their normal cell.

The babies, although residing with their mother, are not prisoners and therefore can be taken out of the prison and may visit relatives for example. Galloway *et al* (2014) report that there is little known about the effect of a prison environment on a child and great care needs to be taken in order to meet the needs of the baby/child.

Organizations such as Birth Companions (BC) provide support to women on MBUs, currently with volunteers visiting women and their babies. Marshall (2010), group coordinator at BC, speaks of the importance of incarcerated pregnant women birthing and post-natal women feeling like 'normal women' rather than just prisoners, giving this group of women with complex physical and mental health needs an identity. Marshall (*Ibid*) also stresses the importance of continuing this care and support post-release, reducing the mother's feelings of isolation and therefore empowering her to parent her baby in a positive way. The Birth Charter for pregnant women champions this concept.

Birth Companions

As already noted, Birth Companions (BC) was set up by a group of North London ante-natal practitioners inspired in 1996 by the late Sheila Kitzinger MBE following the highlighting of a case of a mother giving birth in chains. BC supports pregnant women in three English prisons, pre and post-release. This involves facilitating pregnancy groups, supporting labour, post-natal and post-release support. The support is non-judgemental and unconditional, whether a woman keeps her baby or is being separated. BC often attend appointments and the births of women who are in prison (They can be on 24-hour call when allocated to a mother to be near to her due date). This can be especially important for women who are located many miles from family or who have no family contact. The birth companion is there for the woman as her support. The service is valued by mothers and staff alike:

'When I first came to prison I was about eight weeks pregnant with my third baby and absolutely petrified...the groups seemed to pull everyone together and helped us build strong friendships...we could share previous pregnancy/birth experiences and even offload problems/concerns and BC would reassure us and make us feel better'. (BC Report 2013)

Not Always a Happy Ending ... Separation

Not all mothers however are lucky enough to secure a place and the preparation for separation is intense and must be managed sensitively and with compassion and understanding—another justification for a pregnancy PSO which would highlight and make recommendations for good practice, for example ensuring a mother is not in a single cell immediately following separation or whilst access to support is facilitated.

Case Study 3: Keira

Keira was 29 weeks pregnant with her first child when sentenced to six years in prison for attempted murder. She had her case presented at the assessment board to attempt to keep her baby and gain a place on the MBU. At 36 weeks pregnant, she learnt that she had not gained a place. This meant that she would need to have her baby removed soon after birth.

Plans were made for Keira's mother to have temporary care of the baby with input and support from social services. When she was transferred from her cell at 3 am to the local hospital, she wanted her Mum to be with her. The prison officer on bed watch was a woman who Keira knew and felt happy to be with her. Keira was able to hold and be with her baby son for the first eight hours. After this, her baby was taken away with her Mum and social worker. She was transferred back to prison, to her shared cell, 24-hours after giving birth.

Pause for Thought

What must it have felt like for Keira knowing she wouldn't see her baby develop? — Knowing he would be taken from her? — What must it feel like dealing with that alone? — Or for mothers knowing the baby is going into care and not with family? How can midwives and the prison help women deal with this? Manage this? — What do we need to watch for?

All pregnant women in prison are entitled to apply for a place on an MBU where they are able to live with their babies up until around 18 months. Women who do not gain a place are separated from their babies in hospital following birth. This knowledge increases stress placed on pregnant women in the last three months of their pregnancy, which has been shown to have a negative effect for both the mother and her baby (Schetter and Tanner, 2012). There is limited knowledge and understanding of the impact of enforced separation of a baby and mother (Galloway *et al*, 2014). Nevertheless, it is undoubtedly the most painful thing a mother can go through and why, as seen in both the Psychotherapist chapter (*Chapter 7*) and Social Work chapter (which deals with child protection) (*Chapter 3*), women may seek to fill the void and become pregnant time-and-again. BC work with women who are separating, often attending their birth and supporting the woman in the post-natal period. This can extend to court visits and hearings:

> 'Unfortunately all good things come to an end...I had to go to court as social services wanted to take my daughter at birth. Someone from BC came and sat with me the day before court, she gave me words of encouragement and a great big cuddle. The following day someone also came with me to court and she held my hand and made me feel so good in a stressful situation' (Mother supported; BC Annual Report 2013–2014)

It is clear that at times a separation may be necessary in order to protect the baby. However, compassion at a time of potential deep distress for a woman can make a difference and may influence her future and future children. There is little known about how care givers can best provide support for vulnerable women who are separating and Galloway *et al* (2014) recommend that research is funded to enable those with a responsibility for these mothers to be armed with the best knowledge to be able to provide appropriate evidence-based care and support. Baldwin (2015c) (and see also the closing chapter of this work) suggests this needs to be something offered to all women separating from their children, particularly if this separation is being 'enforced'; as highlighted in the Social Work chapter (which deals with child protection)(*Chapter 3*) — this is an area where support for mothers is lacking and inconsistently available — but one that can have huge implications for mothers and subsequent children. Charities such as BC should be consulted as to their philosophy of care and their experience of working with vulnerable separating women in order for specific guidance to be produced.

Labour and Birth

Labour and birth is an exceptionally important and emotional time for a woman. Research has demonstrated the significance of birth support for mothers and babies (Hodnett *et al*, 2012). Where a woman is giving birth alone, without any emotional and practical support, this may have a detrimental impact on her. Many women in custody will want a member of their family with them and, if so, as soon as a woman starts to labour, family members should be called at the timeliest possible opportunity, increasing the likelihood that they will get to the hospital in time—especially if they have to travel some distance.

It is recognised that some women in prison will have complicated lives and may not have family available to support them. This can be because relationships are fragile, or a woman is being held too far away from home for that to be possible. In these cases it is important that women have access to an alternative form of support. This could be via BC, or because of the availability of funding for specialist training and support for existing doulas. Uvnas Moberg (2014) identifies the vital importance of kindness and compassion being shown towards labouring women to reduce stress and increase the flow of oxytocin (an important hormone which encourages bonding, attachment, relaxation and love). Having a known supporter will ensure that stress is reduced, improving outcomes and experiences of labour and birth.

Prison protocol dictates that a woman is accompanied by one to two POs for hospital admissions, appointments and birth. Their role is to guarantee that the prisoner remains in secure custody whilst away from the prison. Nevertheless, a woman's dignity and privacy should be maintained where possible—particularly during the birth and breastfeeding. Prison officers may be uncertain of their rôle especially when a woman is in labour. Clear guidance and training could help maintain dignity and support prison officers. A specific and clear pregnancy PSO should help clarify roles and responsibilities as well as best practice. Revisiting the PSI

(2011) would be useful in informing guidance but working with organizations such as BC and the Royal College of Midwives may enhance awareness and knowledge.

Due to the trauma a woman may have suffered in her life, labour can trigger unpleasant and intrusive memories for her. Abbott (2001) reports that women who have suffered previous sexual abuse or assault have the potential to suffer distressing flashbacks during labour. This can manifest itself by the woman withdrawing into herself or becoming hyper vigilant and panic stricken. She may also regress back to childhood. BC work on the premise of trauma-focused care where universal precautions are adopted and an assumption that all women may have suffered trauma means that sensitive care and support is given. Midwives and health professionals need to be mindful that a woman may have suffered in her past and be careful not to re-enact abuse by assuming consent for intimate examinations (as an example).

Pause for Thought

The pregnancy listening service? — Especially following 'separation'. A specific and clear pregnancy PSO should help clarify rôles and responsibilities as well as best practice. Revisiting the PSI (2011) would be useful in informing guidance but working with organizations such as Birth Companions and the Royal College of Midwives may enhance awareness and knowledge.

Case Study 1 Yasemine: An Update

Yasemine started to have contractions when she was 41 weeks pregnant whilst she was on the MBU. One of the women who had three children on the outside and a six-months-old baby with her was able to support her and was very calming and reassuring. She felt very scared about leaving the MBU and going to the hospital but also was very worried that her baby would be born in prison. An ambulance was called to transfer her and a female prison officer accompanied Yasemine to hospital where she remained on bed watch. She was supported by a midwife and student midwife who respected her wish not to have internal examinations. This helped Yasemine relax and she was able to spend some of her labour in the water pool which was very calming and seemed to speed up her labour. The student midwife stayed with her all night and acted as a birth support. Yasemine gave birth to a baby girl who was small at 2.5kg. She was able to have skin-to-skin contact with her daughter and breast fed her with encouragement from the midwife and student. The prison officer remained with her despite her shift being finished and was visibly moved by the birth. She returned to the MBU after 48-hours on the post-natal ward. The midwife visited her there and spent an hour with her supporting her with breastfeeding and giving encouragement. Yasemine did not have any visitors when she was in hospital.

▎▎ Pause for Thought

How might such a positive and calm birth experience help Yasemine? How does having her choices and wishes respected and facilitated empower Yasemine? How might Yasemine's experience have been had she not benefitted from such kindness?

Following the birth of a baby to a mother during her sentence there can be little doubt that for some mothers and their babies they have an opportunity to bond in a 'safer', and to some extent, more protected environment than if they were giving birth 'outside' (Abbott 2015). Mothers will have access to 24-hour support and even practical supplies such as maternity pads, breast pumps, sterilising equipment etc. — which perhaps would have proved difficult to obtain on the outside. Also, in part because by the time they give birth many mums, especially the younger mums, have built up trust with MBU staff and are willing and able to ask for advice and guidance, this thereby builds their confidence as mothers and makes them less likely to engage negatively with services once they leave prison (Abbott 2015). A 'knock-on' effect of this positive engagement and support creates an increased chance that a mother will choose to breast feed her baby. Hungerford and Elliot-Honepa (2012) found that babies born to imprisoned mothers and living outside of prison (i.e. not in an MBU) face disruption in terms of loss of breastfeeding and having many different caregivers. Women who are given access to clear, accurate information about the benefits of breastfeeding and then supported in whatever feeding choices they make.

Conclusion

Whatever the 'rightness' or 'wrongness' of whether babies are born to mothers in custody The Department of Health (D of H) policy: Midwifery 2020 (D of H, 2010) and Galloways 'All Babies Count' (2014) report outlines the need to create seamless maternity services for women with complex social needs. This is not nor should it be any different for mothers in prison. Francis's report (2013) like North's (2006) 'Maternity Alliance' paper before them recommend that service users should have greater involvement in the planning of their care and that there is a need for a cohesive mandatory service-wide response to pregnancy in prison. However, there are currently no pregnancy specific policies or guidelines or a Prison Service Order (PSO) outlining the unique needs of pregnant and childbearing women in prison and how they should be provided for (Galloway *et al* 2014). Rather, they are 'tagged-in' and mentioned within policies such as NICE guidance and recommendations for pregnancy and childbearing care are made by Corston (2007), North (2006) and Gullberg (2013) and the PSI previously mentioned.

Price (2005) described the services available for women in prison as inconsistent and variable, reliant on voluntary organizations such as BC supporting women in Holloway, Bronzefield and Peterborough Prisons—again a nationally accepted Birth Charter and pregnancy-specific PSO would address this inconsistency.

Together with Supporting Women Against Prison (SWAP) who continue to campaign for the implementation the Corston Report (2007) the RCM (2008) advocate that the UK develops a PSO specific to childbearing women; encompassing a minimal standard of care for pregnancy, intrapartum care and post-natal care. A PSO for pregnant women is called for by Galloway *et al* (2014) and BC have been campaigning for a PSO for a number of years. It would give clear and transparent guidance for best practice and mean that the women's estate would be working to a benchmark when a pregnant woman is in prison. At the time of writing, a meeting between BC and the RCM has been arranged to discuss how we can link together to recommend and achieve implementation of a detailed pregnancy PSO and a Birth Charter.

NICE guidance for pregnant women in prison should exist, alongside guidance from organizations such as the RCM. Specialist training and expertise is required for all those involved with pregnant women as recommended by Albertson *et al* (2012) consultation. Training for POs could be delivered by specialist midwives and a reciprocal arrangement could exist so that midwives and staff in hospitals and communities understand the complex security issues and rules and regulations around the prison system. It is clear that by providing supportive and nurturing environments such as those evaluated by Hungerford and Elliot-Honepa (2012) and described by Marshall (2010) that bonding, attachment, mental well-being and optimal nutrition for babies result.

The scarcity of research regarding the needs of pregnant and post-natal prisoners is apparent. Albertson *et al* (2014) and Galloway *et al* (2014) urge that funding for research is prioritised. My own doctoral research will, I hope, go some way towards providing evidenced-based research in order to inform change and facilitate effective practice.

A final word from Yasemine:

'I leave today Miss—Thanks for everything, I won't be back—I know it will be different this time, well fingers crossed!'

CHAPTER 9

Parental Supervision
Unravelling Positivity from Complexity; Community Supervision of Mothers

Lucy Baldwin and Susie Atherton

'[B]efore I came here my head was a shed, I couldn't function and I couldn't even think about a future ... I was stuck in the past, stuck in a way of living that I thought was "good enough" for me and I didn't even realise it wasn't.... This place gave me my life back.' (Mary: 2015 — Alternative to custody women's centre)

This chapter focuses on community-based supervision and support of mothers who break the law. Women and therefore mothers tend to commit crime at the 'lower end' of the risk of harm spectrum (Carlen and Worrall 2004; Corston 2007; Hedderman and Gunby 2013); subsequently four out of five women are sentenced by a magistrates' court rather than in the Crown Court. Most women in the CJS are therefore, at least in the vast majority of cases, 'eligible' for community sentences within sentence guideline parameters (whether this occurs is entirely another matter and was discussed in the Courts chapter (*Chapter 5*) and Prison chapter (*Chapter 6*)). This chapter focuses mainly on mothers' law breaking in the bracket that would normally be dealt with by magistrates only.

It is not the aim here to outline the full range of community disposals or of 'opportunities' for supervising women and mothers, rather to focus on the positives community supervision and support partnerships can bring when managed holistically for existing women law breakers and those women who are 'vulnerable' to entering or becoming further entrenched in the CJS — together with an understanding of the 'harm' to women and mothers when those alternatives aren't used.

The chapter comprises a 'whistle-stop' tour of some of the historical external and influencing factors in relation to community sentences, women and mothers. It pulls together aspects of attitudes to women/ mothers as offenders as discussed in other chapters, i.e. lack of consideration of the complexities related to female offending, including motherhood. It is additionally informed by case studies illustrated via vignettes based on reflections from practice and research of the authors. The 'Pauses for Thought' ask readers to critically reflect on their personal and professional thoughts, feelings and responses — and the wider implications in terms of the system's responses, policies and practice in relation to women and the implications for mothers and their children.

Historical Context to Community Supervision

Probation has undergone a great deal of change as perhaps one should expect over a period of 100 or so years, but never more so than now as the transforming rehabilitation (TR) agenda kicks-in. The service is unrecognisable from that of its origins when preventative and rehabilitative work with law breakers, vulnerables and vagabonds was undertaken — largely from philanthropic and religious motivations which required its missionaries and early probation officers to 'advise, assist and befriend.' The last 30 years, particularly, have seen shifts in thinking, policy and practice that have deeply affected the way in which all 'offenders' — but particularly for the purpose of this chapter — mothers have been supervised in the community. These changes, arguably often politically and media-driven have affected every aspect of supervision from the 'labels' practitioners have given supervisees, to the supervision 'requirements' and responses to breach. I recall when, under 'The New Choreography' (the strategic plan for Probation Service delivery between 2001 and 2004) 'we' as probation officers were directed to refrain from calling our service users 'clients' and instructed to call them 'offenders' because 'that is what they are.' The New Choreography opened its introduction with:

'Probation staff must make offenders face-up to the degree of harm that they have done and the impact of their crimes on the lives and well-being of others. They will be vigilant in their supervision, always assessing continuing risk of re-offending and the potential for dangerousness. Through the rigorous enforcement of community sentences and post-custody licences they will bring offenders to understand that this behaviour is unacceptable and that it will not go unpunished' (HMO 2001:4).

Prior to 1998, social workers and probation officers shared the same training, and arguably values and principles, educationally there were some specialist modules in each field, but on qualification a career in either social work or probation was permitted (and remains the case with the Certificate of Qualification in Social Work (CQSW) or Diploma in Social Work (DipSW) qualifications). Following the two year 'Howard Gap' during which no probation officers were trained and new qualification routes established; trainee probation officers followed a career specific programme focused on risk-assessment, public protection and enforcement. Various studies have since identified differences in the attitudes of probation officers and questioned their ways of working related to when they qualified and how they 'trained' (Mawby and Worall 2013; Justice Committee 2013). The New Choreography opening statement above gives a very clear message that the welfarist approach and previous social work-style of probation was a thing of the past.

Jordan (2013) has called breach action a 'narrative decision' and reflects on how practitioner autonomy and discretion can, and does, have an impact on women and mothers' navigation through the CJS. The implementation of the 'new' National Standards in 2000, particularly in their early days when their 'interpretation' was 'rigid' resulted in an increased used of breach—arguably the legacy for many was profound. Jordan (2013) suggests, '[I]f women are imprisoned for breach the ripple effects of trauma can be colossal' (2013:9), which is very obviously the case when those women are mothers, like Helen.

Helen: A 23-year-old single mother of four under the age of nine

Helen had been a single parent with little contact with her children's father but she was a more than capable woman who had no need for any statutory involvement with the children. She was under the supervision of the

Probation Service on a community order with a condition to complete 'Think First' (her original offence had been assault on an ex-partner whom she assaulted as she had found out he had hit one of her children). She had been sentenced to the community order 'by the skin of her teeth' the magistrate had told her, because she had previously unpaid fines and two breaches of bail conditions (for minor public order offences, one for urinating in a public place and another following a scuffle with door staff at a club). Her 'failure to comply' the magistrate stated demonstrated her 'wanton disregard' for the direction of the court.

Helen was making progress, had engaged well, she was gaining some benefit from both the Think First course and her parallel supervision with her probation officer. She had struggled to get to the Think First sessions on time and had been 'warned for lateness'—anything after 15 minutes at that time was considered breachable. However she lived a bus ride away and had three children to drop-off at school and one to a friend before she got to the sessions—which began at 9.30. Helen experienced financial difficulties during a mix up with her housing benefit payments—which she was in the process of sorting out—however she turned up an hour late for her Think First session—the reason being she had had to walk, as she hadn't got the bus fare.

Because of her warnings the programme facilitators 'had no choice' but to breach her and a breach report was prepared for court. Despite her probation officer appearing in court and asking for a continuation of the order the court declined—stating it was obvious she 'had no intention' of complying with community orders and re-sentenced her to eight months in prison. During her period of incarceration, Helen lost her home and her children were all placed in foster care. On release from prison she felt she had nothing and no reason to 'keep trying when there's always someone to bring me down' and quickly re-offended and was returned to prison—which obviously meant her children were now subject to long-term fostering with the intention for the youngest to be adopted.

> ## ❙❙ Pause for Thought
>
> What are your immediate thoughts about this? — This was a real outcome of a 'policy' implementation in which the probation officer had no real autonomy (although to some extent professional autonomy or professional discretion has been 'gifted' back to probation officers)?— What does this tell us about policy and policy-makers and their 'trust' in practitioners? — What of the legacy for Helen and her children — and possibly their children? Policies affect people — really affect people — especially when they are wrong … it's important to not get it wrong … especially for mothers — How might TR go 'wrong' for mothers?

It is important to note that these transitional factors have indeed affected all those supervised via the Probation Service — but, as we have seen throughout this text, outcomes and impact can be very different for women and mothers in the CJS than that of their male counterparts. TR will see 'a revolution in the way we manage offenders' (MOJ 2013). It would be remiss, however, not to state here that many aspects of the TR Agenda, particularly the pace of implementation, were opposed by many front line staff working in probation (NAPO 2014), with very real concerns raised about the motivation and rationale for change, i.e. was it financially-driven or by a genuine desire to improve the CJS? Feelings of being 'de-skilled and demoralised' (*Ibid*) have been described amongst probation staff during the transition and early implementation. Additionally, concerns have been raised with regard to the moral position in relation to the expansion of the privatisation of criminal justice agencies and the survival of smaller more specialist units — particularly for women and within a climate of deferred payments and 'payment by results.'

Questions have been raised about the decision to spend billions on an overhaul of an award-winning, internationally acclaimed system that was arguably 'working' (i.e. probation) as opposed to finding suitable alternatives to a system that arguably isn't 'working' quite so well, i.e. prison, and again, especially for women and mothers (See special edition on TR in the *British Journal of Community Justice* 2013:11:2/3 for full discussion). In undertaking the 'the most comprehensive overhaul of the CJS yet' perhaps it would have been pertinent to also demonstrate a commitment to re-examining a system that still sends pregnant teenagers to prison on the date they are due to give birth for shoplifting £5 worth of goods (Sharpe 2015); or where hundreds of prisoners are still forced to 'slop-out' every day. That would perhaps indicate a more full commitment, socially, economically and arguably morally thereby genuinely being a 'comprehensive overhaul' (Despite being banned in 1996 more than ten prisons in the UK still have no in-cell sanitation with 'no plans' to rectify this situation due to the 'astronomical' cost of facilitating this in older prisons) (Ministry of Justice 2015).

Pause for Thought

In a climate of uncertainly as practitioners — whether in a changing service or in a service with uncertain funding — or insecure long-term funding — how do you as professionals make sure fears and 'work-related stress' isn't passed to service users? — Is this possible? What about transparency? — How do service users feel when 'systems' change around them?

There are many non-custodial options open to sentencers. These include fines, unpaid work, supervision with requirements to complete courses, supervision without conditions, curfews, and suspended sentences to name but a few. Research has shown that, for women, breach of original community-based court orders has been a factor contributing to the rise in the female prison population and will be a factor in the future supervision of women on licence (Prison Reform Trust 2013; Jordan 2013; Stanley 2009; Hedderman 2012). Rex and Hosking (2013) have stated that their fear is that TR may return us to an inflexible and excessively prescriptive way of working — particularly within the less experienced private sector resources — which could lead to a rise in the number of breaches, enforcement and an increased prison population. Baldwin (2015d) has suggested that for women and mothers, if the 'holistic' approach to community supervision does not come to fruition as promised, then the 12 month period of supervision following a custodial sentence may simply create more opportunities for breach, so that

TR may well prove to be a ticking time bomb in relation to the prison population in general (Prison Reform Trust 2013), but particularly for women. TR is heavily focused on outcomes, results and measurability; in part because of the complex pathways into offending for women this is especially challenging, evaluating what is effective and when something is effective for women and mothers in relation to desistance with such complex needs is complicated by definition.

Desired 'outcomes' may be much less obvious in terms of measurement than they are in terms of being an observable intervention—how will it be possible to measure internal impact of 'effectiveness'? There are concerns that this challenge to measurement and explicit outcomes will 'put off' providers from investing in women's services or that because of unclear 'results' existing services will be deemed to be 'underperforming' and have funding limited or withdrawn. There needs to be an acceptance that very often the 'expert by experience' offers the most valid voice in relation to 'what' and 'when' something is effective—and these are the voices that ought to influence funding and policy decisions. Voices—like Mary's who you will meet later in this chapter—or Maxie's from the Substance Misuse chapter (*Chapter 10*), they are able to recognise how and why and what 'worked' or made the difference in their worlds. Significantly and key to their positive change in relation to the process of desistance was the facilitation of 'emotional safety' mentioned in *Chapter 1*.

Why Community-based Support and Supervision 'Works' for Women and Mothers

'All prison did for me was to confirm I was a bad person and a rubbish mother—I lost my house and my kids and came out of prison to nothing.' (Mary 2015—Speaking at a women's community resource post-sentence)

Whilst the focus of this text is on mothers; within a frame of exploring the 'costs and benefits' of sentencing mothers to custody or to a community disposal one cannot ignore the 'cost' or impact of incarceration on children (which will then directly and indirectly affect the mothers).

Far more in-depth research exists (Barnados 2013; Murray and Farrington 2008) in relation to the impact of parental incarceration than we are able to cover in this chapter, although more is needed. However, to fail to acknowledge this 'harm' to children here would be negligent (although as Baldwin 2015a and 2; Reed 2014; and Epstein 2012 suggest, this is exactly what the courts do!). As has been stated throughout this book, the female prison population in the UK has more than doubled since 1995 and 66 per cent of that population are mothers of children under 18. The Prison Reform Trust and Barnados suggest that this results in over 200,000 children every year losing their mothers to custody, even if only temporarily in some cases. The Courts chapter (*Chapter 5*) highlights some of the financial costs of imprisoning mothers (Reed 2014; PRT 2014), together with the secondary costs associated with 'looking after' children who are taken directly into the care of the local authority as a result of maternal incarceration (14 per cent).

In addition to the comparison between £56,500 per annum for a female prison bed as opposed to £2,800 per annum for an average community order, when 'looked after children' costs are added, a single relatively short-term custodial sentence of a mother of three children, can as Reed (2012) puts it in a 'quick back of the envelope calculation', 'end-up' quite simply 'staggering' (in excess of £500,000 for a child with multiple needs). If one was to add in further costs in terms of re-housing and re-settlement following release—quite aside from the 'known' psychological 'harms' causes to mothers and their children—it becomes quite simply a sentence that keeps on punishing.

Patience: Mother of a four-year-old Mercy, four months pregnant at the point of being sentenced

The father of Mercy and her baby was not 'on the scene'. Patience was a 22-year-old woman who had been offending and using substances since the age of eleven. She had Mercy when she was just turned 18, and although there had been 'concerns' expressed by nursery staff, Mercy was not subject to any statutory intervention, nor did Patience receive any support. Patience regarded herself as, 'a good mum - just with a shit life', and loved Mercy dearly. She had previously been supervised by the youth offending team (YOT) and had several public order cautions and breaches of curfew orders. She had been in care as a child, had attempted suicide aged 14 and had no contact with her own family or the baby's father; but was very close to her friends and peer group.

Patience was four months pregnant when she was sentenced to three years and six months in custody for theft, benefit-related fraud and drug-related offences (cannabis and an offence of assault committed against a member of the public who had been accusing Patience of being a bad mother as she was out late in the evening with Mercy asleep in a pushchair). The judge commented to her, 'To think that you acted in such a violent way in front of your child is horrific and reveals exactly what type of mother you are.' Patience entered prison very anxious, depressed and scared. She had left her daughter in the care of a friend, as she had not expected a custodial sentence. Staff at the prison contacted social services and Mercy was taken into 'temporary' foster care.

On being received into custody her personal officer and the prison probation officer encouraged Patience to apply for a place on the Mother and Baby Unit (MBU). Although the process took some time and there was some opposition, Patience was eventually given a place. She had difficulties in relation to her pregnancy—during which time she was taken back-and-forth to outside hospital appointments for scans in handcuffs, something that distressed her greatly and would often trigger self-harm incidents.

Once allocated to the MBU it would be possible for her to keep her baby with her in prison until her child was 18–months-old. Staff had thought that Patience would be relieved and excited at securing her place and initially she was—however they noticed her mood getting lower and saw signs of self-harm on her face, arms and legs. Staff tried to engage with Patience who eventually confided to them that she didn't want to stay on the MBU and was going to give-up her baby at birth—She said she couldn't bear the thought of loving and caring for her child for 18 months—then having to let her 'go outside' to be placed in foster care and in reality to be adopted, as at that point as she would still have time to serve , saying she 'would rather not love it all.' She subsequently had her baby who was taken from her to foster care six hours after its birth; Patience was discharged back to 'normal' location in the prison in a single cell. The child, a girl, was identified as likely for adoption, which would possibly mean her sister would be placed with her as social services preferred to place sibling groups together and babies are 'easier to place.'

▌▌ Pause for Thought

What are your immediate thoughts/feelings about Patience and her sentence? — Do you think Patience made the right decision? — What does this say about her? — Can you imagine what this felt like to Patience and the impact on her long-term? — What might the risk factors be viewed from a probation officer/community supervision perspective when Patience leaves prison? — What can/should a probation officer/ community support do to enable her to complete a successful licence period? — Would you feel equipped to supervise Patience? — If not, why not? — What would help you in the supervision of Patience — What would help Patience? If Patience's children stay 'in care'- what do we 'know' from research in terms of their vulnerability and cycles?

As previously noted, between 1995 and 2014 the female prison population more than doubled and as has been indicated in other chapters this rise occurred despite evidence suggesting time-and-time-again that prison for many, but especially women, is actually ineffective. For over 30 years, feminists, criminologists, academics, campaigners, practitioners and women themselves, have argued this point (Carlen 1983, 1990 and 2002; Dobash and Dobash 1996; Gelsthorpe *et al*, 2007; Corston 2007), suggesting there a strong case for using alternatives to custody, where this is appropriate (Corston, 2007; Prison Reform Trust 2011; Epstein 2012; Baldwin 2015a and 3; Reed 2014). Calls for change in relation to reduced use of custody more generally, but especially for women and mothers who break the law is supported by prison reformists and a plethora of informed and supportive organizations like the Howard

League for Penal Reform, the Prison Reform Trust, Women in Prison, Make Justice Work and Women's Breakout, to name a few. The Prison chapter (*Chapter 6*) and Courts chapter (*Chapter 5*) have explored the characteristics in relation to offending associated with women and sentencing patterns but it will not hurt to reiterate in this chapter that a gendered approach to sentencing is or rather should be a significant part of any rethinking of criminal justice for women and mothers (Corston 2007; Caddle and Crisp 1997; Minson 2014; Carlen and Worrall 2004; Worrell 1990; Reed 2014; Baldwin 2015; Mezoughi 2015).

Work from the Gatekeeper

Sentencing decisions of the judiciary is an area relatively under-researched for mothers who break the law but receiving some attention (Epstein 2012; Reed 2014; Hedderman and Gunby 2013; Baldwin 2015a; Minson 2014; APPG 2015). A significant factor to recognise is that the rise in the prison population is not due to an increase in prevalence or seriousness of crimes being committed by women, but to sentencing decisions (Hedderman 2004) — which, arguably, particularly affect the sentencing of mothers (Reed 2014; Baldwin 2015; Epstein 2012). There are in existence theories offering some explanations such as double deviancy (e.g. Eaton 1993; Hedderman 2004; Heidensohn and Silvestri 2012) or a moment of chivalry (e.g. Pollak 1961). Minson (2014), Marougka (2012) and Hedderman and Gunby (2013) have provided extensive and useful discussion relating to women, mothers and sentencing. The Courts chapter (*Chapter 5*) in this book highlights the 'failure' of sentencers to take into account 'the rights of the child' when sentencing mothers (Epstein 2012) and the 'cost' and 'harm' of imprisoning mothers (Reed 2014) — which will be revisited in the closing chapter amongst proposals for change (Baldwin 2015). This chapter therefore focuses on positive community supervision — both on licence following a custodial sentence and via alternatives to custody, specifically for women and mothers.

Following the implementation of TR, community supervision of offenders on community orders and those on licence will be split. The task of low/medium risk supervision has been 'sold off' to the private sector and that of 'offenders' assessed as such will be undertaken by privately owned community rehabilitation centres (CRCs). High risk 'offenders' will be supervised by probation officers under the National Probation Service (NPS). Much of the work of the NPS and CRCs and therefore community supervision and community support for women and mothers in the CJS is framed not only by government policy but additionally as we have seen by the judiciary and judicial decisions. There is a strong and ever-increasing argument towards the case for using community options and alternatives to custody where this is appropriate — and, in relation to women offenders, there almost always is (Corston 2007; Prison Reform Trust 2011; Carlen and Worrall 2004; Baldwin 2015a). There is a huge amount of evidence-based research and an unusual breadth of agreement and support concerning the need to reduce the use of custody for women and mothers who break the law. Scotland appears to be at the vanguard of moves towards a more systematic response, advocating a holistic approach to women and criminal justice. Demonstrating Scotland's commitment to a more effective response to women who break the law, Justice Secretary Michael Matheson announced he would be releasing a further £639,500 to be awarded to 12 projects committed to working with women who offend in Scotland:

> 'I have already made it clear that I believe Scotland needs to take a new and bold approach to the way we treat female offenders and support them towards more positive futures…Scotland already has the second highest female prison population in Northern Europe, doubling between 2002 and 2012. This is totally unacceptable and does not fit with my vision of how a modern and progressive society should deal with female offenders.' (Speaking at Willow Women's Project, Glasgow 10 June 2015).

Despite opposition, Matheson made the bold decision to scrap plans to build a 'bigger' more modern prison to replace Cornton Vale and instead committed to a women's prison of 'no more than 80 spaces' together with five smaller units of around 20 beds — which will also include outreach and holistic services, modelled on excellent community-based resources like the Willow Project and Glasgow 218. Women for Independence representative Maggie Mellon spoke for many when she said:

'We look forward to building a different and more progressive justice system for women in Scotland. We congratulate Mr Matheson for listening to those opposed to the new prison and for having the courage to change course on this issue. Despite undoubted pressure, he has shown courage, confidence and principles to do the right thing for some of Scotland's most vulnerable women.'

Matheson was apparently 'persuaded' in his thoughts not only by evidence-based research and accounts from a panel of experts, academics and policy-makers who have long called for change all over the UK, but additionally by speaking with women and mothers using services such as the Willow and the 218 Projects; as well as listening to sentencers who value both services and again who had been to the projects and listened to front line staff and the voices of the women themselves. Both Willow and 218 provide extensive, valuable holistic responses and are a real alternative to custody for women in the Scottish CJS.

This stance is something that along with changes to sentencing frameworks (as outlined in the closing chapter) is something that arguably needs to be adopted across-the-board in relation to women and mothers in the CJS.

Pause for Thought

What are your thoughts on this system? — What is the resistance in the rest of the UK?

Complexity Unravelling ... Partnerships in Practice

It is important to remember that supervision of women does not only occur as a result of an enlightened sentencer handing down a community disposal. Women and mothers are also supervised on licence and, in the case of many women's centres, can additionally be referred to services because they are 'vulnerable' to entering the CJS. Indeed many women's centres will accept self-referrals too. Following the implementation of TR (above) in February 2015, anyone who now serves a prison sentence of more than one day will be subject to supervision on licence of at least 12 months (MOJ 2013), given that most women sentenced to custody are serving less than 12 months then this will be of huge significance.

It is early days in terms of the TR provision for women, and evaluative research can only be in its very early stages. Certainly there are fears partly due to the pace at which TR was implemented and partly to the lack of specific consideration in the consultation of women's needs and criminogenic needs as lawbreakers, that women's needs will not be met (Senior 2013; Women in Prison 2013; Women's Breakout 2013).

Women have been described as presenting 'particular challenges' in the CJS by the Justice Select Committee Report (2013) in relation to the TR process, implementation and provision — however, as Gomm (2013) quite rightly points out it is not women presenting the challenge to TR — it is TR 'presenting the challenge' to women; women and mothers that are already known to be disadvantaged and as having complex individual circumstances which have impacted not only on their lived experiences, but additionally on their responses to previous court disposals, the options open to them at court and their ability to move forward positively (or rather under TR the ability to be seen and 'measured' as moving forward positively).

Obviously, desistance from crime will be a 'measurable' quantifiable result that will qualify for 'payment by results'. However, Gomm (2013) suggests, particularly in relation to women, 'desistance is a process' — which cannot actually begin until there is 'attention to essential support needs, and there are high levels of unmet needs for women offenders' (Gomm 2013:154). Such need and complexity has been highlighted already in this book; these 'contextual factors' include domestic abuse, violence, trauma, addiction, mental distress, poor socio-economic position and poverty (Corston 2007). Additionally, however, there are further complex factors in relation to 'managing' all of this. Mothers in the CJS are often dealing with the aforementioned lived experiences whilst 'caring' for dependants or after the trauma of being separated from children due to incarceration or as result of intervention; this presents additional challenges for women and mothers. This is not to say that they are all 'victims' and should be responded to as such — that is not the case at all, for many women 'survival against the odds' is what they have achieved, but to fail to address the complexities of issues surrounding women and mothers who break the law is to fail *them*.

Leanne: A 27-year-old single mother of two aged eight and ten

Leanne is under supervision for offences of possession of drugs with intent to supply. She narrowly escaped a custodial sentence and was 'spared' jail by a sentencer who accepted her mitigation that she was 'forced' to hold the drugs on behalf of her violent drug-dealing partner who used violence and sexual assault against her if she refused. Her partner was sentenced to custody for drugs offences and also a violent assault on her and Leanne only felt able to report the violence once her ex-partner was remanded in custody. The last violent act was one of many that had previously gone unreported—this had resulted in her arm being broken so badly that it was permanently bent and had limited use—meaning she found it difficult to work.

Leanne had previous convictions for prostitution (soliciting), behaviour which again she reports she was forced into by her violent ex-partner, using threats of sexual assault on her if she refused, and again the sexual assaults were not reported to the police. Following her latest injury a Victim Support worker encouraged her to submit a claim to the Criminal Injuries Compensation Authority. She did so and was 'awarded' compensation for her injuries eventually bringing the letter to her probation supervision at the women's centre to have its contents explained. The outcome was, because she was also a convicted offender, and despite explaining the circumstances of her offences, that her 'award' was refused and would not be 'paid out'. She was also told that even if she had not had the latest conviction for the drugs offence—because of her previous convictions her award would have been significantly reduced 'by way of remuneration to the criminal justice system' for the cost of prosecuting her offences.

Leanne felt devastated by this letter feeling it made her a 'non person' and questioning whether there was any point in abstaining from drug use or offending as to escape them seemed 'impossible' to her, in fact at one point she questioned whether there was any 'value' to her life and talked of ending it all or 'naffing off with no trace 'cos the kids are better off without me.'

❚❚ Pause for Thought

What do you think this decision will feel like to Leanne? — How would you feel about it — is Leanne more of a 'victim' than an 'offender'? — Both? — How would you manage this in supervision? — What do you think of Leanne's ex-partner? Have you assumed the ex-partner was male? — This is not the case she is a female. Is that a surprise? — Why? What are the challenges and aims for supervising Leanne? — Would reporting to a probation officer and dealing with only her offending behaviour meet her needs? — If not why not? What can you as a supervisor do and how will you facilitate a positive relationship with Leanne? Will you need to 'balance' your personal and professional view/response, if so how? — Does a women's centre resource with multi-agency responses and a 'safe place' to address all of her issues feel to you like it may have 'more of a chance' to affect positive change than reporting weekly to only a probation officer — whilst having a long wait to see a psychologist via the NHS? ... Would Leanne think so?

Leanne: Update

Leanne worked positively with staff who tried hard to create a space of emotional safety with Leanne and one in which practitioners were able to work with her using a trauma-informed practice model. Through a number of supportive engagements with a range of staff, a psychologist, a counsellor and a drugs worker Leanne was enabled to recognise the pathways into her offending and her life choices — by acknowledging traumatic experiences in her life, allowing herself to understand her choices with understanding (of herself) rather than judgement (of herself), gradually accepting she actually was a person with 'power' in relation to moving forward positively. Additionally, particularly in relation to her letter, Leanne felt supported by other women at the centre who understood how it made her feel, indeed some had had similar experiences and were able to motivate and support Leanne to not let it 'knock her back' and to think positively about her future. Leanne saw others succeed at the centre and became determined to do the same. Three years after her conviction Leanne was a successful single parent with no child services involvement and she went on to become a support worker in a national organization for women leaving custody.

Emotional Safety: Strength-based and Trauma-informed Models of Working ...

In a report on women's compliance with community sentences, Jordan emphasises the 'inter-related series of traumas endured throughout women's lives' (2013:3), adding to already stressful experiences like experiencing custody and also contributing to women's *inability* to comply with their community orders (partly because of cycles referred to previously). Jordan's findings (*Ibid*) highlighted the prevalence of mental illness and substance misuse, attributed in some case to a form of 'complex post-traumatic stress disorder' (PTSD) (Herman 1992), which manifests as self-harming, self-destructive behaviours, loss of self-esteem, attachment disorders and poor decision-making. Recommendations from this study include gender-focused training for practitioners so that sentencers and probation workers see 'beyond' the act of breach and consider what has led to this, making use of their professional judgement and discretion to consider the welfare of the women, mothers (and therefore children) that come before them.

Jordan (2013) also recommended a need for services for women in the community to have 'trauma recovery programmes' in order to begin to address the complex needs presented, so women in these situations may be able to take advantage of education, employment and support offered as part of their community sentence, or licence condition. Access to such programmes requires an identification of need, available and appropriate services in the community and clear lines/routes of referral and access. The centres have to some extent relied on the courts to refer people to them for their continued existence and funding, however Baldwin outlines clear proposals in the closing chapter for how current frameworks could be adapted to require magistrates to consider resources like women's centres at sentencing—particularly for mothers of dependent children.

Jordan (2013), Baldwin (2015c and f) and Gomm (2013) have advocated the trauma-informed models of practice—which are already utilised successfully in a number of community settings for women (Women in Prison 2013; Women's Breakout 2013). Trauma informed practice (TIP) is clearly an important model for working with women and mothers with complex needs and requires further research in relation to its 'place' in the CJS. Roger Grimshaw of the Centre for Crime and Justice Studies (CCJS) is embarking on important new research in relation to 'harms' of the CJS to women and TIP models of working. Baldwin (2015c), however, suggests that prior to trauma work with women and mothers in the CJS, there are pre-conditions which facilitate successful and effective trauma work with women and mothers. From reflections as a practitioner and confirmed in early findings in her doctoral research, she finds that 'emotional responsiveness' is only possible after first creating an environment of 'emotional safety'. This is paramount before any kind of real trauma-informed work can take place. It perhaps additionally raises the question of whether it is appropriate for 'agents of the state' i.e. probation officers and prison officers to undertake this work, given what women and mothers are telling us of the power imbalance in the relationship, which arguably inhibits 'emotional safety' (think about Ursula in the Prison chapter (*Chapter 6*)). It is suggested therefore that although this type of work can and should be undertaken as part of community disposals or indeed in prison this should be with the caveat that careful consideration is given as to 'who' delivers it and in what format.

An interesting point to note and reflect on is in relation to the 'power' of language. We mentioned earlier the change of label from 'client' to 'offender', and I recall having many conversations with service users in supervision whereby they strongly objected to the use of the term 'offender' because it suggested 'current status' when for many they wanted it to be something they had left behind them. Similarly, although used more prolifically and successfully in the USA (Covington 2007, 2008, 2012) the word 'trauma' can I think feel 'too big', 'too scary', and 'too obvious' for some women somehow, perhaps to do with British conservatism about feelings, but certainly it is a term I use with caution and mindfulness. In sharing this very conversation with a support worker in a women's centre/alternative to custody resource in a discussion extolling the virtues of trauma-informed models, I shared my view on the 'word' and the fact I prefer the term 'emotional management'. The practitioner agreed wholeheartedly. 'Absolutely,' she said and further stated:

> '[W]e had a groupwork session called "managing trauma"—no-one attended—yet when we changed the name to "managing emotion"—the floodgates opened, everyone came—the word "trauma" scares women, they don't want to be reminded of trauma—they lived it.' (Staff facilitator at a women's centre: Baldwin 2015c)

Mary below attended such a group:

Mary: A mother of twin boys Ryan and Regan aged 12 when she was sentenced to 14 months for theft

> Coming here, to the women's centre saved my life—prison did nothing for me other than just reinforce that I am bad—here I am listened to, I know I'm not judged but I still know I did wrong—the difference is here they help me see why and deal with it—I only stole things to get drugs and it had become such a normal thing for me to do, I'd done it for years and years. I stopped thinking about why I was taking drugs in the first place—which I suppose was the point. But it's not just about the drugs, there's so much more, I couldn't talk about it to anyone till I came here. Even being in prison just added to the failure that was my life, I'd lost my kids, obviously they had to go into care when I went to prison, my mum tried to have them. But she just couldn't cope.
>
> The boys? Well they kind of went off the rails a bit when I was locked-up. At first I used to want to know what they were up to, was desperate to know in fact—but, when they started getting into bother, I didn't want to know—well actually it wasn't that I didn't want to know I just found it all too much—it was just more guilt—I knew they were playing-up

because they'd lost me. They felt like they got punished too, and they did really—and now they both have criminal records—we may as well all have got sent down together, we ended-up in the same mess. I even took drugs in prison, I just wanted to not feel guilty and not think about when I was little. I started working with the drugs workers in prison and they set it up for someone from the women's centre to come in and see me in here. I went to groups and then when I went outside it wasn't as scary going to the centre because I'd met some of the staff in prison.

Facing up to what happened in my past and dealing with it in a safe way in a safe place with safe people has helped me see that I don't have to take drugs—at the end of the day I can't change my past—but I can change my future—that's what being here has taught me. I'm healthy and drug-free. I have a chance to get my kids back and that means more to me than anything—but I'm not just doing it for them—I'm doing it for me too—I want to be good person—then even if I don't get them back—when they come find me, when they leave care and are a bit older—which I know they would do, I can look them in the eye and say 'I changed,' The staff here have helped me turn it all around. I'm sad not to come here anymore but they have given me the 'tools' they call it to manage on my own. I have a counsellor and the outreach workers when I need them but I have enrolled for a hairdressing course at college, and I take care of my appearance now—in fact I take care of 'me' now—they gave me my life back.

▌▌ Pause for Thought

What do you think of the approach to supporting Mary on her desistance journey? — Had she been able to benefit from working partnerships between the prison, community services and probation, how might her story have 'played out'? — How could/can this be improved on? What If Mary hadn't been 'ready' to move forward independently at the end of her supervision period? — How can long-term support be facilitated?

In working with Mary, and mothers like her, to create a space of emotional safety it is important to recognise the additional traumatising effects of self-punishment and guilt that many law breaking mothers describe. Enabling Mary to see that to take responsibility where appropriate for offending behaviour doesn't need to further punish or undermine her self-confidence. Both the Mental Health chapter (*Chapter 2*) and Prison chapter (*Chapter 6*) discussed the difficulty in creating a safe space for honest and constructive conversations, particularly within relationships where there is a power imbalance like prison officer or probation officer. However, women's centres work hard to create environments where boundaries are firm and fair but where power is not explicit or overwhelming to the women who use the centres (Women's Breakout 2014; Glasgow 218 2015). In the years since the first Corston report (2007) much has been achieved (Hedderman and Gunby 2013), with a great deal of expertise, knowledge and good practice shared from evaluative research such as that from the Together Women Project (Jolliffe *et al*, 2011). Hedderman and Gunby state:

'The funding and development of one-stop shop women's centres were particularly welcomed because they provide the courts with strengthened community sentences as an alternative to custody (Corston 2011:4), while offering holistic support to women whose complex social problems put them at risk of offending and reoffending' (2013:426).

The APPG (2015) is clear that evidence related to partnership working, utilising the expertise knowledge and experience of women's centres is key to working with women who have complex needs. The multi-professional make-up of many of the women's centres, particularly those now working in partnership with the Probation Service offer comprehensive opportunities to facilitate not only desistance in women and mothers but also in relation to preventing criminalisation in the first instance—or when a mother has become criminalised, preventing her from becoming embedded and immersed in offending behaviour and the CJS. Furthermore as Gomm re-iterates:

'Women in the CJS do not appear to have a separate "offending life" and a separate "life" of experiencing chronic stress and abuse (both ongoing and past experiences)' (2013).

In moving forward with women in terms of their desistance process it becomes vital to ensure that not only are they not further' harmed and traumatised by aspects of the CJS itself—but that strength-based and trauma-informed models of holistic practice are applied to working with and supporting women and mothers in the community. To further illustrate the strength and value of partnership working we will re-visit Abbi, whom you 'met 'in the Courts chapter (*Chapter 5*).

Abbi: A 24-year-old mother of three, Jayden seven, Petra four and Archie one

You will recall Abbi was remanded to custody following several breached court orders—She is scared and distressed at her reception into custody. Her eldest child is with her mum; her two youngest have been taken into temporary foster care. Abbi has a long history of substance misuse, unconfirmed experience of domestic violence, had witnessed her ex-partner, Jayden's father killed in front of her, and she was supporting her alcoholic father at the time of her remand.

Abbi was nervous of being in prison as she had 'enemies' (following the trial of her ex's killer) and was 'terrified' of losing her children whom she loved very much. Social services had had previous concerns about her parenting and maturity but there was no doubt of her love for her children or theirs for her. You were asked in the Courts chapter (*Chapter 5*) to consider the likely outcome of her remand—her 'risk factors' and a 'management plan'. Abbi was on remand for five weeks during which time the prison made a referral to Anawim women's centre. A key worker visited Abbi regularly in the prison and began her assessment. Anawim worked with Abbi and with the drugs workers in the prison formulating a plan for support and desistance in the community via the drugs workers at Anawim Women's Centre. Anawim also referred Abbi to the Re-Unite project and Abbi's Re-Unite worker supported her whilst she was in custody, facilitating carers for Jayden to allow Abbi's mum to bring Petra and Archie to the prison to visit.

Re-Unite were able to establish with social services that their 'preferred outcome' was to see Abbi enabled to be a mature and responsible full-time mum in as short a time as was reasonably possible and via a phased return. Anawim and Re-Unite supported Abbi through the parenting assessment and the difficult process of accepting why she couldn't have her children as soon as she was released — Re-Unite remained involved with her whilst she was in custody and when she was released after five weeks on remand with a community order — to be supervised via Anawim. Abbi in addition to the drugs worker and Re-Unite worker received counselling for PTSD (as a result of the murder she witnessed) during which she also revealed she had been violently assaulted by Jayden's dad when he was alive.

Abbi has a long road ahead of her and obviously a complex set of issues to work through, relapse is not unheard of in women's centres, but the philosophy is on honesty, transparency and support — which experience informs staff is often enough to prevent 'old behaviours' and choices from becoming irretrievably entrenched. At her review Abbi had stated, 'I am desperate for my kids back, and I know with the help of this place I'll get them — I'm learning patience, if it was me on my own, I couldn't have done this, I know I would have given in and took stuff because I wouldn't have thought I could do it — but they believe in me here — and that makes me believe in myself.'

▌ Pause for Thought

What are your feelings about this case? — What do you think of Abbi's remand? — Should remand ever be used to gain access to services? — What does it say about 'systems' that Abbi 'had to offend' to have this support? — What opportunities had been missed? — What do feel about Abbi's future and her children's future? — What was 'key' in Abbi's successful engagement? — How could it have 'gone wrong'?

Abbi needed, like so many of the women and mothers in the CJS, to feel safe. Jordan (2013) has emphasised the multiple needs of mothers who break the law, revealing recurrent themes of mental distress and a lack of safety in their lives, alongside experiencing abuse in their early lives. Among the women in her study were incidences of complex PTSD, which Herman (1992) suggests creates barriers and resistance to 'treatment' for women, as they see it as 'too difficult, too painful and too challenging.' Jordan (2013) noted the potential for women who had experienced abuse in childhood facing further abuse and engaging in self-destructive behaviours, such as self-harm and substance abuse leading directly to cycles of offending. It is not unheard of for there to be 'intergenerational factors' in mothers' lives, who have faced abuse, and who break the law and end up with a custodial sentence, and then find they are putting their own children at risk, in a legacy of 'intergenerational transmission of trauma experiences' (Courtois and Ford 2014:178). In these circumstances, Jordan describes prison as 'becoming the abusive partner' (2013:30). In relation to double deviance, Jordan's (2013) work showed incidences where women were penalised for their criminality and yet somehow remained invisible as victims. In addition, she found women often having little understanding of being cared for. For many women and mothers, women's centres not only address their offending behaviour but the complex pathways that have influenced offending choices in the first place. Women's centres are a place of safety but also a place of learning what 'being safe' actually means, providing opportunities to understand how to change their lives for the better (Van der Volk 2001).

There are so many excellent examples of women's centres, it is a challenge to choose which to 'showcase' here. Abbi has helped to illustrate the strengths of women only multi-agency services when working positively with women to reduce re-offending and address root causes of offending behaviour in women. The point was made earlier about Scotland being at the vanguard of positive and contemporary change, however the Glasgow 218 centre, originally Turning Point, Scotland's Time Out Centre has actually been established since 2003. It is used as a true alternative to custody and women can be bailed to the centre to one of the 12 residential beds by the courts, or referred to the centre as part of a community order and /or attend it as someone who has been referred because they are vulnerable in relation the CJS. Additionally women can in self-refer.

The courts value the project, funding is secure and 'permanent', the local sheriffs (magistrates) visit and value the project, indeed the Scottish Minister visited the project extolled its virtues, recognised the worth of such projects and decided to halt the building of a planned super prison for women—wishing to divert the funds and energy into projects such as 218 instead. The centre is staffed by a team of centre-based and visiting practitioners who all contribute to the genuinely holistic approach to reducing offending—whilst maintaining firm beliefs about responsibility, accountability, choices and justice. The centre offers a range of services in-house, which has benefitted its users, who could access a range of services in one place, particularly important for those with multiple and complex needs. Women referred to the centre are vulnerable to becoming involved in the CJS or are already involved in it. The Glasgow 218 Centre takes a 'holistic' approach, working jointly with other services, which include healthcare, forward-looking housing and employment support, exit plans for sex workers and support for problematic drug and alcohol users, trauma-informed models of working and therapeutic interventions, mothering supportive group and one-to-one work and a whole a range of skills-based activities and additional confidence building all of which include mothers accessing the service. Following an evaluation (Louck *et al*, 2006) found that 83 per cent of women reported a reduction or cessation of drugs and/or alcohol, which had a positive impact on other aspects of their lives. Fundamentally, the 218 Centre has developed a model of intervention and support specifically geared to meeting the needs of women and mothers, providing services to tackle the causes of their offending behaviour.

A Specific Response

Women's Breakout, the third sector umbrella organization represents not only Anawim and Re-Unite but 56 voluntary and community sector organizations in total working with women offenders and mothers at risk of involvement in the CJS—all in gender sensitive environments. One such resource is the Asha Women's Centre in West Mercia that works with the Probation Service, to provide woman-centred approaches, through a range of non-residential programmes aimed at supporting and empowering women involved in the CJS. Asha can work with 110 women at any one time, linking women and mothers isolated by disadvantage to resources and support and providing a wide range of women and mother supportive interventions designed to promote desistance, confidence and positivity. Women whose supervision has been via the Asha centre felt it had benefitted them considerably and was effective in securing a reduction in re-offending (Roberts 2002, 2010; Rumgay 2004).

The examples of good practice presented in this chapter have embraced calls for a women-centred approach and alternative, radical changes (Carlen, 2003; Gelsthorpe and Sharpe 2007; Corston 2007). There is some optimism that services for women who break the law, including mothers are improving and acknowledging the failures of the past, as well as campaigns which support reducing the use of custody overall, and recognising many groups of offenders have multiple needs (Gelsthorpe *et al*, 2007). Alternatives to custody for women are not a 'quick fix' and emphasis has to be placed on addressing the wider inequalities and disadvantage women face across-the-board — there has to be some recognition of the benefits of early intervention — preventing women and particularly mothers from being criminalised when other options are known to be more effective and could avoid children being punished for the crimes of their mothers. This will be further discussed in the closing chapter. There are many faces and forms of 'punishment', it stands to reason that if women's 'pathways into offending are complex' and 'different' to their male counterparts — then surely their 'pathways out of offending are complex too,' and therefore are unlikely to be met via custody as best illustrated in a final case study via Polly.

Polly: A 45-year-old mother of one, Roy, 28. Last sentence, eight weeks, for breach of a community order

I've been to prison on and off for years, most of my life really — all my boy's life — he got used to it I think. I used to think he and his dad were better with me out of the way anyway, least Roy wasn't seeing violence if I was inside. I usually go away because I've mouthed-off when I've had a drink, or I haven't paid my fines 'cos I've had no money, or breached my order because I've had a drink and forgot to go—I'm not usually away long, the longest I've ever done is nine months, and I'll be honest with you I got put away on purpose for that one, I smashed up the Post Office. I wanted to get away from him for a bit. You get to the point where you can't take it no more. I thought they'd sent me here this time because I was a lost cause, I so didn't want to come. I don't know what it was, but after the first appointment I just changed my mind—something made me keep coming back.

I'm still living with abuse but it's harder to when it's your son doing it—you can hit your husband back when he beats you—but not when it's your son—something holds you back—it's your child even if he is a six foot 26-year-old-man. I feel like I should just take the violence—it's my fault he's violent anyway—I never left his dad and he saw it all so I take the violence from him because I deserve it, I didn't protect him from it.

I've told him to stay away since the last time, but I feel guilty for saying it. I know I have to work on all this and here the psychologist is helping me do that—I know I have to deal with the pain in my life so I don't fall back into drink to hide it and I've got as far as believing my husband was wrong to hit me, I didn't 'need' it like he said—I can see it all linking together now—why I put up with it—why I blamed myself when he hit me—but with my son—well that's different—but here they tell me its OK to take it day-by-day or a 'bit at a time'—and that's what I'm doing to change everything…'a bit at a time'…We watched a film here the other day, all the women like, and there was a line in it, it said something like…'It'll be alright in the end…and if it's not alright …it's not the end…' We all just looked at each other because that's what we feel like being here, that we will get there in the end… When we came here, nearly all of us I think thought this was us, our lot for life…we might not end up brain surgeons (well we might!), but we will end up something.

> **▎▎ Pause for Thought**
>
> How easy is it to see Polly's 'pathways into offending'? Why might trauma-informed and strength-based models of working prove more effective to her than prison? — Which intervention do you feel might have the 'best' long-term effect? What is being achieved for Polly via attending the centre — for herself?

Baldwin and Epstein are currently undertaking further research in relation to the 'failures' of the CJS pre-TR in relation to women and mothers, remand and short sentences — which it is anticipated will additionally reveal early evaluations of the impact of the new licence requirements for women leaving custody. It remains to be seen whether TR will build on the strong foundations of knowledge and expertise meaning community support and supervision will flourish and develop in a climate of new found flexibility, creativity and innovation — or whether as feared the specific needs of women will be subsumed and shoehorned into services designed largely with men in mind.

It is hoped that this chapter and the cases throughout have demonstrated that where appropriate — which is in most cases when it relates to women and mothers — community disposals are most often the most effective and productive for all concerned. Prison should be reserved for all but the most serious and should be used as a last resort. Further proposals as to how this can be facilitated are located in the closing chapter (Baldwin 2015.3). The 'last words' for the chapter are given over to an alternative to custody resource manager who told me:

> 'Most women come here traumatised and hurting — they need time, understanding and importantly, opportunities to be able to change.'

CHAPTER 10

Mothers Addicted
Working with Complexity

Lucy Baldwin, Sinead O'Malley and Kayley Galway

'I just wanted it all to go away—It doesn't—so best way is to feel nothing and make it.'

The primary aim of this chapter is to present an insight into being a mother and being addicted. It is not the purpose here to explore in detail policies, initiatives or the rights and wrongs of imprisoning addicted mothers, more to explore the realities and the complexities involved when working with mothers who misuse substances or of being an addicted mother—whilst highlighting key factors of positive working. It reflects the research, knowledge and experience of its co-authors and therefore includes the perspectives of practitioners who share certain aspects of the lived experiences of some of the women in the chapter.

Many years of experience inform what follows, coming from practice, working directly and indirectly with vulnerable mothers and mothers who have become addicted to substances. The chapter aims to provide some insight into the lives of addicted mothers and the challenges they face both personally and within 'systems' that struggle to deliver what mothers may need in order to recover and move forward positively.

The authors are based in the UK and Ireland, therefore the chapter is informed by information from both those countries. Approaches and interventions unique to each are presented and we attempt to draw together good practice and lessons learned. In order to provide such mothers, and ultimately their children, with the best opportunity to succeed and progress, the chapter reflects on experiences and practice in both custodial and non-custodial settings.

The first step to change is understanding, and the journey towards real change in relation to addiction must surely begin by attempting to understand the person who is addicted — how and why they became so — how that addiction led to immersion, ultimately therefore to understand the 'addict' — and arguably as important, if not more so, to assist the addicted persons to understand themselves.

The chapter is illustrated by case studies based on the experiences and practices of the authors and is additionally supported by 'Pauses for Thought' which encourage the reader to critically reflect on the chapter material — but perhaps more importantly ask the reader to consider the perspectives of both the mothers and the practitioners working with them. It advocates a strengths-based approach, with human rights and social justice providing the cornerstone of practice, influenced by trauma-informed models of working. Within this is an ultimate belief that allowing voiceless, often vulnerable mothers — who are frequently labelled 'selfish' and thereby rejected by society — to be heard; thus providing the mothers and their children with hope. Belief in the 'ability to change' and a 'hope for change' are primary motivating prerequisites for practitioners working with addicted mothers and the primary instruments for mothers too in working towards affecting change and creating opportunities for a different life if this is what they are able to choose.

This is no easy task — for mothers or for practitioners working with them — as mothers using substances are widely regarded as 'failing' — by themselves and others, and overcoming 'internal damage and distress' from judgement, suspicion, fear and rejection together with the trauma of past experiences can quite simply feel 'too big.'

> 'The female criminal, the prostitute and the female drunk were held up as the very negation of the feminine ideal: a warning to other women to conform.' (Zedner 2010:320)

Creating a space of emotional safety (Baldwin 2015e and f) is a fundamental part of working with mothers who use substances.

Context and Prevalence

This book has already highlighted the position through time of women, especially mothers, being required to be meet ideas, ideals and stereotypes of femininity and maternal representation — and so this chapter will not be repetitive in relation to women, mothers, criminality and society. However, there is a whole new 'layer' of judgement when it comes to pregnant mothers and mothers who parent whilst misusing substances. Victorian England, not known for its lack of moral judgement, often in relation to women, associated alcoholism with prostitution and vice-versa. Dr Norman Kerr a social reformer in discussion on the use of alcohol by prostitutes stated:

'…by drink, the unfortunates deadened their conscience and stifled stir-rings of remorse, thus fortifying themselves to ply their hideous calling.' (Zedner 2010:331)

A prison chaplain at Millbank women's prison made similar observations that women were only able to cope with the horror that was their living existence by being 'intoxicated' (*Ibid*); an early description perhaps of what was to become known as part of the complex picture of substance misuse in women — 'escapism' and 'retreatism' (Freidman and Alicea 2001), i.e. misusing substances as a means of masking the pain of past or current lived experiences (Woods 2007).

Even before drug use was evident in research or even in women's lived experiences in the same way it might be now, alcoholism was seen to have potentially serious moral, emotional and practical consequences when present in women, more so if they were mothers — 'because of women's responsibilities for home life and child care' (MacLeod 1967). Early studies laid blame and moral judgement on mothers who 'drank' rather than making any attempt to understand the background of why women might 'need' to numb their minds and bodies in the first place. This was especially the case in relation to mothers. According to Dr Kerr (1880):

'…Mothers are the more general transmitter of the hereditary alcoholic taint I have little doubt.' (Zedner 2010)

Mothers who drank were condemned and judged, especially if they drank during pregnancy — it was suggested that drunk women were giving birth to 'ever increasing multitudes of social failures' and women themselves who drank were seen as failures. Failures not only as mothers, but as wives and 'homemakers' — they were seen as slovenly, selfish, neglectful, frivolous with housekeeping funds, and absent as mothers, wives and daughters (Kerr 1880; Westcott 1903; Zanetti 1903; Macleod 1967). Zedner (2010) makes the point that the:

> '...lack of sympathy for women who sought to escape the miseries of destitution in drink is all the more marked when one notes the relative lack of comparative censure in men.' (2010:332)

It wasn't until the late-1970s and early-1980s that drugs started to appear more prominently in the research or concerns related to vulnerable families and offending behaviour (Advisory Council on the Misuse of Drugs (ACMD) 2003). The 1960s had seen the increase in the use of 'recreational drugs' especially amongst young people, and there had been some concerns regarding sleeping-pills and diazepam addiction amongst the older more 'middle-class' populations — but drugs use and mothers was not something that had drawn a great deal of attention. However, in contemporary society, drug misuse has become an ever-increasing issue with an astronomical rise in occurrence. The ACMD (2003) suggest for example that the number of people addicted to heroin 'increased ten and 15 fold respectively between 1980 and the late-1990s' (2003:7). Many of those represented in these figures are parents, and it is suggested between 250,000-350,000 children are affected by their parents' drug use (*Ibid*).

The 2003 and 2007 ACMD reports 'Hidden Harm' were commissioned to look into the effects of parental drug use on children. They state that no drug use is 'entirely harmless' but also that 'not all drug use is incompatible with being a good parent.' The focus was very much on 'problematic drug use' which they define as:

> '...drug use with serious negative consequences of a physical, psychological, social and interpersonal, financial or legal nature for users and those around

them. Such drug use will usually be heavy, with features of dependence' (2003:07).

Agneta: A 38-year-old married mother of two, Ophelia four and Pierre two

Agneta is a successful business woman who is married and lives with her husband who is a partner in a law firm in the City. They live in rural countryside, but within commuting distance. She had not wanted children at all and had focussed very much on her career, however her husband had desperately wanted children and so at 34 Agneta had Ophelia followed accidentally later with a son Pierre. Agneta and her husband keep an apartment in the City as they both often need to stay away from home for work, for entertaining or work-related functions. Agneta and her husband both use cocaine, which they describe as 'social use'. She uses sometimes up to three times a week if her work is busier and she is attending lots of functions, her husband less so.

After a particularly busy week Agneta had stayed 'in town' for four consecutive nights and so asked the nanny to bring the children to the apartment for a visit as she would need to be away that evening too. The children would not ordinarily be at the apartment. Whilst she was taking a work phone call and the nanny was helping Pierre with the toilet, Ophelia found some white powder. Assuming it was sherbet she consumed it.

Immediately the nanny and Agneta realised what had happened they rushed Ophelia to the hospital, by which time she was quite unwell. The circumstance of Ophelia's admission meant the hospital social worker was called and the family were advised there would have to be an investigation and they would need to undergo an assessment. Ophelia was in hospital for two days then released into the care of her parents. The police were obliged to investigate, when Ophelia admitted immediately it was cocaine and that it was for her own personal use. She was dealt with by way of a 'police caution.' Following the assessment it was concluded that the incident was a 'one off', that Agneta was not in a 'weak financial position and therefore did not need to offend to fund her usage' and that she and her husband's cocaine use were 'lifestyle choices' (she had asked for the word 'habit' to be replaced by 'usage' in the report). The assessment required that Agneta attend an appointment at least once with a drugs counsellor to assess her usage and discuss her choices. Agneta attended the appointment but felt she did not require further appointments as she was 'in control of her life and her usage and could make choices about her lifestyle herself.'

The assessment concluded the children were 'healthy and well-cared for' and 'not at-risk', social services therefore closed the case and withdrew.

Pause for Thought

What are your 'feelings' about this case? About Agneta? — Do you think you have/would have reacted differently with an alternative socio-economic background? — Do you think the agencies involved would have? Why? Agneta maintains she does not use substances around her children — is it possible to be a 'functioning addict' and a 'good mother'? — Is substance misuse always incompatible with mothering? — Is 'social use of cocaine' different to 'social use of alcohol'? — Maybe in front of or with their children present? — What about nicotine addiction and parents who smoke in front of their children? — Why might Agneta feel she 'needs' or 'makes the choice' to take cocaine — is there a difference? — Why did she want the word changed from 'habit' to 'usage'?

Agneta was 'lucky' in that her use of cocaine was something she could afford (at least financially) — What about when this is not the case? Criminality is often associated with substance misuse and many of the women and mothers who come into contact with the CJS do so because of offending to fund their addictions, and often their partners addiction too (Malloch 2004, 2000; Taylor 1993; Carlen 1985). We have seen already that criminality is seen as a 'deviation from femininity' adding misuse of drugs and alcohol elicits further moral questioning and judgement, which in turn 'is considered even more problematic if the woman is pregnant and/or is a mother' (Malloch 1999; Perry 1991). Malloch suggests this additional stereotyping for mothers who break the law and misuse substances results in defining mothers as 'triple deviants' (*Ibid*).

In the prison population, the Prison Reform Trust inform us that over half reported committing offences connected to their drug-taking, 48 per cent of women prisoners said they had offended to support the drug habit of 'someone else.' Of those prisoners who had used heroin, women stated they had required up to £50 a day to support theirs and/ or someone else's habit (£30 for men). In relation to alcohol, 46 per cent of female prisoners stated they believed their alcohol to be a 'big problem', with 58 per cent stating they believe alcohol was a factor related to their offending behaviour (Prison Reform Trust 2014).

Addicted Mothers — Multiple Choice — Or Limited Choices?

It is accepted that there are more male drug users than female ones and there are some common difficulties faced by both sexes, commonalities in low levels of formal education, poverty, homelessness and unemployment for example (Neale 2004). Nonetheless the stressful life circumstances and complexities of intertwining issues for women and mothers who use illicit drugs or misuse alcohol provides an extremely heterogeneous picture between male and female drug users. Women have often been portrayed as 'dependant on men for their continued supply of drugs and the finance to support their habit' (Malloch 2004), However, Taylor (1993) found evidence in research to challenge this perception suggesting that in daily life it was often the woman who has the 'responsibility' to 'score' or 'graft' in order to fund addictions (although there is no presumption that coercion is not a feature of this responsibility). Women drug users are much more likely to generate income from prostitution, and have poorer physical and mental health than their male counterparts. The most significant dissimilarity however is that female drug users are statistically more likely to have suffered physical and sexual abuse by a relative, family friend or partner, and have a partner or, interestingly, a mother with drug or alcohol problems. They are also more likely to still have parental responsibility and have at least one child living with them than fathers who use drugs (Neale, 2004). Historically, as previously discussed, even as recently as the 1960s to 1980s women's offending was often viewed as 'pathological.' Factors related to offending behaviour of women and ergo mothers was often associated with depression or relationship problems; 'problems leading to medical or psychiatric disposals' (Malloch 2004; Worrell 1990). Although as suggested earlier — in the Victorian era — offending by way of prostitution was often associated with alcohol misuse (Sim 1990) and Malloch (2004) suggests there has been a developed recognition that women's offending and offending of mothers is increasingly linked to poverty and/or drug use;

> 'If I didn't take drugs there's no danger, no way I would be in here. I wouldn't be stealing or soliciting, I wouldn't be doing anything to keep the habit — because I wouldn't need it.' (Malloch 2004:252)

Arguably the increasing gap between the 'haves' and the 'have nots', unemployment and benefit sanctions have all placed increased pressure on those already most disadvantaged in society and have played a significant role in the increased use of substance misuse. Parenting in poverty is something Ghate and Hazel (2002) suggest takes a 'great deal of coping energy':

> '[I]t is not unreasonable to speculate that when parents are faced with other problems — a difficult, tiring child, fatigue, emotional stress and so on — on top of the demands already presented by raising a family in conditions of material poverty, they may have rather depleted personal resources upon which to draw ... It was clear from our data that the individual costs of a constant struggle against multiple adversity could be substantial, characterised for many by high levels of emotional and physical stress, depression, fatigue, and occasional feelings of desperation. Small wonder then, that dealing with a difficult or demanding child could feel like the last straw for struggling parents.' (Ghate and Hazel 2002: 216)

Sian: Aged 22 and a single mother of four children, Reece seven, Rhiannon five, Rhona three and Ria one; the children's father is involved but often absent due to repeat jail sentences

Sian lives in a small ex-mining town in Wales. She left home at 15 when she had her first child due to physical abuse from her stepfather who had hit her whilst she was pregnant. Sian has a closer relationship with her mother now that her mother has finally left the man who had been abusive to her for years. She has a very good relationship with her dad. She has recently been referred to the women's centre as someone who is 'vulnerable' of entering the CJS following a caution for possession of cannabis and a fine for shoplifting children's trainers and meat. Sian said in her statement, 'I have been a good girl I have mainly—I know I had my kids young and that but, well I've looked after 'em. But I can't manage on what I have coming in, the boy he's always wanting new this and that and I can't keep up with him and his mates and what they have—I feel terrible I do. Me Dad, well he has a drink and a smoke you know he said to me, 'Here Sian this will help you cope, smoke this before you go "grafting" today—you won't look so edgy.'

Sian's father had been unemployed for many years, since the pits closed, consequently he had become depressed and unable to work, he often spent all of his own money on alcohol so she was supporting him with money for his gas and electric meters and making sure he ate. She had tried to get work and was employed as a carer in a nursing home, her mum looked after her children—and Sian had loved her job. However, uncertain of the regulations surrounding a zero hours contract and the hours she was allowed to work, Sian had inadvertently gone over her allowed hours by 15 minutes—as a result her benefits were sanctioned and she had not enough money to cover her bills. Terrified of the situation repeating itself Sian had reluctantly given up the job. Disappointed and depressed she had confessed to her drugs worker that her cannabis use was increasing 'to cope with the stress of my stupid life' and she was starting to drink alcohol daily and was now on bail for further offences of shoplifting and was scared that her return to court might mean prison for her.

> ## ❚❚ Pause for Thought
>
> What are your feelings and fears for Sian? — What do think of her as a
> mum? As a drugs worker in a women's centre how would you approach
> working with Sian? — Are there other services' professionals in the team
> that might need to be engaged also in working with Sian? What are the
> strengths on which you can build work with Sian — where do the 'vulner-
> abilities" lie? What do you think will/should happen when Sian goes to
> court? — If she were to get a custodial sentence how do you think that
> might play out for her — for her children? — And if she doesn't, how it
> might be different?

As we have seen, women who use illicit drugs can be viewed by some
as unclean, immoral and unfeminine, especially if that drug use has escalated into 'harder' drugs like heroin or meth amphetamine. Would you
have viewed Sian any differently if it had been heroin in her vignette?
Arguably, mothers who use illicit, and harder drugs not only carry the
weight of the aforementioned labels but also transcend the accepted cultural norms of what it is to be a good mother, and can become judged
and categorised as an 'unfit' mother—both formally and informally
(Woods, 2007). The Irish Constitution (*Bunreacht na hÉireann*, 1937),
provides special recognition of a woman's life and rôle within the home
and as a mother (Article 42.2.1-2). This constitutional platform on which
motherhood is placed provides a clear ideological and cultural representation of the good Irish mother which is engrained in the psyche of the
Irish people, but perhaps the principles in relation to 'mothering' and
'good' mothering are more universally and even internationally applied.

It is agreed that while motherhood is both produced and influenced
by local culture (Hays 1996), the argument about what constitutes a
'good enough' mother umbrellas any varied cultural contradictions of the
construct of motherhood (Doane and Hodges 1992). Considering this,
some argue that real practical and emotional conflicts exist between a
mother's ability to provide for her child(ren) while managing her addiction (Silva *et al*, 2012). According to Winnicott (1953), a child cannot
positively progress through life 'unless there is a good enough mother.'
In fact, 'success' in infant-care depends on the fact of 'devotion from

their mother' (p.97). Devotion, defined as a 'profound dedication', or an 'earnest attachment to a cause, person' (*Oxford Dictionary*), suggests it is impossible to be a good enough mother considering you cannot completely devote yourself to the care and attention required by your child(ren) while a substantial part of your life is consumed by addiction (Think of the Social Work chapter (which deals with child protection) (*Chapter 3*) here too).

As described by Enos (2001), mothers in the CJS will often lay claim that their offending does not contradict their ability to be a good mother, or even that if offending *to provide for their children (by way of prostitution or theft of consumable goods for example)*, then this actually 'proves' they are a good mother. However Enos (*Ibid*) found that, even within the closed and apparently united environment of a prison, judgements would be made against mothers for whom drugs were a significant part of their lives and offending. One mother of three serving time for fraud said:

'[Y]ou can be a good mother and be involved in crime and shoplifting and stuff, but with drugs, that's another thing (Enos 2001:118).

Mothers themselves will, often through guilt (Sutherland 2010 and Enos 2001) suggest mothers themselves at least initially minimise the 'harm' or 'risks' associated with problematic substance misuse. 'I've done drugs, but I've always had food … [for them]' or as another mother in the research undertaken by Enos said:

[Y]ou know what? I never put them in jeopardy when I was on the streets. I did drugs. Yes I did, but at that time I wasn't into heroin. I was doing a little coke, snorting it. Nothing to make me drowsy or anything. Just to make me very hyper where I'd pay attention to them. I would feed them and do my motherly thing. Then when they went to bed I would snort…'. (2001:118)

When working with mothers who misuse substances, it is often very obvious that they are already deeply traumatised, often not only by whatever it was that prompted their misuse in their first place but also by the additional guilt they feel as 'failures' as mothers 'for putting my needs over theirs.' Enos (2001) gives voice to two women in her research who describe the reflection and realisation that substance misuse, particularly once labelled 'problematic', simply can't not affect their children or relationship with their children in some way:

> **Belinda:** 'Some women say, yes you can be an addict and be a mother, but overall to be honest with you, no. The drug overcomes the parent—and that's why my kids are where they are now.'

> **Margaret:** 'I see myself going downward because of the drugs, it messed up the kids because I still wanted the drugs more than I wanted my kids' lives. That bothers me a lot. That's the real hurting thing…So I can't say that I didn't shoot-up or bring them to the coke house. I did it all…right in front of my kids and everything—the worst things.' (2001:124)

Although in working with mothers who misuse substances 'responsibility' is a key factor of moving forward positively, additional blame and judgement are not effective, and in fact are damaging. What is important is to acknowledging the courage and the strength of honest reflection—drawing the strengths from a desperate situation can sometimes be a challenge—but it is an important part of moving forward positively and of breaking the 'cycles' of an unhealthy coping strategy that facilitates ongoing substance misuse. Maxie and her description of her 'cycle' illustrates this point.

Maxie: Aged 29, a mother of one, George aged three

> I started drinking heavily when I was 14, after my mam died. I was raped when I was younger by a family member but didn't go to the police because my family asked me not to—I used to get flashbacks all the time. I started using 'wobbly eggs' (diazepam), I wanted to block out the world—I didn't want to feel anything and that's what they did—they made me feel 'nothing'. I got pregnant, I don't know who his dad is, I really tried not to use when I was pregnant but I couldn't help it, it was too much. If I didn't use I started to hate the baby inside me and I didn't want to, I wanted

to love it—and I could love it if I didn't think how it got there, through sex—which makes me feel dirty—so I started taking 'smack'.

My baby was born addicted and that nearly broke me, well it did really I was so ashamed, the hospital, everyone I could feel them judging me—but they don't know my life...the social helped me and I got off smack for a while and went on methadone, they let me have him with me- the wain, and I tried to stay off it I really did—but then one day I just couldn't cope and so I took him with me to dealers to score—he asked me if I wanted to sell my baby!! Can you believe that the dirty scumbag wanted to buy my baby..? I gave him to my dad after that. I realised I couldn't keep him, I couldn't take him to the places I went or to see the people I see—my dad is straight as a dye he is , so I gave my bairn to him, I wasn't even paying attention to him half of the time, I was away with it...I know it was the right thing to do, but I didn't even want to wake up in the mornings...I felt so disgusted with myself for giving him up. I felt guilty but then I know I'd have felt more guilty if I'd kept him with me.

I wanted to get off drugs for my dad and for my son, but every time I tried I couldn't cope with the stuff in my head, the rape, my mam dying, the guilt—everything it's just too much, it gets too much so I use to block it out—Then I went to prison and after you've been to prison well you just think 'what's the point'. My dad would be broken if anything happened to me but drugs make you selfish...I got remanded, but I used what I could in there to cope and on my first day out I scored big time and nearly died—I think that's why the drugs court judge gave me this place this time—he said I need holistic care or something. I'm trying I really am, but it's hard, I want a life, I want a job, I want what everyone else has, I just don't know if I can have it, but this place gives me hope—I haven't had that in a long time...

‖ Pause for Thought

What do you feel about Maxie's story? What do you think will be key in working with her? Do you see the fact that she 'gave' her son to her father as a strength? — What other strengths would you help Maxie pull from her story? — How would you go forward with her? — Does anyone else need to be involved? Think about emotional safety from *Chapter 1* — How can that be achieved? Will trauma-informed practice models help Maxie move forward? Why will that be 'better' than simply a methadone programme and reporting requirements?

It can be very difficult, for mothers, especially, to recognise or admit that their children are/have been affected by substance misuse; many mothers declare they always provided their children with everything they needed, but often focus on materialistic provision. Mothers reiterate, 'My kids were never without,' however often the hardest and most painful thing to acknowledge is that the need and want from children is/was a mother's time and attention, or as is mentioned in the Social Work chapter (*Chapter 3*) her 'emotional availability' which was/is not always compatible with problematic substance misuse. Maxie's honesty is not an isolated story, many drug-using parents tend to spend less time with their children (Tarter *et al*, 1993 in Silva *et al*, 2012, p.359).

It is acknowledged that often views on 'good mothering' derive from the position of white middle-class women who rarely experience the social marginalisation, deprivation and vulnerabilities of drug invested communities (Rich 1970; Rotkirch (2009); Thurer 1995). Nonetheless, there are moral, practical, ethical and professional complexities practitioners must respond to when working with mothers who are also misusing substances. As seen in other chapters, this highlights the importance of working collaboratively and professionally with supporting agencies and practitioners in ways which obviously are mindful of child protection and child welfare — but are additionally supportive of mothers. Also and importantly, recognising that they, as practitioners are part of a process than can harm mothers further and must therefore ensure they are doing all they can to 'minimise' that further harm. Mothers and families can and are being positively supported to move forward by facilitating holistic, multi-faceted strength-based approaches to working with mothers. Trauma-informed practice can be a key feature in addressing the issues present in mothers like Maxie. Working with them to manage and reduce the impact of trauma from previous events — which may have contributed to the first trigger of substance misuse — and has subsequently begun an emotional merry-go-round of 'not coping' (emotional management) = using = guilt from using *plus* not coping = using = 'not coping' and so it goes on. The Social Work chapter (*Chapter 3*) highlights the potentially devastating consequences for mothers who are not supported in desistance — i.e. the loss of their children — which can then result in withdrawal of, or withdrawal from, support services and therefore increased substance misuse — sometimes before the repeat of another cycle with potentially another child.

❚❚ Pause for Thought

Is it 'easy' to see how cycles can develop? — What are the challenges to 'breaking the cycles' — for mothers and for practitioners? — How difficult is it to balance the needs of the child against the needs of the mother? — Given what is known about 'relapse' in relation to substance misuse, what is important in terms of support? — Are your personal feelings at odds with your professional feelings in any way or vice-versa? — How will you/do you deal with this? — Do 'drugs workers' have a different perspective to other professions — for example social workers? (It is acknowledged it is possible to be both).

Adams' (1999), research on the attitudes of social workers toward drug users reported that 99 per cent of participating social workers believed that drug-users are entitled to the 'same respect' as everyone else, while 68 per cent believed that many drug users are 'good enough' parents, 24 per cent were uncertain and eight per cent disagreed. Paradoxically, 63 per cent believed that parents living with children should not use drugs. Thirty-two per cent of respondents agreed that social workers discriminate unfairly against drug-using parents, 39 per cent were unsure of their response while 29 per cent disagreed. However, only 18 per cent agreed that drug-using parents get treated as fairly as non-drug-using parents in the child protection system with 35 per cent uncertain and 47 per cent believing that drug-users are treated less fairly (in Woods 2007). This attitudinal 'snapshot' highlights the kind of issues that can surround some of the challenges of working with mothers who misuse substances and would arguably produce different results again if the same questions were posed to police officers, magistrates or doctors for example. Given that effective positive work with mothers who misuse substances will very often involve more than one agency this highlights some of the additional challenges mothers themselves may face and the differential ways in which they might be responded to. Further evidence, were it required, of the value of 'women's centres' like the Anawim resource or the Glasgow 218 Centre mentioned in other chapters—where a multitude of agencies come together (e.g. psychologists, probation officers, drugs workers, counsellors, nurses and advocates)—all with a deep professional and personal understanding of the complex needs of women and mothers who offend and/or misuse substances.

Donna: A 34-year-old mother who has five children, Donovan 13, Shannon 11, Seamus ten, Niemh five and two-year-old Nessa

'Always remember, never forget, I've loved you since the first day we met'—This is what Donna says to all of her children when she calls them from prison.

Donna's three eldest live with her mum and the two youngest live with their paternal grandma. She is currently one year into a three year sentence for drug-related offences. Donna wasn't using drugs when she had the first three children, she began using substances around the time of the birth of her ten-year-old, whose father was very violent towards her and as a result of that violent relationship Donna's mother took the children back to live with her, however Donna continued to see them daily. She felt guilty as she felt she was 'choosing her partner over her children'. However she believed they were happier with her mother and she didn't believe in divorce. Her husband however died from an alcohol-related illness and she struggled to cope living alone. Within her circle of friends many were already taking drugs and, following her husband's death, Donna turned to heroin 'to block it all out'. It quickly became apparent that she could not 'afford' her new habit and began to offend to fund her addiction.

Donna met a new partner and successfully weaned herself away from heroin, and had two more children with her new partner. However on the birth off her youngest child she was visited by social services, who informed her that her partner of over five years, whom she loved and whom had been nothing but good to her, was a convicted rapist. Furthermore he had served seven years in prison before he met Donna. She was devastated, confused and angry that neither he nor social services had told her sooner. Her partner refuses to discuss the matter with her. He was forced to move out pending assessments. Donna returned to heroin use, which she describes as 'harder than ever'. Stating, 'Social services told me all that, and as a drug addict, when someone tells ya that the person ya love is a rapist, what are you supposed to do only turn to drugs..

During this time Donna's older children remained living with her mum and she signed a two week voluntary care order for the two younger children which she agreed would give her time and space to think and absorb what she had learnt. However, in the meantime social services learned of her return to substance misuse and visited Donna's home. She by her own admission was heavily under the influence of heroin at the time and can't remember any details of the visit. On waking after that visit she made the assumption that her children had now been taken from her and placed into care — and so she failed to collect them. Social services contacted the police following the visit as they believed drugs were in the house. Hence Donna now found herself in prison as a result of being caught with heroin in her possession, though she was bailed initially. However this understandably did not help her presenting situation regarding her wish to have her children home. She was not allowed contact with her children, whose father was trying to resume contact with her. During her prison sentence she has not seen any of her children, she won't let her mother bring her eldest children to the prison and she thinks it is 'wrong.'

There is no social work involvement with Donna's three eldest children, they are doing really well, and they have always lived in her mum's house and with Donna for the first few years of their lives. They don't understand why they cannot see their two younger siblings as they had a close relationship with them — they miss them as well as their mother. The social worker for the two youngest children has told Donna that it is 'unlikely but not impossible' that she will regain custody of her children, but her chances will be reduced if she doesn't 'engage' with the supportive services both during and after her sentence or if she takes her ex-partner back... Donna is however terrified to re-establish a connection with social work, stating, 'I don't know where to start.' She feels that if she tries to get her children back and 'fails' or the contacts with the social workers do not go well, then she will fall back into substance misuse — even whilst in prison — whereas if she doesn't try — then at least she has some control.

The women's centre prison outreach workers are currently trying to engage with Donna prior to her release in a few months' time. She will be subject to licence supervision following her release — via the women's centre, obviously if she were to breach her licence conditions she would be returned to custody.

Pause for Thought

How can the outreach workers increase the chances of engaging Donna pre-release? — What are the 'strengths' drugs workers and other practitioners can take from Donnas history, to work with her? — How do you see her future unfolding? — How can trauma-informed practice help Donna? — What needs to occur before TIP can begin? — What kind of support and from where could Donna be most effectively supported?

The Fear Factor...

This book throughout aims to illustrate the complexities and inter-connectedness often (but not always) present in the lived experiences of women and mothers who are engaged in one way or another with social and criminal justice agencies. It highlights that early intervention can be key in responding to mothers with complex needs. However, this is not so straightforward when it comes to substance misuse. Understandably perhaps, it is difficult when struggling with temptation or even after beginning the journey of 'using to cope' to imagine a mother, especially a young mother (think of *Chapter 1*) even contemplating asking for help—for fear of 'consequences' in relation to her parenting. It is likely that her ability to parent and protect will almost automatically be at least assessed at worst called into question. It is therefore more often than not that issues for mothers in relation to substance misuse only come to light because of a secondary intervention of some sort (e.g. illness, pregnancy, arrest) rather than early voluntary and preventative intervention (ACMD 2003).

The ACMD suggests challenges lie in engaging parents and mothers, but engagement is key to working effectively to reduce the risk of 'harms' to children, however they acknowledge that substance misuse alone is rarely a singular issue and that by the time a mother may come to the attention of the services, issues facing both mothers and their children are somewhat embedded or immersed.

> 'Problem drug use in the UK is characterised by the use of multiple drugs, often by injection, and is strongly associated with socio-economic deprivation and other factors that may affect parenting capacity. It is typically chaotic and unpredictable. Serious health and social consequences are common. Parental problem drug use can and often does compromise children's health and development at every stage from conception onwards.' (ACDM: 2003:10)

It is, by its very nature, difficult to proactively intervene or measure the prevalence of illicit drugs, particularly 'hard' drugs use by mothers, as the vast majority are consumed in covert situations and 'hidden' due to their illegality. The illegality obviously makes it difficult for addicted mothers who might want help and support to withdraw from substances possibly due to their pregnancy as highlighted above, and therefore they may prefer to conceal the problem out of fear of intervention from statutory agencies who may question the care they are able to provide for their children while immersed in addiction (Woods 2007). Studies suggest that very often the extent of addiction may only come to light in most cases when the mother has to go to the hospital to give birth, and it is at this point she is then unavoidably exposed to 'public scrutiny, which could include legal challenges to [her] mothering status' (Murphy and Rosenbaun 1999:102). This may be the case particularly when, as illustrated in the Social Work chapter (*Chapter 3*) and Psychotherapist chapter (*Chapter 7*), this same situation has occurred before and a mother has lost previous children to the care system because of substance misuse and lifestyle choices.

Pause for Thought

How can agencies attempt to work positively and proactively with mothers abusing substances? — What is your view on anonymous 'clean needle exchanges' for example? When a mother is pregnant whose needs come first the mother's or the child's? Is it possible to meet the needs of and protect both?

Francine: Eight months pregnant with her first child

Francine began using drugs not long after arriving in the UK as an asylum seeker. She fled the country of her birth after her family all bar her aunt were killed as a result of civil war in her country. They were granted asylum and housed in an area where drugs and social deprivation surrounded them. Francine had progressed from cannabis use to meth amphetamine within an eight month period and in part due to her chaotic lifestyle she had not realised she was pregnant until she had been arrested and remanded and tested in the prison following a drugs raid at a 'crack house', she was six months pregnant on reception into remand and in poor health physically, mainly due to malnourishment. She had been in possession of quite a large amount of meth amphetamine and had admitted it was her intention to sell this (not realising the significance of this admission).

Francine had been given a three year sentence of which she would serve half. She has engaged positively with the drugs workers in prison who have supported her application for a place on the mother and baby unit. If granted she will be able to keep her baby until the end of her sentence if all goes well (babies are allowed to stay in prison usually for 18 months to two years depending on the circumstances: see the Midwife chapter (*Chapter 8*)). The plan would be for Francine to maintain her drug-free stance in prison with the support of the prison team—she would eventually meet a prison in-reach worker to support her abstinence who would also work with her outside following her release. She will be supervised on licence via the women's centre where she will have additional support, access to childcare, support groups and will see her probation worker via the women's centre.

Pause for Thought

What do you think should be the outcome of Francine's application? How do you feel about babies in prison? — If Francine is refused, her baby will be fostered — how might this affect Francine? — Or the baby? — Short-term? — Maybe long-term? — What are common 'outcomes' for children who enter the care system? — On this occasion prison may have given Francine a reprieve from her chaos and an opportunity to withdraw from substances — but was prison the most appropriate outcome? — Should prison ever be used as a means of accessing services? — What does it say about access to services that magistrates have described using prison in such a way?

There are conflicting arguments for the presence and use of facilities that mean children can remain with mothers serving a sentence, with some opposition focusing on the fact that obviously the child is an innocent (Dwyer 2009). Conversely prison and enforced separation of a mother from her children, especially young children has long since been proved to be a major disruption to the mother-child relationship (Irish Penal Reform Trust 2011; Barnados, 2013). A possible alternative might be community-based residential programmes for pregnant convicted mothers, such as Women and Infants at Risk (WIAR). The WIAR programme transferred substance-dependant pregnant prisoners to an alternative facility which allowed their babies to remain with them. The woman participated in therapeutic and educational programmes to help with childbirth, child-rearing, mother-child bonding and social skills. The aim was to replace the inadequate health and drug treatment services provided in prisons and achieve better birth and development rates for children and babies. Kubiak *et al* (2010) conducted a ten year longitudinal examination on the 'outcomes' of the WIAR programme. The study concluded that 45 per cent of mothers who were transferred to a WIAR programme in the community remained arrest free in the ten years following the birth of their child. This compared to only 25 per cent of the comparison group who did not receive the same interventions. Additionally, 43 per cent of the children of the comparison group did not return to the care of their mother after their release, whereas 100 per cent of the children from the mothers who were transferred to the WIAR programme remained with their mothers after the programme had ended. Mother and baby units within prisons currently offer a similar range of supportive and therapeutic inputs which will hopefully be 'carried' on in the excellent examples of women's centres like the New Dawn New Day Centre in Leicester, the Anawim Centre in Birmingham and the 218 Centre in Glasgow—who all work successfully and effectively from a holistic, trauma-informed, women-centred model of working. The Midwife chapter (*Chapter 8*) (*Chapter 8*) also demonstrates how some mothers are additionally supported via organizations such as Birth Companions.

Ashleigh House in Dublin follows the WIAR Model. It is part of the Coolmine Therapeutic Community Dublin and provides the only drug rehabilitation residential unit in Ireland accommodating children alongside their mothers. Ashleigh House accept referrals directly from the Dóchas Centre and holds a waiting list of hopeful incarcerated mothers, predominately pregnant women, who wish to be transferred to the treatment centre from prison.

Ana Liffey and Merchants Quay work specifically with addiction in the Dóchas Centre and Limerick Prison (serving the two prisons in Ireland that accommodate women). These services support mothers and predominately deliver from a capacity that the mother and the key-worker hold a previous therapeutic relationship prior to her committal and the key worker 'follows the mother in' in order to continue working with her during her incarceration period and again post her release providing a continuation of care. In addition Merchants Quay provides two part-time addiction counsellors in the Dóchas Centre who remain linked with mothers post-release to provide an integrated service provision. Current and ongoing research around mothers in prison (O'Malley 2013) is reporting that influxes of women are now receiving drug treatment in prison and are also reducing their methadone prescriptions for the first time. Governor O'Connor explained:

> 'It's a team effort…we're a prison, we're not a therapeutic community, and yet we're providing assistance…which is enabling them to move on with the therapeutic programme.'

As highlighted throughout this text, in working with women it is of key significance to recognise that women in the criminal and social justice systems often have complex needs, which may be compounded by past or current trauma—substance misuse is hardly ever seen, even by the people who 'misuse', as a 'long-term' solution. It is very often a 'coping strategy', a short term, immediate 'solution' to intruding, unwelcome, difficult emotions, thoughts, feelings and sometimes memories—however the nature of addiction is that this 'short-term' solution becomes a habit (physically and mentally), one that brings temporary relief—to be asked to be or to be without that relief is scary, sometimes overwhelming and exposing. Creating a space of 'emotional safety' (Baldwin 2015e and f) for mothers is a key foundation on which trauma-informed models of working can be built—in doing so addressing the triggers and causes of substance misuse in its first instance, and thereby creating strong foundations which will ground mothers and facilitate an ability and confidence to move forward positively, for themselves and their children.

Update: Francine

Francine was given her place in the mother and baby unit—she also 'worked' in the gardens of the prison and undertook an agricultural course whilst she was there. Following her release, she kept to the conditions of her licence and, with the help of her advocate at the women's centre, her aunt and her baby girl, Liberty, were re-housed. She is now attending college full-time and intends to become a landscape gardener. Liberty is the apple of her mother's and her aunt's eyes—and she knows it!

CHAPTER 11

Summary, Conclusion Proposals and Best Hopes …

Lucy Baldwin

'I will spend the rest of my life looking through a lens of a mother who's been to prison — every bad decision they […my children]…make or wrong turn they take, I will wonder if it is my fault, if it is because I went to jail…any sentence for a mother is a life sentence really…' (A Mother)

It is hoped that *Mothering Justice* will generate a fresh understanding and recognition of the additional layer that motherhood adds to the existing complexity that is 'women' in criminal and social justice settings. This chapter pulls together the themes, messages and conclusions from the book along with proposals for change.

The opening chapter explored the 'motherhood messages', the social construction of motherhood and the motherhood script in relation to its ideals and expectations. Expectations of motherhood, mothering and mothers are both internally and externally generated. Within the 'self' women and mothers have expectations of what makes us a good mothers or not — almost a checklist if you like of what will help us define ourselves as a 'good' mother — Will we love our child(ren) enough? Will we buy them enough? Will we 'make' them fashionable, sociable, likeable, successful? — Will we be organized enough? Protect them? Have a mothers 'instinct'… and on the list goes? Similarly, there are external pressures in a comparable vein of what constitutes good mothering or a good mother — these exist for all women (Rich 1970; Oakley 1993; Mahon 1995). It is perhaps not surprising then that in the face of such expectation mothers often feel insecure about their mothering ability, or indeed that as Sutherland (2010) suggests mothering is almost synonymous with guilt — particularly when women 'fail' to meet-up to such high ideals and expectations. The impact of these ideas and ideals of motherhood both internally and externally generated have been illustrated and explored in the context of social and criminal justices services throughout the chapters of this text.

Arguably, mothers who are already facing multiple challenges and obstacles that may impact on mothering, such as poverty, mental health issues, domestic abuse, past trauma, substance misuse — and being in the criminal/social justice systems — may be more likely to feel they are 'failing as mothers' simply because of circumstance; and therefore more likely to feel a sense of 'guilt' or 'shame', as explored in the opening chapter (Sutherland 2010; Corston 2007; Sharpe 2015; Enos 2001). This internal feeling of 'failure' and the subsequent guilt, is a recurring theme and something that has been highlighted and illustrated in the 'voices' of the mothers throughout the chapters. It is therefore reiterated here that the unique status of 'motherhood', regardless of how it plays out for women, has emotional consequences and ergo a bearing on practice when engaging with mothers professionally. These emotional consequences need to be actively 'factored-in' in relation to our understanding of practice with women who are mothers — not least because of the ideals, expectations and commitments that come with 'motherhood'. Recognising motherhood, recognising past trauma and where and how the 'motherhood script' fits in terms of professional working relationships with mothers — both from the practitioner and service user perspective — is key in relation to both engagement and outcomes. The impact of failing to support mothers in this rôle or failure to recognise the centrality and importance of motherhood (and all that goes with it) — particularly for those mothers facing challenging circumstances — is quite simply vast. Poignantly demonstrated by Fiona Anderson who, unable or unwilling to ask for help for fear of being judged a bad mother, took her own life and the lives of her children, at least in part because in her words, 'A mother doesn't abandon her children.' *Chapter 1* therefore identified the importance of reducing the barriers to support and engagement, by 'laying the foundations' and creating a space of emotional safety on which to build positive moves forward for mothers who are vulnerable. Particularly those mothers who have a lived experience involving trauma, mental distress fear and disadvantage — which are all too familiar experiences for those coming to the attention of the social and criminal justice systems. Systems, which by definition can potentially harm, judge and sanction such mothers.

A theme identified by all of the contributors was the 'legacy' of historical, patriarchal and religiously influenced ideas and ideals of motherhood, womanhood and femininity, vividly demonstrating the perceived 'deviancy' of women who do not conform to or confirm such ideals. Mary Carpenter, a respected Victorian authority on women who broke the law, summed up in one sentence (also found in the Courts chapter (*Chapter 5*)) the 'fear' of apparently and supposedly deviant women which to a greater or lesser extent retains influence in contemporary society:

> 'The very susceptibility and tenderness of women's nature renders her more completely diseased in her whole nature when this is perverted to evil; and when a woman has thrown aside the virtuous restraints of society and woman is enlisted on the side of evil, she is far more dangerous to society than the other sex.' (1864b; 1:31-32)

The historical reflections throughout the chapters have also highlighted that this fear of 'contamination' from deviant women is exacerbated and exaggerated when it relates to women who are mothers (Zedner 1991; Davie 2010). Unfortunately this fear factor that 'bad mothers' contaminate and create a further generation of deviants and delinquents has not been constrained to Victorian times and indeed has continued to have impact, as we have seen within the foregoing chapters in relation to various professional assessments, sentencing decisions expectations and judgments. Both the Mental Health chapter (*Chapter 2*) and the Social Work chapter (which deals with child protection)(*Chapter 3*) highlighted the challenges faced when presented with competing and sometimes conflicting priorities. It can be very difficult for example to meet the needs of both a mother and a child in child protection circumstances — but it is short-sighted in the least, and as we have seen in this book, potentially fatal to focus only on the needs of one party — most often the child. Despite the complexity, the challenge and the apparent immediate cost, there has to be a renewed focus on the 'whole' (i.e. the mother *and* her child(ren) or future children. This does not necessarily mean always keeping a family together (in the short-term at least) — nor does it mean allowing the needs of individuals to be subsumed by the 'whole'. What it does mean is that there shouldn't be 'winners and losers' in terms of intervention, focus and support. All parties should be supported for the best possible outcomes to be achieved. For example, all too often in situations where there are competing needs and priorities we are told, 'It is in the interests of the child' or the 'interests of the mother,' however where possible, it is suggested, despite its complexity, there is often a path that covers the interests of both. That path may involve multi-agency working, may be intense for a period of time, and may on the face of it be expensive — but most often in the long-term mothers, children and therefore society will benefit (including financially).

What is vital in all circumstances but particularly in circumstances of conflicting need is that the 'voices' of mothers are 'heard' and enabled to be heard. Think of Tania Clarence highlighted in the opening chapter. Her children had been assessed as in need of a huge 'range' of services and they were rightly so provided. Yet were Tania's needs as a mother and a person taken into account? She used her 'voice' to ask to retain a social worker she 'knew and trusted' — and was ignored. Perhaps if she hadn't been ignored her children might still be alive.

The Mental Health, the Psychotherapist, Midwife and the Social Work chapter particularly all highlighted the potential further 'harm' caused to mothers and their children by only *partially* responding to mothers with complex needs. Responding to a mother with 'complex background' factors that may have led to abusive relationships, poor choices, substance misuse or criminal activity simply by assessing her as a 'failed mother' and removing her child — without offering ongoing support and understanding — is short-sighted and likely to result in a cycle of repetition. Quite apart from the human moral 'rightness' of understanding and supporting women and mothers through the complex mire of challenging factors that may have led to their coming to the attention of social and criminal justice agencies in the first place; additionally there are the absolute benefits both long and short-term, for children, mothers and society. Primary, preventative and early intervention saves hearts, minds and economies in the long run, and has to be given priority in terms of funding and resources in order to effect positive change for mothers (and therefore their children) who come to the attention of social and criminal justice services.

The need for strength-based and trauma-informed models of working with women with complex histories and needs are a further theme presented throughout the chapters. Each chapter in its own way illustrates that in each of the 'services' mentioned in the book, the immediate 'presenting' issue — whether it be offending behaviour, domestic abuse, a forthcoming baby, substance misuse, or a court appearance — in none of these presentations was *either* the fact the women was a mother, or her complex, often 'troubled' (at the least) background irrelevant. Culminating, at least in the UK, in the Corston report (2007), the need for more gender specific responses to women in the CJS is highlighted throughout the catalogue of research on women and criminal justice. Research, particularly from the USA (Covington 2007, 2008, 2013; Covington and Bloom 2008) has recognised the 'need' for more holistically informed models of working with women — models that take into account and address their often lived experiences of trauma. Recognition in the UK has been slower, perhaps because as I have suggested at least in part because of British fear of labels such as 'trauma' (see *Chapter 10* for further discussion) together with women's coping strategies of 'avoiding' that which feels 'too difficult to face.' However, as Sheehan *et al* (2007), Malloch and Loucks (2007), Pearce (2007) and Gelsthorpe, McIvor *et al* (2007) have suggested — if women are supported through positive women-centred, needs-led resources — places where 'emotional safety' is facilitated by supportive relationships and intervention — then trauma-informed and strength-based models of working can be successful and appropriate. Trauma-informed practice (TIP) in relation to women in the CJS is garnering increasing interest in the UK, which can be evidenced by the ongoing work of Dr Stephanie Covington in partnership with HM Prison Service to ensure that all existing frontline prison staff (in the female estate initially) are trained in working from a trauma-informed perspective. My own continuing research relates to TIP and emotional management specifically in relation to mothers but further research is currently being undertaken by the Centre for Crime and Justice Studies (Roger Grimshaw, Research Director) which will explore the additional 'harm' caused by the imprisonment of women and hopes to generate proposals for addressing and reducing the impact of trauma for women in the CJS. Existing services that already utilise trauma-informed models of working have described it to me also as 'mindfulness' (Baldwin 2015.3), a women's worker in a residential alternative to custody resource stated:

> '[W]e do "searches"—but no woman is ever naked or undressed in front of anyone and no woman has hands laid on her. It's about respect and recognition of who they are and what they might have come from.'

It is imperative that systems endeavour to not add to the 'harm' already experienced by those who come to their attention. In relation to the CJS there is an increasing questioning of the appropriateness and effectiveness of cognitive behavioural skills programmes for women (Malloch and Loucks 2005)—not least because such programmes were designed for men, to be delivered within a system with primarily male offenders in mind. Pearce, Sheehan, McIvor *et al* (2007) suggest interventions for women need to be 'tailored to women's experiences and needs' (2007:302), favouring holistic, women-centred interventions in women only resources in line with the Corston (2007) recommendations. Whilst there are very real concerns about the negative impact of the transforming rehabilitation (TR) agenda on women and mothers, it could be argued that this is an opportunity like never before to facilitate the innovative use of gender specific resources, from which women and mothers, children and therefore society will genuinely benefit; reducing re-offending or further interventions by truly addressing the root causes and pathways into offending for women. Many services like this, as detailed in the book, already exist (Glasgow 218, Anawim, Asha, New Dawn New Day (NDND), Women in Prison (WIP), etc.). What is required is increased and consistent use of referral to these services—including by sentencers (which will be re-visited shortly) together with committed funding—as has been demonstrated by Scotland. It is clear from the chapters in the book that key to working with women and mothers from such perspectives is the ability of practitioners to overcome barriers to engagement, which requires positive and supportive relationships in the first instance. A fundamental, key element of services such as those described above and in the various chapters of this book are 'positive supportive relationships' (Sheehan *et al*, 2007; O'Keefe *et al*, 2007).

During a visit to one such resource a service manager and a service user said to me, respectively:

'…Here we model what we are teaching—we don't have one way for us and one way for the women that come here—there is just one way for us all—and that is about mutual respect.' (Service manager 2015)

'It's not like prison here, there you are just a number—here you are a person—[in prison] it's not their fault they don't have time for you, and you don't always have enough time to serve to be bothered to engage yourself to be honest—but here there is time and there is "space." It just feels safer… don't get me wrong it's not always perfect and there are run-ins with staff and other women—but we respect each other. We learn how to live with each other and we learn how to trust each other.' (Tanya. Mother, resident, service user)

Power and relationships between practitioners and mothers was another key theme evidenced in all of the chapters and in the voices of the women and mothers throughout the book. There is of course no escaping the fact that, very often, agencies have power over service users in criminal and social justice settings, and as we have seen where mothers and children are involved the outcomes, sanctions, assessments and judgements within these power-based relationships have enormous significance and consequences in relation to their lives. Additionally, there is no escaping the fact that there will be occasions when outcomes are not positive in the eyes of mothers. For example, decisions to remove children, prosecution decisions or access to services, however as described and highlighted in all of the chapters (but particularly perhaps the Prison chapter (*Chapter 6*) and Social Work chapter (which deals with child protection)(*Chapter 3*), professional relationships undertaken with honesty, understanding, transparency, kindness, compassion and respect are the ones that prove the most fruitful and most importantly are the least damaging and harmful. The Home Office (1984) suggests, 'It is well-known that relationships are at the heart of prison life.' Liebling suggests that relationships in prison are 'decisive in shaping prison's social and moral culture.' Research around prisoner/officer relationships although it can present a challenge is nevertheless vital to demonstrate the 'harmonising of welfare and discipline—of care and control' (Liebling 2008; Crawley 2004)

Listening to service users in relation to their views and experiences within systems is vital to shaping effective and appropriate resources—particularly where 'power' is a feature—for example from my own early findings in relation to TIP in prisons it is clear there are challenges to those with 'explicit' power being 'able' to easily facilitate the emotional safety required for trauma-informed models to work. Plans to train prison officers for example in working with TIP may need to specifically include and reflect the position of women in prison and their view on this—as Ursula said in the Prison chapter (*Chapter 6*), 'How can they be caring if they have the keys?' No one is suggesting that skilled and experienced prison officers ought to be 'turnkeys' only, or that communication where appropriate between agencies would not or should not occur—however, perhaps as my research suggests, women and mothers in prison would feel 'emotionally safer' (as they have described matters in this book) if third sector workers were 'coming-in' to deliver the more in depth 'therapeutic work' related to trauma. However that is not to say that all front-line officers (and indeed staff) ought not to be trained in working in a trauma-informed manner (Baldwin 2015f) which will serve to not only empower officers but lead to vastly improved services for the women themselves. Partnership working and third sector involvement is seen to be especially successful and is evident in the engagement of women and mothers in services such as the Re-Unite projects, Coaching Inside and Out, Birth Companions, Hibiscus and the many inside-outside substance misuse-related programmes making a difference for women in prison.

Of course with any intervention or service response the foundation to any positive engagement with women and mothers is the 'relationships' between mother and 'service identities' as a whole, and between individuals as practitioners and as mothers. The importance of the 'quality' of the relationships between individual mothers and practitioners was a key theme across all of the services in the chapters—not specifically or only prison relationships.

It is via these relationships that women and mothers are 'heard', or not heard as the case may be. 'Voice' was another theme that shone (or shouted?) from the pages of this book via the mothers in most of if not all of the chapters. The largely missing but acknowledged voice from the book is the voice of the children. It is vital that research is supported and facilitated to assist and inform resources for children and families of mothers in the CJS, work like that of Barnados, the National Society for the Prevention of Cruelty to Children (NSPCC), Parents and Children Together (PACT), Children of Prisoners Europe (COPE) and Prison Reform Trust (PRT). Key to supporting children of prisoners is to work proactively to reduce the number of parents, specifically mothers, going to prison in the first instance (Epstein 2012; Baldwin 2015a; Reed 2014; Prison Reform Trust 2014; Howard League 2015; APPG 2015).

Emphasis on the importance of listening to 'user' voice, service users' and 'experts by experience' is not a new phenomenon. The third sector particularly has an excellent track record in designing resources, policy and practice which accommodate 'experts by experience'; organizations such as Women's Breakout, Women in Prison and Women's Aid for example actively encourage service users to speak out and they facilitate ways in which voices can be heard, in terms of engagement, means of exchange and provision design. The Care Quality Commission (CQC) is actively working with care providers in order to ensure user voices and experiences are embedded in care service (CQC 2015). However, in the CJS and statutory services particularly this has been less visible (or audible?). The Police chapter (*Chapter 4*) and Courts chapter (*Chapter 5*) via mothers like Jane Clough and Fiona Pilkington demonstrated very clearly the importance of listening to women and mothers and hearing their story and what it means to them, rather than focussing solely on the bare facts—without listening to the 'background noise,' the feelings and the emotions that outside of our professional world we would completely accept as the bigger picture may render full understanding and assessment incomplete.

The Psychotherapist chapter (*Chapter 7*), Midwife chapter (*Chapter 8*) and Mental Health chapter (*Chapter 2*) all refer to the importance of 'creating space', creating situations with the right conditions to facilitate engagement—conditions Fiona Anderson didn't feel and the agencies surrounding her failed to create. Certainly the women reporting domestic abuse and quoted in the opening caption of the Police chapter (*Chapter 4*) would not have felt they had any 'space' or opportunity to be really 'heard'.

Paula Harriott previously director of User Voice, now of Equal Voice spoke at a Women in Prison national event stating that when a woman, especially a mother, goes to prison there ought to be a 'serious case review'. Whilst she may not have meant this quite literally, what she was suggesting—and evidence supports her—is that by the time a women or mother goes to prison there have often been many 'missed opportunities' for more positive, less intrusive and less harmful and more effective interventions to have occurred than imprisonment. Independent Police Complaints Commission (IPCC) and serious case review (SCR) findings and inquests are often littered with statements such as 'there were missed opportunities to support or engage,' 'missed opportunities to communicate with other agencies' and clearly in cases like Jane Clough, Fiona Pilkington and Tania Clarence—'missed opportunities for the voices of mothers to be heard.' Many of the IPCC and SCR reports referred to in this book, and many more that haven't been included, found that circumstances surrounding the subject of the report were 'unique and unpredictable.' Concluding therefore there are 'no grounds for misconduct or disciplinary action' but that 'lessons must be learnt.' However, often by stating the obvious in relation to 'sets of individual circumstances', such reports actually fail to connect the common themes that connect almost every SCR report or IPCC inquiry—failure to communicate between agencies, missed opportunities to listen or to act on fear/views/opinion of the 'victim' and therefore, particularly, where there is 'no cause' for misconduct or disciplinary action, lessons are not learned at all.

Assistant Chief Constable, Dawn Copley of Greater Manchester Police stated she was 'puzzled' by the findings of the inquiry into the deaths of Jael Mullings' sons that 'police neglect had contributed to their deaths'(see the Police chapter (*Chapter 4*)), 'when two IPCC [investigations] had not founds grounds for misconduct.' Quite how Ms Copley could be 'puzzled' when two little boys died following calls to the police of a mother in distress, a mother who was known to have mental health issues and it was a GP stating this was an emergency situation—and yet not every effort was made to establish contact with Jael Mullings—is actually something that truly puzzles me.

In order for all of the correct 'lessons to be learnt' and real change to be implemented as a result of some of these SCR and IPCC reports perhaps there ought to be a concentrated piece of research which closely examines and reviews many such reports, identifies the solid key themes and failures with a view to making cross-agency recommendations and real proposals for positive change.

Probably the most significant themes (aside from the impact of motherhood and lack of 'voice' of course) running throughout the chapters was the relevance and impact of 'background' experiences, 'womens position in society', trauma and the unnecessary criminalisation and imprisonment of women especially mothers. Furthermore it feels very much like a 'welfarist' gap has developed in statutory provision, particularly in relation to the CJS. A key message contained within this book is that far too many women and mothers are being sent to prison in the first instance and it is that, together with an increase in women's only, gender specific community provision of services *has* to be addressed for anything to change. As has been repeatedly stated for 30 years plus there has been agreement that fewer women should be sent to prison and that prison is not the most effective means of dealing with women law breakers. The facts are that over 80 per cent of women are in prison for short sentences for non-violent offences—that, shockingly, over 60 per cent of these women are mothers of children under 18—this book and much research, many reports and the voices of mothers and children themselves have highlighted the impact and the need for change. Baroness Corston (2007) talked of the 'catastrophic impact' of mothers being imprisoned in relation to their children and the inappropriate use of custody in the face of the multiplicity of problems many women face even before going to prison — which is often only further compounded by prison. Surely to continue to ignore such strong evidence-based opinion is not only negligent but arrogant.

Minson (2012), Marougka (2012) and Hedderman and Gunby (2013), Reed (2012), Epstein (2012) and Baldwin (2015a) have all explored and questioned why, in the face of such consistent opposition, magistrates still sentence so many women to custody — as discussed in the Courts chapter (*Chapter 5*) — and again as stated in that chapter, despite all of the detailed research and the reasons sentencers themselves give (see particularly Minson, Marougka and Hedderman) — the answer remains 'because they can' (see again *Chapter 5*). I would suggest that this 'absolute discretion' is addressed and that in recognition of the negative impact of custody for women and children, that magistrates rather than being 'encouraged' to use increased community disposals (use which we have seen is at best inconsistent and at worst non-existent), instead that they become formally *required* to consider alternatives to custody for women and especially mothers — and then to use imprisonment only if all other avenues have been explored and discounted — because of the seriousness of the offence and risk of harm.

Punishment can have many faces and to minimise use of custody for women and mothers as a rule rather than an exception is not flying in the face of justice. Legitimate restrictions to absolute freedom and liberty are possible in response to the retributionists amongst us, even when delivered in the community as part of a comprehensive women-centred holistic approach to desistance. Technically, magistrates are 'required' as per guidelines issued in relation to the sentencing of mothers (see the Courts chapter (*Chapter 5*) for discussion) to take account of the affect of sentencing on children. However this is not currently monitored or it appears to be unenforceable — what I am proposing is a change to the sentencing process for mothers by the adaption of existing services. Should these proposals be adopted there would be an *immediate and significant reduction* in the number of women in custody (given 66 per cent are mothers of under 18s). Furthermore, I propose that these changes are

implemented wherever possible by gender specific courts where magistrates with expert knowledge, training and experience sit and are able
to base sentencing decisions for women and mothers on increased and
specialist knowledge. This would in theory remove some of the 'inconsistency of sentence decisions' found in sentencing research in relation
to women and mothers. In relation to children, Reed (2012) suggests it
is vital their voice and presence is heard at court and she too proposed
the use of guardians ad litem (GALs) to facilitate this.

As an ex-probation officer and social worker I am all too aware of
the fact that changes can be and are implemented swiftly when need
be — furthermore as an ex-practitioner who has worked within these
'systems' and 'processes' I do not believe I am proposing anything that
is either impossible or unreasonable, whilst accepting there would be
challenges and resistance — however I don't feel that would be a reason
to carry on ignoring evidence and relying on the inevitable inconsistency
that without structured change to sentencing frameworks would prevail.

Following the Macpherson (1999) report, probation officers were
required to identify and extract pre-sentence reports (PSRs) where there
was any kind of racial element, similarly this occurred with sex offender
PSRs — these had to then be written only by experienced and knowledgeable staff with awareness of pertinent issues and best practice sentencing
decisions and awareness of resources (Ergo directives *can* be given in
response to need which then allow an 'audit trail' facilitating monitoring
and accountability). What I am proposing is that at first court appearance (where remand to custody would be avoided if at all possible and
certainly where custody is ultimately unlikely), referrals would be made
that will trigger a chain of events similar to that described above.

I propose that in all cases where custody is a possibility a PSR be made
mandatory in relation to, ideally, all women — but specifically mothers with children under the age of 18 (or more broadly anyone who is a
lone carer for children or dependant adults). At this point, in relation to
mothers a referral to a GAL (or a criminal justice team social worker: see
below) with a view to seeking an independent report in relation the circumstances of the children and the potential impact and provision for
the children in the event of a custodial sentence being imposed on the

mother. I propose this report be secured over an adjournment period of four weeks—and it would then be used to assist and inform the court in relation to impact and (therefore proportionality of) punishment. This would assist sentencing decisions in perhaps the same way a psychiatric report might—certainly the format and the principle is the same. This period of adjournment would also facilitate the PSR in relation to the woman/mother and allow time for the PSR writer (who ideally would have specialist gender specific knowledge) to establish the criminogenic and holistic needs of the mother and again gather the most useful and relevant information in order to inform the court and advise on the most appropriate and comprehensive community disposals, including identification and availability of local resources. If custody is to be advised—in appropriate cases only—then the report would focus on the requirements for custody-based and licence supervision requirements—i.e. would the mother lose her home, her children to care, etc.—and how will that be addressed post-sentence (forward planning and consideration given to things like child visits would reduce the further harm and importantly the disproportionality of punishment of the CJS).

It is acknowledged that this would result in a delay in proceeding and create some additional costs—however, on balance, the cost (as demonstrated in the Courts chapter (*Chapter 5*)) would be offset by the significant reduction of mothers in custody, children in care and successful desistance. Importantly also, it would facilitate proper investigation into what arrangements or provisions might or might not need to be in place for children. The result would be two comprehensive reports presented to the sentencer to assist in making truly informed and importantly (as per human rights requirements) balanced sentencing decisions. This framework could arguably be readily accommodated and built into magistrates' training and made subject to monitoring with measures of accountability.

A logical consequence of implementation of these proposals and steps would be a reduction in the number of women in custody and—given that 66 per cent of women in prison are mothers of under 18s this would reduce the number of mothers in custody significantly, which in turn would reap benefits for women, children and society—socially, economically, psychologically and emotionally (Baldwin 2015a).

The last theme that was observed throughout the chapters as something 'missing' from contemporary statutory services is the 'welfarist' response, particularly one that can 'bridge the gap' between services and assist in joining the dots by providing at least advocacy in a mire of multi-agency responses to women and mothers in often disconnected and disjointed systems. O'Malley (2013) throughout her research has firmly argued for a prison-based worker at best, and a prison-based advocate for women at least. Mothers in prison, we have seen, often lose their children and their homes, but particularly in the case of children outside there are child protection proceedings going on parallel to a mother's sentence—and these are proceedings where most often the mother has no voice. O'Malley (*Ibid*) suggests that meetings often occur where decisions are made, significant decisions about mothers' and children's futures, with no advocate for the mother—no-one to report on her progress or her plans. This is not acceptable.

Not only do I concur with O'Malley in relation to a prison-based social worker, but I would argue there is a real need for a statutory 'bridge' to address the often wide gap between services—particularly when one of those services is a prison; a gap that would be filled by a criminal justice social work team (CJSW team). The farther that probation has been forced to move away from its original social work roots the less probation officers have the time or remit to become involved with offenders' lives—home visits are rare and the focus in supervision has become much more on risk factors, reducing re-offending and the 'here and now', particularly with the onset of 'offending behaviour programmes'; which we have seen are, particularly for women, questionably effective (Malloch and Loucks 2007). Within the many SCR and IPCC matters mentioned earlier there are 'failures to communicate' between services—very often I would argue a criminal justice social worker (CJSW) would be a means to bridge that gap. Third sector support like Re-Unite would for example have a direct contact with a CJSW and would be able to plan for release or liaise for contact. In place of the GAL, a CJSW could be the 'team' a court would go to for a report to assist in relation to sentencing.

It may be the case that referrals are made relating to mothers who misuse substances and there might be joint-working from a supportive perspective in relation to mothers and the CJSW teams—which would have specific knowledge and training in relation to mothers who are also law breakers. For example, in the case of mothers who misuse substances—there would be knowledge that relapse may be a feature of recovery—but that relapse doesn't always have to be dealt with as absolute failure and agencies could work together to increase support in order to bring about full child protection intervention—whilst at the same time ensuring the safety of mothers and their children. It is an idea floated here that would require further research and exploration as the last thing women and mothers need in relation to their experiences of the systems are yet more experts to take away their voices and choices but at the very least I do believe there is a gap and a rôle for at least an advocate in relation to women, especially mothers, in the CJS.

If there should remain an absence of desire to create a 'new' service then I would revert back to adapting the frameworks and systems currently in existence and reiterate the sensibility of the combined gender-specific pre-sentence report, time delayed informed court proceedings, representation of children via a GAL and gender-informed magistrates who are required to consider alternatives to custody first.

Twenty Proposals: A Focus for Positive Change

1. Review the sentencing framework specifically in relation to mothers and explicitly *require* magistrates (and where apposite judges) to consider alternatives to custody for women—together with training and development to support them in this process.

2. Increase recognition of and 'factoring-in' across social and criminal justice agencies of the impact and influence of motherhood.

3. Reduce the number of women and mothers entering custody in the first instance, abolish short sentences and restrict remands in custody to only the most essential circumstances.

4. Reduce the number of women and mothers entering the CJS by early and preventative intervention that will stop the criminalisation of some women and mothers.

5. Follow the lead of Scotland in relation to smaller units for the few women who do need to be in prison — modelled on the success and expertise of projects like Glasgow 218 and Anawim.

6. Again as in Scotland introduce a 'presumption' against prison sentences of three months or less (but with discretion to impose below three months where the circumstances of the case are such that this is the only possible outcome).

7. Create gender specific sentencing policy, via specific 'women's courts' where 'expert' knowledge is brought together and valued.

8. Create a rôle of prison-based social worker and criminal justice social work teams or at least prison-based advocates for women, who will be the 'link' to community resources and particularly social services — especially in child protection proceedings.

9. Require childcare proceedings to secure the views wishes and representation via an advocate for the mother even when the mother is currently imprisoned.

10. Make continuing and increased use of third sector partnerships between prisons and relevant agencies — expand projects like Peterborough's First Day Out joint working initiative, Re-Unite, Women's Breakout and Women in Prisons in-reach work.

11. Carry-out close monitoring and review of the impact of Transforming Rehabilitation (TR) on women/mothers with opportunities to develop gender specific, research-informed support and supervision.

12. Expand police projects in relation to mental health and triage cars to pilot something similar in relation to domestic abuse—increase links with the third sector, particularly following reporting.

13. Issue a specific pregnancy Prison Service Order (PSO) containing guidance for officers working with pregnant prisoners with outlines for standards for care provision.

14. Conduct a review of why prison Mother and Baby Units (MBUs) are consistently under-occupied and have a high level of rejection of applications. (As opposed to the situation in Scotland: see *Chapter 8*). If it is found that the key to rejection is shortness of 'time left to serve' than this needs to be fed into a sentencing review along with questions around why pregnant women are on short sentences or sentenced to custody at all (except maybe for serious violence).

15. Where good practice and benefits are identified (e.g. Born Inside, Coaching Inside and Out, Re-Unite projects) look at ways in which they can be expanded or replicated.

16. Improve support for and recognition of the re-traumatising effects of court for vulnerable witness—ensure more consistent access to existing Crown Prosection Service support resources.

17. Continue with increasing awareness and commitment to inform practice from strength-based and trauma-informed models of working with women and mothers.

18. Truly listen to the 'voice' of service users in considering (e.g. children, *family*) developments—and secure input from the 'voice' of those affected—directly, via advocates and via agencies that represent them (e.g. Women's Breakout, Women In Prison, Barnados, Parents and Children Together, etc.)

19. Embrace and extend third sector partnership working, particularly with agencies where 'power' may have a potentially 'silencing' or 'restrictive' effect—so that more third sector input and support for women and mothers in prison for example is utilised, particularly after the removal of any children.

20. Support practitioners in their support of others—recognition of impact of 'secondary trauma'—both informally and formally—and promote and actively engage staff in 'resilience' awareness and training.

The voices of the mothers, shared via their narratives and the vignettes in this book, together with the views and experiences of the chapter authors provide a clear message about what is important, nay essential in relation to working positively with women and mothers in social and criminal justice settings. Not least is the need to immediately reduce the number of them sentenced to custody, and it is hoped that the proposals outlined above, if adopted, will go some way towards addressing the disruption of motherhoods and childhoods by often unnecessary, unjust, devastating and wasteful imprisonment of women. However, most significantly of all is the need to recognise, understand and importantly 'factor-in' the additional layer motherhood brings to existing complexities. Motherhood has a centrality to it that is never irrelevant to engagement or outcomes—whatever a mother's circumstances, whether she has her children with her or not—and the motherhood script leaves an emotional footprint in the hearts and minds of mothers that, in best efforts to engage with mothers, needs at the very least to be acknowledged. In order to afford justice to many women in social and criminal justice settings, we must 'do' justice to motherhood.

Appendix: Student Online Resource Bank

Acts of Parliament

Great Britain. Children Act 1989 (England). London: HM Government.
➜ www.legislation.gov.uk/ukpga/1989/41/contents

Great Britain. Mental Health Act 1983: Elizabeth II. Chapter 20. (1983). London:
HMSO. ➜ www.legislation.gov.uk/ukpga/1983/20/section/3

Great Britain. Mental Health Act 2007. London: HMSO. ➜ www.legislation.gov.uk/
ukpga/2007/12/contents

Great Britain. The Human Rights Act 1998. London: HMSO. ➜ www.legislation.gov.
uk/ukpga/1998/42/contents

Great Britain. Policing and Crime Act 2009. London: HMSO. ➜ www.legislation.gov.
uk/ukpga/2009/26/contents

Home Office

Hamlyn, B. and Lewis, D. (2000). Women Prisoners: A Survey of their Work and
Training Experiences in Custody and on Release. *Home Office Research Study, 208*.
London: Home Office. ➜ webarchive.nationalarchives.gov.uk/20110218135832/
http:/rds.homeoffice.gov.uk/rds/pdfs/hors208.pdf

Kershaw, C., Nicholas, S. and Walker, A. (2008). *Crime in England and Wales 2007/08.
Home Office Statistical Bulletin*. London: Home Office.
➜ webarchive.nationalarchives.gov.uk/20110218135832/rds.homeoffice.gov.uk/rds/
pdfs08/hosb0708.pdf

HMSO (1998). *Supporting Families* (Green Paper). London: The Home Office.
➜ www.parentinguk.org/resources/supporting-families-a-consultation-document/

Ministry of Justice

Hedderman, C., Palmer, E. and Hollin, C. (2008). *Implementing Services for Women
Offenders and Those 'At Risk' of Offending*. London: Ministry of Justice.
➜ webarchive.nationalarchives.gov.uk/+/http:/www.justice.gov.uk/docs/together-
women.pdf

Ministry of Justice (2012b). *Prison Population Statistics: Population and Capacity Briefing
for Friday 03/02/2012*. ➜ www.gov.uk/government/uploads/system/uploads/
attachment_data/file/218317/prison-population-3-02-12.xls on 26/08/2015

HM Inspectorates

HM Inspectorate of Constabulary (HMIC) (2014). *Everyone's business: Improving the police response to domestic abuse.* ⮕ www.justiceinspectorates.gov.uk/hmic/publications/improving-the-police-response-to-domestic-abuse/

HM Government (2011). *A cross-government mental health outcomes strategy for people of all ages.* Department of Health, London. ⮕ www.gov.uk/government/publications/no-health-without-mental-health-a-cross-government-mental-health-outcomes-strategy-for-people-of-all-ages-a-call-to-action

HM Inspectorate of Probation, HM Inspectorate Crown Prosecution Service and HM Inspectorate of Prisons (2011). *Equal but different? An inspection of the use of alternatives to custody for women offenders.* London: HMI Probation. ⮕ www.justiceinspectorates.gov.uk/probation/wp-content/uploads/sites/5/2014/03/womens-thematic-alternatives-to-custody-2011.pdf.

HM Government (2013). *Working Together to Safeguard Children: A guide to Inter-Agency Working to Safeguard and Promote the Welfare of Children.* London: Department for Education. ⮕ www.gov.uk/government/uploads/system/uploads/attachment_data/file/417669/Archived-Working_together_to_safeguard_children.pdf

Prison Service Orders

(See generally ⮕ www.justice.gov.uk/offenders/psos)

HM Prison Service (2008). *Prison Service Order 4800, Women in Prison.* London: Home Office.

HM Prison Service (2008). *Prison Service Order 4801, Management of Mother and Baby Units.* London: Home Office.

Halsbury Law Exchange Articles

Baldwin, L. (2015.1). Mothers Confined — Part 1: Over the threshold? *Halsbury Law Exchange* ⮕ www.halsburyslawexchange.co.uk/mothers-confined-part-1-over-the-threshold/

Baldwin, L. (2015.2). Mothers Confined — Part 2: Time for Action. *Halsbury Law Exchange.* ⮕ www.halsburyslawexchange.co.uk/mothers-confined-part-2-time-for-action/

Baldwin, L. (2015.3). Mothers Confined — Part 3: Lead by example: transforming rehabilitation. *Halsbury Law Exchange.* ⮕ www.halsburyslawexchange.co.uk/mothers-confined-part-3-lead-by-example-transforming-rehabilitation/

Reports from Charities

Birth Companions (2013). *Birth Companions: Annual Report*. (Accessed 01/10/2013) ⬇ www.birthcompanions.org.uk/media/Public/Resources/Ourpublications/AnnualReport0910.pdf

Barnardos (2015). *Sexual Abuse: Facts*. ⬇ www.barnardos.org.uk/what_we_do/our_projects/sexual_abuse.htm

Webb, M. A. and Nellis, B (2007). *Hidden Harm: Addictions in the Family*. ⬇ www.barnardos.org.uk/hidden_harm.pdf Policy and Briefing No, 13, NI: Barnados.

Webb, M. A. and Nellis, B (2007). *Hidden Harm: Addictions in the Family*. ⬇ www.barnardos.org.uk/hidden_harm.pdf. Policy and Briefing No, 13, NI: Barnados.

Greenhalgh, S. and Gibbs, B. (2014). *The Police Mission in the Twenty-First Century: Rebalancing the role of the first public service*. (Accessed 15/9/15 via) ⬇ socialwelfare.bl.uk/subject-areas/services-activity/criminal-justice/reform/1622342 1st_Century_Policing_FINAL.pdf (Reform report).

Reports from the Howard League for Penal Reform

⬇ www.howardleague.org/publications-women/

Report on the Inquiry into Preventing Unnecessary Criminalisation of Women. This report presents the findings of the Inquiry into Preventing Unnecessary Criminalisation of Women run by the All Party Parliamentary Group (APPG) on Women in the Penal System, chaired by Baroness Corston.

'Mitigating Motherhood: A study of the impact of motherhood on sentencing decisions in England and Wales'. This article by Shona Minson explores the impact of motherhood as a mitigating influence on sentencing decisions in England and Wales.

Keeping Girls Out of the Penal System. This briefing by the All Party Parliamentary Group on Women in the Penal System coming out of its inquiry into girls reveals that girls are less violent and committing fewer crimes despite common misconceptions that girls have become increasingly criminal and recommends a return to restorative policing where officers can exercise professional discretion and resolve matters informally and immediately (2012).

Voice of a Child. In 2010 at least 17,000 children were separated from their mother due to imprisonment. This report draws on interviews with children to document the impact that the imprisonment of their mother has on their lives: including long term emotional, social, material and psychological damage, with little or no dedicated support.

Women in the Penal System: Second report on women with particular vulnerabilities in the criminal justice system. This report by the All Party Parliamentary Group on Women in the Penal System chaired by Baroness Corston reviews progress made by the government on implementing the recommendations outlined in the original Corston Report (2011).

Prison Information Bulletin 2: Women and girls in the penal system. The second in a series of bulletins provides facts and figures on the female prison population, sentencing, community programmes and the impact of imprisonment on women, girls and their families. It is an essential tool for all those concerned about women and girls in the penal system (2006).

'Care, Concern and Carpets': How women's prisons can use first night in custody centres to reduce distress. This report argues that the early period in prison custody is a time of heightened risk of self-harm and suicide. It offers practical guidance on how first night in custody arrangements can be used to help reduce distress amongst newly arrived prisoners. (2006).

Advice, Understanding and Underwear: working with girls in prison. This report is essential reading for anyone working with girls and young women in the criminal justice or social care systems. It looks at current provision for girls and provides a useful insight into the impact of imprisonment on the lives of young women (2004).

Suicide and Self-harm Prevention: repetitive self-harm among women and girls in prison. The rate of self-harm is highest among women and girls in prison and many self-harmers will cut and burn themselves day after day. This report uses the voices of women and girls in prison to try to understand their motivations for self-harm and provides strategies for supporting them based on the views of prison staff and policy makers (2001).

A Chance to Break the Cycle: women and the drug treatment and testing order. More than 2,500 drug dependent women each year experience prison. These women could be eligible for the Drug Treatment and Testing Order. Research by the Howard League has shown that the Drug Treatment and Testing Order has the potential, if properly targeted and resourced for drug treatment to break the cycle between drug use and offending (2000).

Life in the Shadows. There is very little known about the prison experience of the women serving life sentences. This report examines what happens to women lifers, how they are treated and the conditions they live in (1999).

Research Reports

Covington, S. (2014) 'Creating gender-responsive and trauma-informed services for women in the justice system.' *Magistrate*, October/November 2014, Volume 70, Number 5, Pgs 2–3. The Magistrates' Association: London, United Kingdom.

Engender Health (2002). Law and Policy, Chapter 4 in *Contraception and Sterilisation: Global Issues and Trends, Engender Health.* ➲ www.engenderhealth.org/pubs/family-planning/contraceptive-sterilization-factbook-praise.php

Gelsthorpe, L., Sharpe, G. and Roberts J. (2007). *Provision for Women Offenders in the Community.* London: The Fawcett Society. ➲ www.fawcettsociety.org.uk

Manchester Metropolitan University (2015). *Equality and Diversity Guidance on Gender: The Women's Timeline.* (Accessed 2015) ➲ www.mmu.ac.uk/equality-and-diversity/gender

North, J., (2005). Getting it Right? Services for Pregnant Women, New Mothers and Babies in Prison. ➲ www.maternityaction.org.uk/sitebuildercontent/sitebuilderfiles/prisonsreport.pdf

Seth-Smith, N. (2013). *Rape in the UK: myths about myths,* 50:50 Inclusive Democracy. ➲ www.opendemocracy.net/5050/niki-seth-smith/rape-in-uk-myths-about-myths

Mezoughi, L. (2015). *Why sentence women to short custodial sentences that don't even work?* The Justice Gap. ➲ thejusticegap.com/2015/02/sentence-women-short-custodial-sentences-arent-working/

Websites

Rape Crisis — ➲ rapecrisis.org.uk

Safe Lives — ➲ www.safelives.org.uk

Women's Aid — ➲ www.womensaid.org.uk

Women's Breakout — ➲ www.womensbreakout.org.uk

Re-Unite — ➲ www.re-unite.org.uk

Anawim — ➲ www.anawim.co.uk

218 Centre — ➲ www.turningpointscotland.com/what-we-do/criminal-justice/218-service/

Asha Women's Centre — ➲ ashawomen.org.uk

Women in Prison — ➲ www.womeninprison.org.uk

Fawcett Society — ➲ www.fawcettsociety.org.uk

Howard League for Penal Reform — ➲ www.howardleague.org

One Small Thing — ➲ www.onesmallthing.org.uk (a project promoting the importance of trauma-informed therapy in prisons)

Other resources

Tracy Chapman's 'Behind the Wall' ➲ www.youtube.com/watch?v=mfeUZJwioio

Information on the 'Care Programme Approach' ➲ www.nhs.uk/conditions/social-care-and-support-guide/pages/care-programme-approach.aspx

Bibliography and References

Abbott, L. (2014). The Pregnant Woman in Prison. *Howard Journal of Criminal Justice*, 23.

Abbott, L. (2015). The Incarcerated Pregnancy: What is the experience of being pregnant in prison? PhD. University of Hertfordshire.

ACPO (Association of Chief Police Officers) (2008). *Guidance on Investigating Domestic Abuse*. London: ACPO/National Policing Improvement Agency.

Adams, P. (1999). Towards a family support approach with drug-using parents: The importance of social worker attitudes and knowledge. *Child Abuse Review* 8 (1): 15–28.

Advisory Council on the Misuse of Drugs (2003). *Hidden Harm — Responding to the needs of children of problem drug users*. London: ACMD.

Albertson, K., O'Keeffe, C., Lessing-Turner, G., Burke, C., Renfrew, M. J. (2012). *Tackling Health Inequalities through Developing Evidence-based Policy and Practice with Child-Bearing Women in Prison: A Consultation*. Sheffield: Sheffield Hallam University.

Aldgate, J. and Statham, J. (2001). *The Children Act Now: Messages from Research*. London: TSO.

Alexander, K. (2014). *Judicial Diversity: Accelerating Change*, UK Supreme Court Blog.

Baldwin, L. (2015.1). Mothers Confined — Part 1: Over the threshold? *Halsbury Law Exchange.* ➲ www.halsburyslawexchange.co.uk/mothers-confined-part-1-over-the-threshold/

Baldwin, L. (2015.2). Mothers Confined — Part 2: Time for Action. *Halsbury Law Exchange.* ➲ www.halsburyslawexchange.co.uk/mothers-confined-part-2-time-for-action/

Baldwin, L. (2015.3). Mothers Confined — Part 3: Lead by example: transforming rehabilitation. *Halsbury Law Exchange.* ➲ www.halsburyslawexchange.co.uk/mothers-confined-part-3-lead-by-example-transforming-rehabilitation

Baldwin, L. (2015a). Rules of Confinement: Time for changing the game. *Criminal Law and Justice Weekly*, 179 (10).

Baldwin L. (2015b). What is the Purpose of Punishment? *Criminal Law and Justice Weekly*, 179 (17).

Baldwin, L. (2015c) Mothers Confined: A study of mothers, grandmothers, emotion and prison. PhD. De Montfort University.

Baldwin, L. (2015d) Emotions Confined: The importance of working with the emotions and voices of mothers in criminal justice settings. (Presentation) Scotland: University of Dundee.

Baldwin, L. (2015e) Motherhood Confined: An exploration of the emotional challenges for incarcerated mothers. (Forthcoming).

Baldwin, L. (2015f) Emotions Confined: Emotion and mothers in criminal justice. (Presentation) London: Women's Breakout AGM.

Ballou, M. and Brown, S. (2002). *Rethinking Mental Health and Disorder: Feminist Perspectives*. New York: Guildford Press.

Barnados (2013). *Working with children with a parent in prison: Messages for practice from two Barnardo's pilot services*, Essex: Barnados.

Barnardos (2015). *Sexual Abuse: Facts*. ➲ www.barnardos.org.uk/what_we_do/our_projects/sexual_abuse.htm

Barnados (2015). *The evaluation of the Community Support for Offenders' Families service*, Essex: Barnados.

Bastick, M. and Townhead, L. (2008). *Women in Prison: A Commentary on the UN Standard Minimum Rules for the Treatment of Prisoners*. Geneva: Quaker United Nations Office.

Bateman, A. and Fonagy, P. (2004). Mentalisation based treatment of borderline personality disorder. *Journal of Personality Disorder*, 18, 36–51.

Bhugra, D. and Gupta, S. (2010). *Migration and Mental Health*. Cambridge: Cambridge University Press.

Birth Companions (2013). *Birth Companions: Annual Report* accessed at ➲ www.birthcompanions.org.uk/media/Public/Resources/Ourpublications/AnnualReport0910.pdf on 01/10/2013.

Bloomfield, L., Kendall, S., Applin, L., Attarzadeh, V., Dearnley, K., Edwards, L., Hinshelwood, L., Lloyd, P. and Newcombe, T. (2005). A qualitative study exploring the experiences and views of mothers, health visitors and family support centre workers on the challenges and difficulties of parenting. *Health and Social Care in the Community*, 13(1), 46–55.

Bosworth, M. (1999). *Engendering Resistance: Agency and Power in Women's Prisons*. Aldershot: Ashgate.

Bourlet, A. (1990). *Police intervention in marital violence*. London: Open University Press.

Bowlby, J. (1970). Reasonable fear and natural fear. *International Journal of Psychiatry*, 9, 79–88.

Brown J. and Heidensohn F. (2000). *Gender and Policing*. Basingstoke: Palgrave MacMillan.

Bushfield, J. (1996). *Men, Women and Madness: Understanding Gender and Mental Disorder*, Basingstoke: Palgrave Macmillan.

Caddle, D. and Crisp, D. (1997). Imprisoned Women and Mothers. *Home Office Research Study Number 162*, London: Home Office.

Callahan, K. (2013). Women Who Kill: An Analysis of Cases in Late Eighteenth- and Early Nineteenth-Century London. *The Journal of Social History*, 46:4, 1013–38.

Canton, R. (2015). Crime, punishment and the moral emotions: Righteous minds and their attitudes towards punishment. *Punishment and Society*, 17 (1), 54–72.

Care Quality Commission (2015).*Experts by Experience Bulletin: Integrated care for older people*, CQC.

Carlen, P. (1983). *Women's Imprisonment: A Study in Social Control.* London: Routledge and Kegan Paul.

Carlen, P. (ed.) (1985). *Criminal Women.* Cambridge: Polity Press.

Carlen, P. (1988). *Sledgehammer: Women's Imprisonment at the Millennium.* London: Macmillan.

Carlen, P. (2002). *Women and Punishment: The Struggle for Justice.* Cullompton: Willan.

Carlen, P. (2003). A strategy for women who break the law? Lock them up, programme them … and then send them out homeless. *Criminal Justice Matters*, 53, Autumn.

Carlen, P. (2004). Risk and Responsibility in Women's Prisons. *Current Issues in Criminal Justice*, Vol. 5(3) 258–266.

Carpenter, M. (1864). *Our Convicts.* (repr. 1969). Montclair, New Jersey: Patterson Smith.

Carrabine, E., Iganski, P., Lee, M., Plummer, K. and South, N. (2004). *Criminology: A Sociological Introduction.* London: Routledge.

Centre for Maternal and Child Enquiries (2011). Saving Mothers' Lives Reviewing maternal deaths to make motherhood safer: 2006–2008. *An International Journal of Obstetrics and Gynaecology*, 118(1).

Chase, E., Simon, A. and Jackson, S. (2013). *In Care and After: A Positive perspective.* London: Routledge

Chase, E., Warwick, I., Knight, A. and Aggleton, P. (2008). *Supporting young parents: Pregnancy and Parenthood among young people leaving care.* London: Jessica Kingsley Publishers.

Chesney-Lind, M. (1997). *The Female Offender: Girls, women and crime.* London: Sage.

Chesney-Lind, M., and Pasko, L. (2004). *The Female Offender: Girls, women, and crime.* London: Sage.

Chesler, P. (1989). *Women and Madness.* San Diego: Harcourt Brace Jovanovich.

Chigwada-Bailey, R. (2003). *Black Women's Experiences of Criminal Justice, Race, Gender and Class: A discourse on disadvantage* (Second Edition). Winchester/Sherfield-on-Loddon: Waterside Press.

Cleveland 1987 (1988). *Report of the inquiry into child abuse in Cleveland 1987* Cm 412, London: Her Majesty's Stationery Office.

Connor, M. and Norman, P. (2005). *Predicting Health Behaviour.* Maidenhead: Open University Press.

Corcoran, M. (2012). Be careful what you ask for: Findings from the seminar series on the 'Third Sector in Criminal Justice.' *Prison Service Journal,* 204.

Corston, J. (2007). *The Corston Report: A report by Baroness Jean Corston of a Review of Women with Particular Vulnerabilities in the Criminal Justice System.* London: Home Office.

Corston, J. (2011). *Women in the Penal System: Second Report on Women with Particular Vulnerabilities in the Criminal Justice System.* London: Howard League for Penal Reform

Courtois, C. A. and Ford, J. D. (eds) (2009). *Treating Complex Traumatic Stress Disorders: Scientific Foundations and Therapeutic Models.* New York: The Guildford Press.

Covington, S. (2001). Creating Gender-Responsive Programs: The Next Step for Women's Services. *Corrections Today,* 63(1):8588.

Covington, S. (2007). Women and the Criminal Justice System. *Women's Health Issues,* 17(4): 180–182.

Covington, S. (2014). *Women@Risk: Becoming Trauma-Informed: A Core Value in Services for Women.* La Jolla, Centre for Gender and Justice.

Covington, S. (2012). Curricula to Support Trauma-Informed Practice with Women. In N. Poole, and L. Greaves (eds). *Becoming Trauma Informed.* Toronto, Ontario, Canada: Centre for Addiction and Mental Health (CAMH).

Covington S. and Bloom, L. (2008). Addressing the Mental Health Needs of Women Offenders. In R. Gido and L. Dalley eds, *Women's Mental Health Issues Across the Criminal Justice System.* Columbus, OH: Prentice Hall.

Coyle, A. (2005). *Understanding Prisons: Key issues in policy and practice.* Milton Keynes: Open University Press.

Craig, S. C. (2009). Historical Review of Mother-Child Programs. *The Prison Journal,* 89.1 Cullompton: Willan.

Crawley, W. (2004). Emotion and Performance: Prison Officers and the Presentation of Self in Prisons. *Punishment and Society,* 6 (4), 411–427.

Dallaire, D. (2007). Incarcerated Mothers and Fathers: A Comparison of Risks for Children and Families. *Family Matters,* 56 (5), 440–453.

Daly, K. (1994). *Gender, Crime and Punishment.* New Haven: Yale University Press.

Davie, N. (2010). Business as Usual? Britain's First Women's Convict Prison, Brixton 1853–1869. *Crimes and Misdemeanours,* 4(1).

Deakin, J., Spencer, J. (2003).Women behind bars: Explanations and Implications. *Howard Journal of Criminal Justice* 42(2): 123–136.

De Beauvoir, S. (1949). *The Second Sex,* translated from the French by C. Borde and S. Malovany-Chevallier. London: Vintage (originally published in 1949).

Department for Education (2011). *A Child-Centred System. The Government's response to the Munro Review of Child Protection.* London: HM Government.

Department for Education (2015). *Working Together to Safeguard Children: A guide to Inter-Agency Working to Safeguard and Promote the Welfare of Children.* London: HM Government.

Department of Health (2004). *National Service Framework for Children, Young People and Maternity Services: Part III Maternity Standard.* London: HM Government.

Department of Health (2010). *Midwifery 2020: Delivering Expectations.* Midwifery 2020 Programme. London: HM Government.

Devlin, A. (1998). *Invisible Women.* Winchester/Sherfield-on-Loddon: Waterside Press.

Dignan, J. (2005). *Understanding Victims and Restorative Justice.* Maidenhead, England: Open University Press.

Dixon, M., Reed, H., Rogers, B. and Stone, L. (2006). *Crime Share: The Unequal Impact of Crime.* London: Institute for Public Policy Research.

Doane, J. and Hodges, D. (1992). *From Klein to Kristeva: Psychoanalytic feminism and the search for the "good enough" mother.* Ann Arbor: University of Michigan Press.

Dobash, E. R. and Dobash, R. P. (1992). *Women, Violence and Social Change.* London: Routledge.

Dodd, T. and Hunter, P. (1992). *The National Prison Survey 1991.* London: HMSO.

Dodd, T., Nicholas, S., Povey, D. and Walker, A. (2004). *Crime in England and Wales 2003/2004.* Home Office Statistical Bulletin. 10/04. London: Research, Development and Statistical Directorate.

Dolman, C., Jones, I., Howard, L. M. (2013). A systematic review and meta-synthesis of the experience of motherhood in women with severe mental illness. *Archives of Women's Mental Health*, 16:173–96.

Domestic Violence, Crime and Victims Act (2004). Available at: ➲ opsi.gov.uk/acts/ acts2004/ukpga_20040028-en_1. (Accessed on 12 November 2008).

Dwyer, C. (2009). Researching Children's Rights in the Context of Northern Ireland. In Davis, J., Gallagher, M. and Tisdall, K. (Eds.). *Researching with Children and Young People: Research Design, Methods and Analysis.* London: Sage.

Eaton. M. (1993). *Women After Prison.* Buckingham: Open University Press.

Eckton, S. (2012). Do the Consequences of Incarceration Problematise the Justification for Women's Incarceration? *Internet Journal of Criminology*, ISSN 2045–6743. ➲ www.internetjournalofcriminology.com/Eckton_Consequences_of_ Incarceration_IJC_July_2012.pdf

Edwards, S. (1989). *Policing 'Domestic' Violence.* London: Sage.

Engender Health (2002). Law and Policy, Chapter 4 in *Contraception and Sterilisation: Global issues and trends, engender health.* ➲ www.engenderhealth.org/pubs/family-planning/contraceptive-sterilization-factbook-praise.php

Enos, S. (2001). *Mothering from the inside: Parenting in a women's prison.* Albany: State University of New York Press.

Epstein, R. (2012). Mothers in Prison: The sentencing of mothers and the rights of the child, *Coventry Law Journal*. December 2012 Special Issue: Research Report.

Ericson, R., Baranek, P. and Chan, J. (1987). *Visualizing Deviance: A Study of News Organization*, Milton Keynes: Open University Press.

Equality and Human Rights Commission (2011). *Hidden in Plain Sight Inquiry into Disability-related Harassment*. London: Equality and Human Rights Commission (EHRC).

Equality and Human Rights Commission (2014). *Preventing Deaths in Detention of Adults with Mental Health Conditions An inquiry by the Equality and Human Rights Commission*. London: Equality and Human Rights Commission (EHRC).

Fawcett Society (2004). *A Report of the Fawcett Society's Commission on Women and the Criminal Justice System*. London: Fawcett Society.

Fearon, P. Kirkbride, J. B., Morgan, C., Dazzan, P., Morgan, K., Lloyd, T., Hutchinson, G., Tarrant, J., Fung, W. L., Holloway, J., Mallett, R., Harrison, G., Leff, J., Jones, P. B. and Murray, R. M. (2006). Incidence of schizophrenia and other psychoses in ethnic minority groups: results from the MRC AESOP Study. *Psychological Medicine*, 36 (11). pp.1541–1550.

Featherstone, B. (1999). Taking mothering seriously: the implications for child protection. *Child and Family Social Work*, 4: 43–53.

Featherstone, B., Morris, K. and White, S. (2013). A Marriage Made in Hell: Early intervention meets child protection. *British Journal of Social Work*, 1–15.

Ferrero, G. and Lombroso, C. (1895). *The Female Offender*. London: T. Fisher Unwin.

Ferguson H. (2011). *Child Protection Practice*. Basingstoke: Palgrave Macmillan.

Ferguson, H. and O'Reilly, M. (2001). *Keeping Children Safe: Child abuse, child protection and the promotion of welfare*. Farmar Press.

Fernando, S. (1991). *Mental Health, Race and Culture*. Basingstoke: Macmillan and Mind.

Fernando, S. (2010). *Mental Health, Race and Culture* (Third Edition). Basingstoke: Palgrave Macmillan.

Fine, M. (1993). *Disruptive Voices: The possibilities of feminist research*. Ann Arbour: University of Michigan Press.

Firestone, S. (1972). *The Dialectic of Sex: The case for a feminist revolution*. New York: Bantam.

Flynn, E. (2015). *Disabled Justice? Access to justice and the UN Convention on the Rights of Persons with Disabilities*. Aldershot: Ashgate.

Forrester, D., Westlake, D. and Glynn, G. (2012). Parental resistance and social worker skills: towards a theory of motivational social work. *Child and Family Social Work*, 2012, 17: 118–129.

Fraiberg, S. (1980). *Clinical Studies in Infant Mental Health: The first year of life*. Basic Books.

Francis, R. (2013). *Report of the Mid-Staffordshire NHS Foundation Trust Public Inquiry.* London: HMSO.

Friedman, J. and Alicea M. (2001). *Surviving Heroin: Interviews with women in methadone clinics.* Gainesville: University Press of Florida.

Friend, J. (1998). Responding to Violence Against Women: A specialist's role. *Hospital Medicine*, 59 (9), 98–99.

Fulton, H. (ed.) (2005). *Narrative and Media.* Cambridge: Cambridge University Press.

Galloway, S., Haynes, A., Cuthbert, C. (2014). *An Unfair Sentence—All Babies Count: Spotlight on the Criminal Justice System.* London: Barnardos and NSPCC.

Gannon, T. A. and Cortoni, F. (eds.) (2010). *Female Sexual Offenders: Theory, assessment, and treatment.* Chichester: Wiley-Blackwell.

Garrett, P. M. (2003). Swimming with Dolphins: The Assessment Framework, New Labour and new tools for social work with children and families. *British Journal of Social Work*, 33, 441–463.

Gerhardt, S. (2004). *Why Love Matters: How affection shapes a baby's brain.* London: Routledge.

Gilbert, B. (2013). Public Protection? The Implications of Grayling's 'Transforming Rehabilitation' Agenda on the Safety of Women and Children. *British Journal of Community Justice*, 11(2–3): 123–134.

Gelsthorpe, L. (2011). Working with Women Offenders in the Community: A view from England and Wales. In R. Sheehan, G. McIvor G and C. Trotter (eds.) *Working With Women in the Community.* Cullompton: Willan Publishing.

Gelsthorpe, L. and Hedderman, C. (2012). Providing for Women Offenders: The risks of adopting a payment by results approach. *Probation Journal* 59: 374.

Gelsthorpe, L. and Morris, A. (2002). Women's Imprisonment in England and Wales. *Criminal Justice*, 2/3, 277–301.

Gelsthorpe, L. and Sharpe, G. (2007). Women and Resettlement. In Hucklesby A. and Hagley-Dickinson L. (eds) *Prisoner Resettlement: Policy and Practice.* Cullompton: Willan Publishing.

Gelsthorpe, L., Sharpe, G. and Roberts J. (2007). *Provision for Women Offenders in the Community.* London: The Fawcett Society. ➲ www.fawcettsociety.org.uk

Ghate D and Hazel N (2002). *Parenting in Poor Environments: Stress support and coping.* London: Jessica Kingsley Publishers.

Goc, N. E. (2007). Monstrous Mothers and the Media. In Scott N. (ed.) *Monsters and the Monstrous: Myths and Metaphors of Enduring Evil.* Amsterdam: Rodopi.

Gomm, R. (2013). What Will 'Count' And Be Transformed For Women In The Criminal Justice System? *British Journal of Community Justice*, 11(2–3): 153–157.

Great Britain. *Children Act 1989* (England). London: HM Government.

Great Britain. *Mental Health Act 1983*: Elizabeth II. Chapter 20 (1983). London: HMSO.

Great Britain. *The Human Rights Act, 1998* (1998). London: HMSO.

Great Britain. *Mental Health Act 2007* (2007). London: HMSO.

Great Britain. *Policing and Crime Act 2009* (2009). London: HMSO.

Greene, S., Haney, C. and Hurtado, A. (2000). Cycles of Pain: Risk factors in the lives of incarcerated mothers and their children. *Prison Journal*, 80, (1), 3–23.

Gullberg, S. (2013). *State of the Estate: Women in Prison's Report on the Women's Custodial Estate 2011–2012.* London: Women in Prison.

Haidt, J. (2012). *The righteous Mind: Why good people are divided by politics and religion.* London: Allen lane.

Halliday, J. (2001). *Making Punishments Work: Report of a Review of the Sentencing Framework for England and Wales,* London: Home Office.

Hamlyn, B. and Lewis, D. (2000). Women Prisoners: A survey of their work and training experiences in custody and on release. *Home Office Research Study, 208.* London: Home Office. ➲ webarchive.nationalarchives.gov.uk/20110218135832/ http:/rds.homeoffice.gov.uk/rds/pdfs/hors208.pdf (accessed 14 Sept 2009)

Hanmer, J. and Saunders, S. (1984). *Well-founded Fear: A community study of violence to women.* London: Hutchinson.

Hannah-Moffat, K. (2003). Getting Women Out: The Limits of Reintegration Reform, *Criminal Justice Matters* 53: 44–5.

Hedderman, C. (2004). The 'Criminogenic' Needs of Women Offenders. In G. McIvor (ed), *Women Who Offend: Research Highlights in Social Work* 44. London: Jessica Kingsley Publishers.

Hedderman, C. (2010). Government Policy on Women Offenders: Labour's legacy and the Coalition's challenge. *Punishment and Society,* 2010 12(4): 485–500.

Hedderman, C. and L. Gelsthorpe, (eds.) (1997). Understanding the Sentencing of Women. *Home Office Research Study 170.* London: Home Office.

Hedderman, C. and Gunby, C. (2013). Diverting Women from Custody: The importance of understanding sentencers' perspectives. *Probation Journal,* 60(4) 425–438.

Hedderman, C., Palmer, E. and Hollin, C. (2008). *Implementing Services for Women Offenders and Those 'At Risk' of Offending.* London: Ministry of Justice. ➲ webarchive.nationalarchives.gov.uk/+/http:/www.justice.gov.uk/docs/together-women.pdf (accessed 14 September 2009)

Heidensohn, F. (1981). Women and the Penal System in A. Morris and L. Gelsthorpe (eds.), *Women and Crime,* 129/139. Cropwood Conference No. 13 Cambridge.

Heidensohn, F. (1985). *Women and Crime.* London: Macmillan.

Heidensohn, F. (1995). Women in Control: The role of women in law enforcement. Oxford: Oxford University Press.

Heidensohn, F. and Silvestri, M. (2012). Gender and Crime. In Maguire, M., Morgan, R. and Reiner R. (eds.), *The Oxford Handbook of Criminology.* Oxford: Oxford University Press, 336–369.

Herman, J. L. (1992). *Trauma and Recovery: The aftermath of violence from domestic abuse to political terror.* New York: Basic Books.

HM Government (2011). *A Cross-government Mental Health Outcomes Strategy for People of All Ages.* London: Department of Health.

HM Inspector of Constabulary (HMIC) (2014). *Everyone's Business: Improving the police response to domestic abuse.* ➲ www.hmic.gov.uk, London: HMIC.

HM Prison Service (2008). Prison Service Order 4800, Women in Prison. London: Home Office.

HM Prison Service (2008). Prison Service Order 4801, Management of Mother and Baby Units. London: Home Office.

HM Inspectorate of Probation, HM Inspectorate Crown Prosecution Service and HM Inspectorate of Prisons (2011). *Equal But Different? An inspection of the use of alternatives to custody for women offenders.* London: HMI Probation.

HM Government (2011). *No Health Without Mental Health: A cross-government mental health outcomes strategy for people of all ages.* London: Department of Health.

HM Government (2013). *Working Together to Safeguard Children: A guide to Inter-Agency Working to Safeguard and Promote the Welfare of Children.* London: Department for Education.

HMSO (1998). *Supporting Families* (Green Paper). London: Home Office.

Hodnett, E. D., Gates, S., Hofmeyr, G. J. and Sakala, C. (2011). Continuous Support for Women During Childbirth. *Cochrane Database of Systematic Reviews Issue 2.* Chichester: John Wiley and Sons Ltd.

Holland, S. (2010). *Child and Family Assessment in Social Work Practice* (2nd Edition). London: Sage Publications.

Hollin, C. R. and Palmer, E. J. (eds.) (2006). *Offending Behaviour Programmes: Development, application and controversies.* Chichester: John Wiley and Sons.

Home Office (2004b). *Women's Offending Reduction Programme (WORP) Action Plan.* London: Home Office.

Home Office (2005). *Offender Management Caseload Statistics, 2004.* London: Home Office.

Home Office (2013). *Multi-Agency Working and Information Sharing Project Early Findings,* London, Home Office.

Horwath, J. (2009). Managing Difference: Working effectively in a multi-agency context. In P. Cawson, H. Cleaver and S. Walker (eds), *Safeguarding Children: A shared responsibility.* Chichester: Wiley.

Hunter, R. (2008). Can Feminist Judges Make a Difference? *International Journal of the Legal Profession,* 7–36.

Roberts, J. V. and Hough, M. (2011). Custody or Community? Exploring the boundaries of public punitiveness in England and Wales, *Criminology and Criminal Justice* 11/2: 181–197.

Hough, M., Bradford, B., Jackson, J. and Roberts, J. R. (2013). Attitudes to sentencing and trust in justice: Exploring trends from the crime survey for England Wales. *Ministry of Justice Analytical Series*, Ministry of Justice: London,.

Hough, M. and Roberts, J. (1999). Sentencing Trends in Britain: Public knowledge and public opinion. *Punishment and Society*. Vol: 1(1): 11–26.

Hoyle, C. (1998). *Negotiating Domestic Violence: Police, criminal justice and victims.* Oxford: Oxford University Press.

Hoyle, C. and Sanders, A. (2000). Police Response to Domestic Violence: From victim choice to victim empowerment? *British Journal of Criminology*, 40: 14–36.

Humphreys, C. and Thiara, R. (2002). *Routes to Safety: Protection issues facing abused women and children and the role of outreach services.* Bristol: Women's Aid Federation of England.

Hungerford, R. and Elliot-Hohepa, A. (2012). Formative Evaluation of Mothers with Babies Units in Prison. Momentum research and evaluation. Independent evaluation on behalf of the Department of Corrections, New Zealand.

Independent Police Complaints Commission (IPCC) (2009). *IPCC Report into the Contact between Fiona Pilkington and Leicestershire Constabulary, 2004–2007.* London: IPCC.

International Confederation of Midwives (2011). *Essential Competencies for Basic Midwifery Practice 2010.* London: ICM.

Irish Penal Reform Trust (IPRT) (2011), *Women in Detention*, IPRT Briefing.

Jewkes, Y. (2008). Media Representations of the Causes of Crime. *Criminal Justice Matters*, 55 (1):26–27.

Jewkes, Y. (2011). Media and Crime (2nd Edition). London: Sage.

Johnson, D. D. and Swanson, D. H. (2006). Constructing the 'Good Mother': The experience of mothering ideologies by work status. *Sex Roles*, 54 (7–8), 509–519.

Jolliffe, D., Hedderman, C., Palmer, E. and Hollin, C. (2011). Re-offending Analysis of Women Offenders Referred to Together Women (TW) and the Scope to Divert from Custody. *Ministry of Justice Research Series 11/11*. London: Ministry of Justice.

Jones, R. S. (1993). Coping With Separation: Adaptive responses of women prisoners. *Women and Criminal Justice*, 5:71–96.

Jordan, S. (2013). *Missing Voices: Why women engage with, or withdraw from, community sentences.* Research Paper, 2013/01, The Griffin Society.

Judicial Diversity Taskforce (2013). *Improving Judicial Diversity: Progress towards delivery of the 'Report of the Advisory Panel on Judicial Diversity 2010.* Annual Report produced by the Judicial Diversity Taskforce.

Justice Committee (2013). *Women Offenders: after the Corston Report, Second Report of Session 2013–14, Volume I: Report, together with formal minutes, oral and written evidence.* London: House of Commons Justice Committee.

Kappeler, V. E. and Potter, G. W. (2005). *The Mythology of Crime and Criminal Justice* (4th Edition). Long Grove, IL: Sage.

Kennedy, D. A. (2012). The Good Mother: Mothering, feminism, and incarceration. *William & Mary Journal of Women and the Law*, 18(2).

Kershaw, C., Nicholas, S. and Walker, A. (2008). *Crime in England and Wales 2007/08. Home Office Statistical Bulletin.* London: Home Office.
➜ webarchive.nationalarchives.gov.uk/20110218135832/rds.homeoffice.gov.uk/rds/pdfs08/hosb0708.pdf

Kesteven, S. (2002). *Women Who Challenge: Women offenders and mental health issues.* London: Nacro.

Kubiak, S. P., Beeble, M. L., and Bybee, D. (2010). Testing the Validity of the K6 in Detecting Major Depression and PTSD Among Jailed Women. *Criminal Justice and Behavior*, 37, 6480.

Laing, B.A. (1990). Error in Medicine: Legal impediments to US reform. *Journal of Health Politics and Policy Law*, 24:27–58.

Laming, W. H. (2003). *The Victoria Climbié Inquiry: Report of an Inquiry by Lord Laming.* Cm 5730. London: HMSO.

Lapierre, S. (2010). More Responsibilities, Less Control: Understanding the challenges and difficulties involved in mothering in the context of domestic violence. *British Journal of Social Work*, 40, 1434–1451.

Layder, D. (2004). *Emotion in Social Life: The lost heart of society.* London: Sage.

Lewis, G. and Appleby, L. (1998). Personality Disorder: The patients psychiatrists dislike. *British Journal of Psychiatry*, 153: 44-49.

Levinson, D. and Harwin, N. (2000). Reducing Domestic Violence … What Works? Accommodation provision. *Crime Reduction Research Series*. London: Policing and Reducing Crime Unit.

Liebling, A. (2008). Why Prison Staff Culture Matters. In Byrne, J. M., Hummer D. and Taxman F. S. (eds) *The Culture of Prison Violence*. Boston, USA: Allyn and Bacon Publishing, 105–122.

Liebling A. and Coyle, A. (2009). *The Role of the Prison Officer.* House of Commons Justice Committee. London: HMSO.

Link, B. G., Phelan, J. C. (2001). Conceptualising stigma. *Annual Review of Sociology*, 27:363–385.

Lishman, J. (1991). *Handbook of Theory for Practice Teachers in Social Work.* London: Jessica Kingsley.

Lishman, J. (1994). *Communication in Social Work.* Basingstoke: Palgrave Macmillan.

Lock, R. (2014). *Serious Case Review: The Anderson family. overview report.* Suffolk Safeguarding Children Board, Ipswich.

Loftus, B. (2008). Dominant Culture Interrupted: Recognition, resentment and the politics of change in an English police force. *British Journal of Criminology* 48, No. 6: 756–777.

Loucks. N., Malloch, M., McIvor, G. and Gelsthorpe, L. (2006). *Evaluation of the 218 Centre*. Edinburgh: Scottish Executive Social Research.

MacKinnon, C. (2005). Pornography as Trafficking, *Michigan Journal of Gender and Law*.

MacKinnon, C. (2011). Trafficking, Prostitution, and Inequality. *Harvard Civil Rights-Civil Liberties Law Review*.

Macnaghten, J. (1938). *Rex v Bourne* [1939] 1 K. B. 687, 3 All E. R. 615 (1938).

MacPherson, Sir W. (1999). The Stephen Lawrence Inquiry. Report of an inquiry by Sir William Macpherson of Cluny. London: HMSO, CM 4262-I.

Malloch, M. (1999). Drug Use, Prison, and the Social Construction of Femininity. *Women's Studies International Forum*, 22 (3): 349–358.

Malloch, M. (2000). *Women, Drugs and Custody*. Winchester/Sherfield-on-Loddon: Waterside Press.

Marougka M. and Cass R. (2012). *Listening to Young Women in Police Custody: Mental Health Needs and the Police Response*. London: Independent Academic Research Series.

Marsh, I. and Melville, G. (2009). *Crime, Justice and the Media*. Florence, KY: Routledge.

Malloch, M. (2004). Women, Drug Use and the Criminal Justice System. In McIvor, G. (ed) *Women Who Offend*. London: Jessica Kingsley Publishers, 245–265.

Marshall, D. (2010). Birthing Companions: Working with Women in Prison Giving Birth. *The British Journal of Midwifery*, 18(4) pp.255–258.

Manchester Metropolitan University (2015). *Equality and Diversity Guidance on Gender: The women's timeline*, accessed 2015 via ➲ www.mmu.ac.uk/equality-and-diversity/gender.

Marshall, J. E. and Raynor, M. D. (eds.) (2014). *Myles Textbook for Midwives*. United Kingdom: Elsevier Health Sciences

Martin, S. (1980). *Breaking and Entering: Policewomen on patrol*. University of California Press: Berkeley.

Marougka, M. and Cass, R. (2012). *Listening to Young Women in Police Custody: Mental health needs and the police response*. London: IARS.

Mason, L., Glenn, S., Walton, I. and Hughes, C. (2001). Women's reluctance to seek help for stress incontinence during pregnancy and following childbirth. *Midwifery*. 17:212–221.

Mawby, R. C. and Worrall, A. (2013). *Doing Probation Work: Identity in a criminal justice occupation*, London: Routledge.

Mawby, R. C. and Worrall, A. (2013). Working With Offenders: Someone has to do it … but not just anyone can, *British Journal of Community Justice*, 11(2–3): 115–118.

McCoy, C., Metsch, L., Chitwood, D. and Miles, C. (2001). Drug Use and Barriers to Use of Health Care Services. *Substance Use and Misuse*, 36, 789.

McCulloch, D. (2012). *Not Hearing Us: An exploration of the experience of deaf prisoners in English and Welsh prisons*. London: Howard League for Penal Reform.

McGibbon, A., Cooper, L. and Kelly, L. (1989). *What Support? An Explanatory Study of Council Policy and Practice, and Local Support Services in the Area of Domestic Violence within Hammersmith and Fulham*. London: Hammersmith and Fulham Community Safety Unit.

McGregor, C. (2015). *Coaching Behind Bars: Facing challenges and creating hope in a women's prison*. Oxford University Press.

McIvor, G. (2004). *Women Who Offend*. London: Jessica Kingsley Publishers.

McSweeney, T. and Hough, M. (2006). Supporting Offenders with Multiple Needs: Lessons for the 'mixed economy' model of service provision. *Criminology and Criminal Justice*, 6(1): 107–125.

McSweeny, T, Turnbull, P. and Hough, M. (2008). *The Treatment and Supervision of Drug-dependent Offenders: A review of the literature prepared for the UK Drug Policy Commission*. Institute for Criminal Policy Research, King's College London.

Mead, M. (1935). Sex and Temperament in Three Primitive Societies. In M. Kimmel (ed.) *The Gendered Reader*. Oxford University Press: Oxford.

Mezoughi, L. (2015). *Why Sentence Women to Short Custodial Sentences that Don't Even Work?* The Justice Gap. ➲ thejusticegap.com/2015/02/sentence-women-short-custodial-sentences-arent-working/

Ministry of Justice (2012b). *Prison Population Statistics: Population and Capacity Briefing for Friday 03/02/2012*, accessed at ➲ www.gov.uk/government/uploads/system/uploads/attachment_data/file/218317/prison-population-3-02-12.xls

Ministry of Justice (2013). *Compendium of Reoffending Statistics and Analysis*, London: Ministry of Justice.

Ministry of Justice/NOMS (2012). A Distinct Approach — A guide to working with women offenders. London: Ministry of Justice.

Ministry of Justice, Home Office and the Office for National Statistics (2013). An Overview of Sexual Offending in England and Wales. *Statistics Bulletin*, January 2013. London: Ministry of Justice, Home Office and Office for National Statistics.

Ministry of Justice (2014). *Costs Per Place and Costs Per Prisoner by Individual Prison, NOMS Annual Report and Accounts 2013–14: Management information addendum*, London: Ministry of Justice.

Ministry of Justice (2015). *Population and Capacity Briefing for Friday*. 15 May 2015, London: Ministry of Justice.

Minson, S. (2014). *Mitigating Motherhood: A study of the impact of motherhood on sentencing decisions in England and Wales*, Howard League for Penal Reform, London.

Morris, A. (1987). *Women, Crime and Criminal Justice.* Oxford: Basil Blackwell.

Munro, E. (2008). *Effective Child Protection* (2nd Edition). London: Sage.

Munro, M., Foster Reitz, M. And Seng, J. S. (2012). Comprehensive Care of Pregnancy: The unmet care needs of women with a history of rape. *Mental Health Nursing.* Dec 33 (12) 882–896.

Murphy, S., and Rosenbaum, M. (1999). *Pregnant Women on Drugs: Combating stereotypes and stigma.* New Brunswick, NJ: Rutgers University Press.

Murray, J. and Farrington, D. P. (2008). Effects of Parental Imprisonment on Children, in M. Tonry, (ed.) *Crime and Justice: A review of research.* Chicago: University of Chicago.

National Institute for Mental Health in England (2003). *Mental Health Policy Implementation Guide Developing Positive Practice to Support the Safe and Therapeutic Management of Aggression and Violence in Mental Health In-patient Settings.* London: NHS.

National Offender Management Service and National Probation Service (NOMS/NPS) (2006). *Delivering Effective Services for Women Offenders in the Community: A good practice guide.* London: Home Office.

National Offender Management Service (2011). *Mother and Baby Units,* PSI 54–2011. London: Home Office.

National Offender Management Service (2014). *Offender Equalities Annual Report 2013/14.* London: Ministry of Justice.

National Offender Management Service Women and Equalities Group (2012). *A Distinct Approach: A guide to working with women offenders.* London: Ministry of Justice.

National Probation Service (2001). *A New Choreography: An integrated strategy for the National Probation Service for England and Wales. Strategic Framework 2001–2004.* London: Home Office.

National Treatment Agency (2010). *Women in Drug Treatment: What the latest figures reveal.* London: NHS/NTA.

National Treatment Agency (2012). *Parents with Drug Problems: How treatment helps families.* London: NHS/NTA.

Neale, J. (2004). Measuring the Health of Scottish Drug Users. *Health and Social Care in the Community,* 12 (3).

Nellis, M. (2000). Creating Community Justice. In K. Pease; S. Ballintyne and V. McLaren (eds.) *Key Issues in Crime Prevention, Crime Reduction and Community Safety.* London: IPPR: 67–86.

New Economics Foundation (2008). *Unlocking Value: How we all benefit from investing in alternatives to prison for women offenders,* London: NEF.

Norman, P., Boer, H., and Seydel, E. R. (2005). Protection Motivation Theory. In M. Conner and P. Norman (eds.) *Predicting Health Behaviour: Research and Practice with Social Cognition Models* (2nd ed) (81–126). Maidenhead: Open University Press.

North, J. (2005). Getting it Right? Services for pregnant women, new mothers and babies in prison, accessed at ➲ www.maternityaction.org.uk/sitebuildercontent/sitebuilderfiles/prisonsreport.pdf on 20/10/2011

North, J. (2006). *Getting it Right? Services for pregnant women, new mothers, and babies in prison.* Maternity Alliance.

Nursing and Midwifery Council (2012). *Midwives Rules and Standards.* London: National Midwifery Council (NMC).

Nursing and Midwifery Council (2015). *The Code: Professional standards of practice and behaviour for nurses and midwives,* London: NMC.

Nursing and Midwives Order (2001). Article 45: Attendance by unqualified persons at childbirth. Statutory Instruments.

Oakley, A. (1974a). *The Sociology of Housework.* Oxford: Martin Robertson.

Oakley, A. (1979). *Becoming a Mother.* Oxford: Martin Robertson.

Oliver, C. (2010). *Children's Views and Experiences of their Contact with Social Workers: A focused review of the evidence.* Children's Workforce Development Council: Leeds.

O'Malley, S. (2013). *The Experience of Imprisonment for Incarcerated Mothers and their Children in Ireland.* Unpublished PhD Thesis.

O'Malley, S. (2015). Maintaining the Mother-child Relationship Within the Irish Prison System: The practitioner perspective, *Childcare in Practice*

Pahl, J. (1989). *Money and Marriage.* Basingstoke: Macmillan.

Parton (2002). *Child Protection and Family Support: Tensions Contradictions and Possibilities.* Routledge: London.

Payne, M. (2005). *Modern Social Work Theory* (3rd Edition). Basingstoke: Palgrave Macmillan.

Perry, L. (1991). *Women and Drug Use: An unfeminine dependency.* London: ISDD.

Phoenix, A. (1996). Social Constructions of Lone Motherhood: A case of competing discourses. In E. Bortolaia Silva (ed.) *Good Enough Mothering? Feminist perspectives on lon e motherhood,* 175–190 London: Routledge.

Phoenix, A. (1991). *Young Mothers.* Cambridge: Polity Press.

Phoenix, A. (1994). Practice in Feminist Research: The interjection of gender and race in the research process. In M. Maynard and J. Purvis (eds.), *Researching Women's Lives from Feminist Perspectives.* Portsmouth: Taylor and Francis.

Pickersgil, M. (2013). How Personality Became Treatable: The mutual constitution of knowledge and mental health law. *Social Studies of Science,* 43(1): 30–53.

Platt, D. (2006). Investigation or Initial Assessment of Child Concerns? The impact of the refocusing initiative on social work practice. *British Journal of Social Work,* 36, 267–281.

Pollak, O. (1961). *The Criminality of Women.* New York: Barnes.

Potts, N.C. (2005). Problem Drug Use and Child Protection: Interagency working and policies in Scotland. *Infant* 1(6): 189–93.

Price, S. (2005). Maternity Services for Women in Prison: A descriptive study. *British Journal of Midwifery* 13(6): 362–368.

Priest, J. (2012). *The Integration of Health and Social Care*. Health Policy and Economic Research Unit. London: British Medical Association.

Priestley, P. (1999). *Victorian Prison Lives: English Prison Biography 1830–1914* (2nd edition). London: Pimlico.

Prison Reform Trust (2010). *Women in Prison, August 2010 Statistical Bulletin*, London: Prison Reform Trust.

Prison Reform Trust (2011). *Reforming Women's Justice: Final report of the Women's Justice Taskforce*. London: Prison Reform Trust.

Prison Reform Trust (2014). *Bromley Briefings Prison Factfile Autumn 2014*, London: Prison Reform Trust.

Pryce, V. (2013). *Prisonomics: Behind bars in Britain's failing prisons*. London: Biteback Publications.

Quamby, K. (2011). *Scapegoat: Why are we failing disabled people?* London: Granta.

Ramsbottom, D. (2003). *Prisongate: The shocking state of Britain's prisons and the need for visionary change*. London: Simon and Schuster.

Rayns, G., Dawe, S. and Cuthbert, C. (2013). *Spotlight on Drugs and Alcohol: All babies count*. London: NSPCC.

Reed, K. (2014). Children of Prisoners: 'Orphans of justice'? *Family Law*, 44, 69

Refuge (2014). *Refuge Response to Home Office Consultation, 'Strengthening the Law on Domestic Abuse'*. London: Refuge.

Reiner, R. (1992). *The Politics of Police* (2nd Edition). Toronto: University of Toronto Press.

Rex, S. and Hosking, N. (2013). A Collaborative Approach to Developing Probation Practice: Skills for effective engagement, development and supervision (SEEDS). *Probation Journal*, 60 (3) pp.332–338.

Rich, A. (1976). *Of Woman Born: Motherhood as Experience and Institution*. London: W. W. Norton and Company.

Rich, A. (1995). *Of Woman Born: Motherhood as Experience and Institution* (2nd edition). London: W. W. Norton and Company.

Roberts, J. (2002). Women-centred: The West Mercia community-based programme for women offenders, in P. Carlen (ed.) *Women and Punishment: The struggle for justice*. Cullompton: Willan Publishing.

Robinson, F. W. (1862). *Female Life in Prison, by a Prison Matron*. London: Hurst and Blackett.

Rock, P. (1996). *Reconstructing a Women's Prison: The Holloway Redevelopment Project, 1968–88*. London: Clarendon Press.

Rotkirch, A. (2009). Maternal Guilt. *Evolutionary Psychology*, 8, 90–106.

Rowe K. (2011). *Unruly Girls, Unrepentant Women: Redefining feminism on screen*. Austin, TX: University of Texas Press.

Royal College of Midwives (RCM) (2008). *Caring for Childbearing Prisoners: Guidance paper*. London: RCM.

Royal College of Nursing (RCN)(2014). *Integrated Health and Social Care in England: The story so far*. London: RCN.

Rubus Services Ltd (2010). *Footsteps to the Future: An evaluation of the work of Anawim: Women working together*. Rubus Services Ltd.

Rumgay, J. (2004). *The Asha Centre: Report of an evaluation*. Worcester: Asha Centre.

Rutman, D., Strega, S., Callahan, M. and Dominelli, L. (2002). 'Undeserving' Mothers? Practitioners' experiences working with young mothers in/from care. *Child and Family Social Work*, 2002, 7, 149–159.

Schetter, C. D. and Tanner, L. (2012). Anxiety, Depression and Stress in Pregnancy. *Current Opinion in Psychiatry*, 25(2), 141–148.

Scourfield, J. (2000). Constructing Women in Child Protection Work. *Child and Family Social Work*, 6, 77–87.

Safe Lives (2015). *Policy and Evidence: About Domestic Abuse*, Safe Lives: Ending Domestic Abuse.

Sandler, M. and Coles, D. (2008). *Dying on the Inside: Examining women's deaths in prison*. London: Inquest.

Senior, P. (2013). Community Engagement: Innovation; Past, present and future. In *Probation Journal*, 60(3): 242–258.

Seth-Smith, N. (2013). *Rape in the UK: Myths about myths*, 50:50 Inclusive Democracy, ➲ www.opendemocracy.net/5050/niki-seth-smith/rape-in-uk-myths-about-myths

Shapland, J., Bottoms, A., Farrall, S., McNeill, F., Priede, C. and Robinson, G. (2012). *The Quality of Probation Supervision—A literature review*. Centre for Criminological Research, University of Sheffield and University of Glasgow.

Sharpe, G. (2015). Precarious Identities: 'Young' Motherhood, Desistance and Stigma. *Criminology and Criminal Justice*, 1–16.

Silva, S. A., Pires, A. P., Guerreiro, C. and Cardoso, A. (2012). Balancing Motherhood and Drug Addiction: The transition to parenthood of addicted mothers. *Health Psychology*, 18:359.

Sim, J. (1990). *Medical Power in Prisons*, Milton Keynes: Open University Press.

Smart, C. (1976). *Women, Crime and Criminology: A feminist critique*. London: Routledge and Kegan Paul.

Social Exclusion Unit (2002). *Reducing Re-offending by Ex-prisoners* London: Office of the Deputy Prime Minister, Social Exclusion Unit.

Stanley, S. (2009). What Works in 2009: Progress or stagnation? *Probation Journal*, 56(2): 153–174

Stanko, E. (2000). The day to Count: A snapshot of the impact of domestic violence in the UK. *Criminal Justice* 1:2

Sugarman, L. (2001). *Life Span Development: Frameworks, accounts and strategies* (2nd edition). East Sussex: Psychology Press.

Sutherland, J. (2010). Mothering, Guilt and Shame. *Sociology Compass*, 4(5), 310–321

Symons, J. (1849). *Tactics for the Times as Regards the Condition and Treatment of the Dangerous Classes.* London: John Ollivier.

Tasca, C., Rapetti, M., Carta, M. G., and Fadda, B. (2012). Women and Hysteria in the History Of Mental Health. *Clinical Practice and Epidemiology in Mental Health*, 8, 110 119.

Taylor, A. (1993). *An Ethnography of a Female Injecting Community.* London: Clarendon Press.

Thompson, N. (2011). *Promoting Equality; Working with diversity and difference.* Basingstoke: Palgrave Macmillan.

Thorne, B. (2004). *Gender Play: Girls and Boys in School.* New Jersey: Rutgers University Press.

Thurer, S. (1995). *Myths of Motherhood: How culture reinvents the good mother.* Middlesex: Penguin Books.

Treadwell, J. (2006). Some Personal Reflections on Probation Training. *Howard Journal of Criminal Justice*, 45(1): 1–13.

Turney, D., Platt, D., Selwyn, J. and Farmer, E. (2011). *Improving Child and Family Assessments: Turning research into practice.* London: Jessica Kingsley Publishers

Ussher, J. (1991). *Women's Madness: Misogyny or mental illness?* London: Harvester Wheatsheaf.

Uvnas-Moberg, K. (2014). How Kindness, Warmth, Empathy and Support Promote the Progress of Labour: A physiological perspective. In Byrom, S. and Downe, S. (eds.) (2014) *The Roar Behind the Silence: Why kindness, compassion and respect matter in maternity care.* United Kingdom: Pinter and Martin.

Van der Volk, B. (2001). The Assessment and Treatment of Complex PTSD, Chapter 7. In, R. Yehuda (ed.) *Traumatic Stress,* American Psychiatric Press.

Waddington, P. A. J. (1999). Police (Canteen) Sub-culture: An appreciation. *British Journal of Criminology,* 39:2 , 287–309.

Waterhouse, L. and McGhee, J. (2009). Anxiety and Child Protection—Implications for practitioner-parent relations. *Child and Family Social Work*, 14, 481–490.

Webb, M. A and Nellis, B (2007). *Hidden Harm: Addictions in the Family.* Policy and Briefing No, 13, NI: Barnados. ➲ www.barnardos.org.uk/hidden_harm.pdf

Welldon, E. V. (2000). *Mother, Madonna, Whore: The idealisation and denigration of motherhood.* Karnac Books, London.

Welsh Assembly Government (2008). *Mental Health Act 1983: Code of Practice for Wales.* Cardiff: Welsh Assembly Government.

Westad, C. and McConnell, D. (2012). Child Welfare Involvement of Mothers with Mental Health Issues. *Community Mental Health*, 48, 29–37.

Westmarland, L. (2001). *Gender and Policing: Sex, power and police culture*. Cullompton: Willan.

Wilson, H. and Huntington, A. (2006). Deviant (M)others: The construction of teenage motherhood in contemporary discourse. *Journal of Social Policy*, 35, 59–76.

Winnicott, D. W. (1967). Mirror-role of the Mother and Family in Child Development. In P. Lomas (Eed.). *The Predicament of the Family: A Psycho-Analytical Symposium* (pp.26–33). London: Hogarth.

Winnicott, D. W. (1953). Transitional Objects and Transitional Phenomena — A study of the first not-me possession, *International Journal of Psycho-Analysis*, 34:89–97.

Women's Aid (2014). *Women's Aid Annual Report*, Women's Aid.

Women's Breakout (2013). *Transforming Rehabilitation: A revolution in the way we manage offenders, Government Consultation Paper CP1/2013, Response from Women's Breakout*. Birmingham: Women's Breakout.

Woods, M. (2007). *Keeping Mum: A qualitative study of women drug users' experience of preserving motherhood in Dublin*. Thesis, Trinity College Dublin.

Wolf, N. (1994). *Misconceptions: Truth, lies, and the unexpected on the journey to motherhood*. New York: Doubleday Press.

Woolf Report (1991). *Prison Disturbances April 1990 — Report of an enquiry by the Right Hon Lord Justice Woolf and His Honour Judge Stephen Tumin*. Cm. 1456. London: HMSO.

Worrall, A. (1990). *Offending Women*, London: Routledge.

Worrall, A. (1999). Twisted Sisters, Ladettes and the New Penology: The social construction of violent girls. In Alder, C. and Worrall, A. (eds), *Girls Violence: Myths and Realities*. New York: Albany Press.

World Health Organisation (2006). *Gender Disparities in Mental Health*. Department of Health and Substance Dependence, WHO.

Zedner, L (1991). Women, Crime, and Penal Responses: A historical account. *Crime and Justice*, 14, 307–362

Zedner, L. (1995). Comparative Research in Criminal Justice. In Noaks, L., Levi, M. and Maguire, M. *Contemporary Issues in Criminology*. University of Wales Press.

Zedner, L. (1998). Wayward Sisters: The prison for women. In Morris, N. and Rothman, D.J. (eds.), *The Oxford History of the Prison: The practice of punishment in western society*, 295–324, New York: Oxford University Press.

Zedner, L. (2010). Pre-crime and Pre-punishment: A health warning. *Criminal Justice Matters*, 81(1).

Index

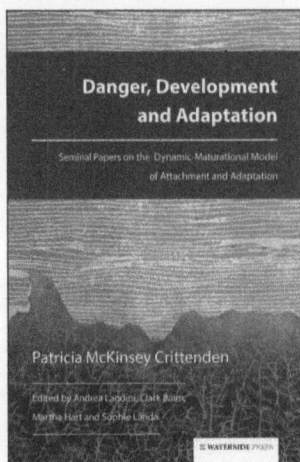

Danger, Development and Adaptation: Seminal Papers on the Dynamic-Maturational Model of Attachment and Adaptation
by Patricia McKinsey Crittenden
With a Foreword by Rodolfo de Bernart
Edited by Andrea Landini, Martha Hart, Clark Baim and Sophie Landa

A collection of writings by leading developmental psychologist Patricia M Crittenden, highlighting her vast contribution to attachment theory and research. It includes her observation of and research into behavioural patterns; application of attachment theory to child maltreatment, parent and child mental illness, and criminality; and the Dynamic-Maturational Model (DMM) of Attachment and Adaptation.

'This volume contains a selection of the seminal works of Patricia Crittenden, one of the most creative and innovative thinkers in the history of attachment theory. Crittenden integrates the fields of developmental psychology and developmental psychopathology in her thought-provoking and insightful research on attachment in normal and atypical development. Her ground-breaking work on attachment and child maltreatment stimulated the field to embark on translational research to prevent attachment insecurity and to promote resilient functioning': Dante Cicchetti, Ph.D.

Paperback & ebook | ISBN 978-1-909976-27-6 | 2015 | 592 pages

www.WatersidePress.co.uk